# Self-Determination Beyond Liberal Legalism

# Self-Determination Beyond Liberal Legalism

## *Ethics, Law, and the Politics of Justice*

Anna Irene Baka

BLOOMSBURY ACADEMIC
NEW YORK • LONDON • OXFORD • NEW DELHI • SYDNEY

BLOOMSBURY ACADEMIC
Bloomsbury Publishing Inc, 1359 Broadway, New York, NY 10018, USA
Bloomsbury Publishing Plc, 50 Bedford Square, London, WC1B 3DP, UK
Bloomsbury Publishing Ireland, 29 Earlsfort Terrace, Dublin 2, D02 AY28, Ireland

BLOOMSBURY, BLOOMSBURY ACADEMIC and the Diana logo are trademarks of Bloomsbury Publishing Plc

First published in the United States of America 2026



Library of Congress Cataloging-in-Publication Data
Names: Baka, Anna Irene author
Title: Self-determination beyond liberal legalism : ethics, law, and the politics of justice / Anna Irene Baka.
Description: 1. | New York : Bloomsbury Publishing, 2026. | Includes bibliographical references and index.
Identifiers: LCCN 2025035919 (print) | LCCN 2025035920 (ebook) | ISBN 9781666965155 hardback | ISBN 9781666965179 paperback | ISBN 9781978771130 epub | ISBN 9798216254676 pdf | ISBN 9798881888558
Subjects: LCSH: Aristotle | Self-determination, National | Self-determination, National—Moral and ethical aspects | Autonomy (Psychology) | Sovereignty
Classification: LCC KZ4042 .B35 2026 (print) | LCC KZ4042 (ebook) | DDC 341.26—dc23/eng/20250804
LC record available at https://lccn.loc.gov/2025035919
LC ebook record available at https://lccn.loc.gov/2025035920

ISBN: HB: 978-1-6669-6515-5
ePDF: 979-8-216-25467-6
eBook: 978-1-9787-7113-0

Typeset by Deanta Global Publishing Services, Chennai, India

For product safety related questions contact productsafety@bloomsbury.com.

To find out more about our authors and books, visit www.bloomsbury.com and sign up for our newsletters.

*To my loving family*

# Contents

# Preface

This book represents a comprehensive revision of my PhD thesis, originally submitted and successfully defended at the University of Hong Kong in 2015 under the title *The Dialectic of the Cave: Self-Determination, Constitution, and the Phenomenology of Deprivation*. Since then, my journey has encompassed significant changes in my personal, academic, and professional life, enriching my perspectives and my current view of that work. After several years as a human rights lawyer and deepening my engagement with Edmund Husserl's phenomenology, early and medieval Chinese thought, Aristotelian and comparative philosophy, I revisit this work with a fresh perspective. Although I might approach some sections differently today, I stand by the core arguments, which I believe remain as relevant today, if not more so.

Identifying myself as an Aristotelian in mind and spirit, I recognize that achieving a sophisticated form of justice on the international stage is unattainable. Indeed, our international legal reality often shows that *de facto* outcomes are far more likely than mediated legal resolutions. This is largely due to the lack of an international legislator or world government to administer justice. Nonetheless, the implementation of corrective justice is an absolute minimum if we wish to ever maintain a world that offers conditions of peaceful exchange. This, I believe, is our best hope. The absence of corrective justice on the international plane does more than create a void; it fosters an environment that, by failing to penalize wrongdoing, implicitly rewards unethical behavior, with grave consequences for global welfare and human morale. Regrettably, the issues addressed in this book are still very pertinent and timely; unrestrained human passions perpetually resurface, and the major conflicts of our time will continue unresolved if the international actors involved persist in their shortsighted and destructive policies.

The realities of my human rights practice and subsequent empirical engagements with governments, national and international human rights organizations, have tempered some of the romanticism of my PhD days. Nonetheless, I firmly believe that even seemingly minor efforts by individuals can spark profound, lasting changes at both national and international levels.

The central figure in this discussion is the legal scholar and practitioner, a recurring subject throughout this work as well as my work in general. Intellectual curiosity, fearless engagement with our world, a deep ethical commitment to understanding others—as well as the implications of our decisions, actions, and omissions—are crucial for those who mostly bear the responsibility and are essential for any realistic hope of change.

Selected sections and ideas from this work, particularly those pertaining to Aristotle, Hegel, and the phenomenology of rights, have previously appeared in a significantly revised form in the *Oxford Handbook of the Sources of International Law*, co-written with Tony Carty and edited by Jean D'Aspremont and Samantha Besson (Oxford University Press, 2017); *The Theory and Philosophy of Customary International Law and its Interpretation*, edited by Panos Merkouris, Jörg Kammerhoffer, and Noora Arajärvi (Cambridge University Press, 2022) and *The Phenomenology of Law and Normativity* (Springer, 2024) which I have co-edited with Panos Theodorou and Pedro Alves.

Treviso, May 7, 2025

# Acknowledgments

The journey for the preparation of this manuscript has been long but has not been solitary. I am profoundly grateful to my mentor at the University of Hong Kong, Tony Carty, whose endless curiosity inspired and constantly challenged me to improve.

I owe special thanks to my PhD examiners—Jean D'Aspremont, Louis Groarke, and Trevor Morris—for their invaluable feedback on earlier versions of this work. Louis, an inspiring Aristotelian, has particularly influenced my interpretation of Aristotle and supported me in numerous ways beyond the PhD, reinforcing my belief in the broader impact of a virtuous individual. I am forever grateful to him.

I wish to thank my parents and my family in Greece and Germany, who have consistently supported me, embracing my dreams and efforts with love and encouragement. I am deeply grateful to all my dear friends in Hong Kong and mainland China, without whose support I could not have completed this journey. I would also like to acknowledge the University of Hong Kong for its financial support and technical assistance, particularly the Hong Kong University Libraries for providing access to an extensive array of primary and secondary sources. Last but not least, I thank my husband, Sotiris Papanikolaou, and my son, Adrianos, whose unconditional love and support have been a profound source of empowerment, inspiration, and hope.

This work was also made possible thanks to a national scholarship from the Greek State (Greek State's Scholarship Foundation, IKY), for which I am especially thankful. I apologize to all my friends and colleagues who have supported me throughout this long journey whom I have not mentioned by name. Any errors in this work are solely mine.

*The monograph has been funded by the European Union, and particularly the ERC grant RECONCILE, project no. 101171645. Views and opinions expressed are however those of the author only and do not necessarily reflect those of the European Union or the European Research Council Executive Agency. Neither the European Union nor the granting authority can be held responsible for them.*

# Introduction

Arthur Schopenhauer once observed that the greatest obstacle to the discovery of truth is not the illusion created by external appearances, nor even the limitations of human intellect, but rather the force of preconceived opinion. Such prejudice, he wrote, acts like a contrary wind, pushing the ship of inquiry away from the direction in which truth lies, rendering the rudder and sail ineffective (Schopenhauer 1974, 15).

Building upon Arthur Schopenhauer, Alasdair MacIntyre suggests a disturbing hypothesis: an immense human disaster has produced a dystopian world in which the fragmentation of knowledge and disorientation are so pervasive that individuals cannot discern the catastrophic state they inhabit (MacIntyre 2007, 1–5). In this Kafkaesque condition, individuals are surrounded by the textual debris of earlier civilizations yet lack the conceptual frameworks necessary to make sense of them. Academic curricula remain oblivious to the disaster, leaving scholars unable to recognize the profound errors in their comprehension of the world. MacIntyre argues that it is not possible to step outside the prevailing dystopia in order to recognize that what is commonly taken as knowledge may, in fact, be nothing more than a distortion or fragment. He critiques both analytical philosophy and the phenomenological tradition for their essentially descriptive orientations, arguing that neither is equipped to uncover the deeper structural disorder of our intellectual condition (MacIntyre 2007, 2). As a potential corrective, he tentatively proposes a Hegelian historical analysis—one that might reconstruct a hypothetical three-stage narrative: an original flourishing of knowledge, its subsequent catastrophic collapse, and a flawed attempt at restoration (MacIntyre 2007, 3). Yet even this framework, he suggests, is likely out of reach, since the disaster occurred without recognition and thus remains undetected. While MacIntyre's scenario is specifically directed at the degeneration of moral discourse, the metaphor he constructs lends itself to a broader analogy:one that powerfully captures the possible disorientation afflicting contemporary understandings of knowledge.

In dystopian scenarios such as those described by MacIntyre, it is not intellectual weakness or mere false appearances that obstruct the advancement of knowledge, but rather our false convictions. False convictions are sustained by the authority ascribed to traditional bodies of knowledge and reinforced by the bureaucratic structure of modern academic curricula. This institutional framework tends to divorce the history of ideas from the history of political and social change, creating a dualistic narrative in which, as MacIntyre notes, "ideas are endowed with a falsely independent life of their own on the one hand and political and social action is presented as peculiarly mindless on the other" (MacIntyre 2007, 61). This conceptual split is particularly pronounced in legal theory, which remains deeply rooted in the Cartesian dualism of mind and body. Within this framework, law is fragmented into three distinct components: rules, understood as the external expression of norms; norms, viewed as the internal cognitive or moral basis of those rules; and facts, treated as discrete elements of social reality. These facts are not engaged with critically, but are instead processed as raw data to be slotted into pre-existing legal categories and typologies.

That ideas tend to acquire an independent life of their own is also anticipated by Saint Thomas Aquinas in the *Summa Theologica*, where he recalls Aristotle's principle that "the soul understands nothing without a phantasm" (Aquinas 1920, 16). This insight highlights the point that our understanding of the world is always mediated through conceptual images and definitional structures that we ourselves construct. As such, errors and prejudices are less attributable to the phenomena under observation than to the interpretive frameworks we impose upon them. Recognizing this epistemic risk is essential, as is the ability to engage in a mode of reasoning that re-establishes a connection between abstract ideas and the empirical data from which these ideas originally emerged.

The central aim of this book is to argue that it is indeed possible to transcend the conceptual distortions entrenched in legal theory and to diagnose the kind of epistemic disorder described by MacIntyre, through a synthesis of Aristotelian logic and phenomenology. My focus starts off from the problematic and under-theorized, relationship between self-determination and constitutional law. From a doctrinal perspective, this relationship remains poorly articulated: There is little consensus on how these two normative frameworks intersect. The absence of a rule of recognition has given rise to fragmented and inconsistent legal discourse, often supplemented by recourse to political theory, particularly contractarianism, in an attempt to fill normative voids.

In addressing these issues, I begin with a narrowly legal positivist lens and gradually broaden the scope of my induction to incorporate philosophical, phenomenological, and interdisciplinary approaches to self-determination. I contend that the complexity of this relationship exceeds the explanatory reach of legal positivism alone. To grasp it adequately requires a revitalized engagement with syllogistic reasoning, particularly Aristotelian induction, and with Edmund Husserl's phenomenology, both of which may enable the identification of the elusive middle term that logically and normatively links these two bodies of law.

Specifically, I address the prominent syllogism that links self-determination with constitutional law—a syllogism currently mired in logical inconsistencies due to its ambiguous middle term, often formulated around the abstract concept of the social contract. The notion of the social contract, along with other abstract political concepts, is frequently appropriated by legal theory to fill in doctrinal gaps. This appropriation aims to construct, or facilitate, syllogistic reasoning, especially inductive inferences within international law. I will argue that the syllogism in question is compromised by the so-called fallacy of the ambiguous middle, stemming from the abstractness and equivocation intrinsic to the concept of the social contract. To counter this fallacy, I strive to inductively identify a concrete middle term that preserves logical precision. Rather than grounding the discussion in abstract legal or political notions, I anchor it in specific social acts, particularly acts of deprivation that have historically shaped the concept of self-determination. These acts, I argue, transform the right to self-determination from a theoretical abstraction into an actionable legal claim-right.

The methodology adopted in this book is both phenomenological and interdisciplinary, aiming to explore the relationship between the legal principle of self-determination and the concrete material realities it purports to regulate. The analysis begins with a critical examination of self-determination from the standpoint of mainstream international legal doctrine, drawing attention to its internal ambiguities and contradictions. After outlining the logical and structural limitations of this doctrinal approach, the inquiry expands beyond closed legal induction to incorporate rational, psychological, and moral dimensions in an open-ended and integrative manner. This shift can be described as a broadly Aristotelian as well as interdisciplinary "open system" approach—one that moves beyond the confines of legal doctrine to consider the concrete social act of deprivation as a key stressor on collective identity through the lenses of reason, psychology, and ethics.

To this end, the analysis engages multiple disciplinary perspectives, including sociology, social psychology, psychoanalysis, social phenomenology, and critical hermeneutics. It incorporates theoretical frameworks concerning social identity, intergroup relations, collective loss and trauma, relative deprivation, and the psychological mechanisms of aggression and frustration. The psychoanalytic component involves a critical engagement with canonical texts by Sigmund Freud and their major critiques (Freud 1945, 1989), alongside Otto Rank's pivotal contributions to existential psychotherapy and trauma theory (Rank 1973). The discussion of social phenomenology draws on the work of Edmund Husserl and Alfred Schütz, while the critical hermeneutic dimension is grounded in Paul Ricoeur's influential writings on memory, history, and forgetting (Ricoeur 2004).

The next, and indeed most analytical, part of this book turns toward empirical terrains, anchoring its analysis in historical and political realities. It undertakes a focused investigation into selected, well-documented instances of collective deprivation and loss. Rather than attempting an exhaustive survey, which would be impractical given the sheer volume of historical evidence, the aim is to present illustrative case studies that reflect the complexity and diversity of the phenomenon. The chosen examples span from the pre-institutional phase of self-determination involving indigenous peoples in North America, through the geopolitical consequences of the dissolution of the Ottoman Empire with particular attention to Palestine, the decolonization of Nauru, and more recent conflicts such as those in Kosovo and Cyprus. These cases were selected to represent a cross-section of modernity, a period defined by the emergence, institutionalization, and normative development of the concept of self-determination.

The section engages with high-profile disputes involving claims to collective self-determination, drawing upon both domestic and international legal frameworks and incorporating a wide range of secondary sources. The overarching objective is to shed light on how acts of deprivation—understood as powerful triggers of collective psychological distress and trauma—have significantly shaped the development of the international right to self-determination. While deprivation constitutes a concrete social act, it is also a multidimensional phenomenon whose meaning and impact are mediated by cultural variables and conditioned by the normative frameworks of international law and the broader discourse of human rights. As will be discussed, deprivation entails a dual structure: it includes an external aspect, where loss is attributed to an identifiable agent or event, and an internal aspect, which reflects the psychological imprint of loss or trauma on collective identity. This duality may intensify the experience of deprivation, though—as will be argued through sociological analysis—the psychological dimension can exist independently of any direct external cause. What is emphasized in this book are those forms of deprivation that have an impact on the collective identity of a people, for it is in such contexts that the legal relevance and applicability of the right to self-determination become most evident.

The concluding section turns to the moral dimension of deprivation, understood—within both Aristotelian philosophy and one of the oldest bodies of law, namely, tort law—as the domain of corrective justice. It then moves to a logical reconstruction of the international legal syllogism, placing at its center the newly identified middle term: the act of objective deprivation. In developing this framework, I engage Aristotle's account of corrective justice, which rests on the idea that the obligation to repair harm is a natural moral duty. The argument advanced here is that the rationalization of international legal reasoning cannot be accomplished in the absence of a moral and ethical theory. On this basis, I advocate for a paradigm shift in international legal thought—one that integrates syllogistic logic with Aristotelian ethics. Such a shift, I suggest, would enable international jurists to become intellectually conscious of the irrational and morally aware of the unjust.

# 1

# Self-Determination and Constitution from the Scope of Law

## Why Self-determination and Constitutional Law

"A society does not have a constitution. A society is a constituting, an unceasing process of self-creating" (Allott 2002, 79). With this formulation, Philip Allott sought to express the evolutionary and dynamic character of constitutional becoming, a notion that remains intelligible within a legal positivist framework, where the demand for legal certainty is a defining feature. Yet, it ought not to be considered unreasonable to expect that a deeper legal understanding of collective selves would begin precisely from the foundational structures of domestic law, where identity, collective consciousness, and distinctiveness are both constituted and, to a significant extent, constitutionalized.

Despite the apparent logic of this expectation, no serious scholarly effort has been devoted to articulating a coherent international legal theory that would systematically reflect it. With few exceptions, there has been little attempt to explore the normative intersections between constitutional law and the international legal right to self-determination. The limited theoretical endeavors that do exist either gesture toward a presumed connection between these two normative orders or focus narrowly on the ontology, validity, and content of what is termed the right—or principle—of "constitutional self-determination." This scholarly oversight has resulted in significant doctrinal confusion. It has encouraged an uncritical acceptance of a Janus-faced conception of the collective right to self-determination: one that appears to oscillate ambiguously between a constitutional and an international legal character. Against this backdrop, some fundamental questions arise: Why, how, and to what extent is constitutional law relevant to the theory of international self-determination? And through what logical and normative processes does such an expectation emerge?

The present chapter argues that a substantive relationship exists between the international right to self-determination and constitutional law, a relationship that requires careful elucidation. Constitutional law becomes relevant in several theoretical and practical contexts where the international right to self-determination emerges as the central legal issue in dispute. By virtue of the classical doctrinal distinction between the "internal" and "external" aspects of the international right to self-determination, it appears evident that the internal aspect—namely, the right of all peoples to unimpeded access to governmental structures and effective participation in the public affairs of a state—is closely intertwined with the constitutional design of that state. Moreover, there are numerous instances in which national constitutions establish juridical elements that are directly connected to, or overlap with, the international right to internal and external self-determination.

Examples of such constitutional engagement include the constitutional definition of "peoples" for administrative or other organizational purposes;[1] conversely, constitutional silence or explicit denial of the recognition of distinct peoples within a state or federation, as exemplified by the case of the Kurds under the Turkish Constitution; the territorial demarcation of administrative units within states, federations, or confederations,[2] a practice that historically triggered the application of the principle of *uti possidetis juris* in both decolonization and post-decolonization contexts;[3] constitutional provisions explicitly granting a right to self-determination to the constitutionally designated people(s) of a state, federation, or confederation;[4] constitutional affirmations of the indissolubility and inviolability of state sovereignty, often accompanied by prohibitions on secession, whether implicit or explicit;[5] constitutional frameworks providing for a right to secession, including the specific processes by which such a right may be exercised;[6] and constitutional provisions establishing autonomy or other special administrative arrangements for particular regions or peoples. More remotely, one might also consider constitutional provisions related to the protection of minorities, as well as those governing jurisdictional relations among federal units, special administrative regions, and central authorities.

Despite these strong empirical indications, it is striking that few mainstream international jurists have attempted to propose an analytical framework capable of relating, or integrating, these crucial constitutional provisions into a unified legal theory of self-determination. Such a unified theory would hardly be a rhetorical exercise, given that the precise content of the post-colonial right to international self-determination remains profoundly indeterminate; contributions from constitutional law and constitutional legal theory would therefore have been particularly valuable.

The limited and fragmented manner in which mainstream scholarship addresses this relationship is largely attributable to the absence of a secondary rule of recognition that could generate specific rules and legal principles to guide legal scholars and practitioners. As will be further suggested, international legal doctrine provides neither a *lex specialis* nor a *lex* generalis upon which legal scholarship or the judiciary could construct coherent syllogistic reasoning regarding the relation between self-determination and constitutional law. The broader debate over monism and dualism, moreover, remains vague, outdated, and offers no definite resolution to the doctrinal problem at hand.

In contrast to the shortcomings of international legal theory, the constitutional perspective exhibits a relative normative 'maturity' in addressing such lacunae. This maturity is attributed to the existence of concrete constitutional laws and principles, which facilitate constitutional interpretation of, for example, the relations among various state jurisdictions, the interaction between state and federal structures, and the interface between international and domestic legal orders. Reference could be made, for instance, to the principle of subsidiarity, which governs the allocation of administrative competences between national and supranational organs in both European and American legal orders.[7]

It follows from the foregoing that, despite the absence of comprehensive theories, there exist strong empirical indications that constitutional law is highly relevant to the international legal discourse on self-determination. Accordingly, a systemic theoretical approach that bridges these two normative fields remains urgently needed. The next two sections aim to elucidate how legal and political theorists, as well as the international and constitutional judiciary, have thus far approached—or failed to approach—this doctrinal relation or gap.

The first section examines the available legal frameworks, along with the most pertinent case-law. It highlights the difficulties faced by international legal scholars in identifying any existing legal rule or principle that could serve as a foundation for a coherent theory of the relationship. It further discusses the emergence of a peculiar duplicate ontology, namely, the postulation of a "constitutional right" (or principle) to self-determination, which is often presented as existing in parallel to its international legal counterpart.

The second section shifts focus to political theory, exploring how theorists have conceptualized the role of national constitutions in relation to the international right of peoples to self-determination. This analysis reveals that, within political theory, national constitutions are seen as accommodating two fundamentally conflicting poles: state sovereignty and self-determination. These two poles correspond, respectively, to two opposing political philosophies:political realism and social contract theory.

## The Legal Perspective

### The Case-law

The research scope of this book generally focuses on the international rather than the municipal legal treatment of the relationship between the international right to self-determination and constitutional law. This thematic focus is primarily justified by the considerable diversity observed in the constitutional treatment of international law across domestic legal systems. Such diversity includes variations regarding the permissibility or prohibition of direct effect within specific constitutional frameworks, differing theories of "transformation," and notable distinctions between the civil and common law traditions concerning the reception of international customary law. Given the complexity and breadth of these constitutional differences, any attempt to provide an exhaustive account within a single work would be impractical. Nevertheless, the present section incorporates an examination of the legal reasoning employed by both international and constitutional courts. This broadening of the research scope in the case-law analysis is warranted for two main reasons. First, the number of constitutional decisions directly addressing the interplay between constitutional law and self-determination remains remarkably limited. Second, in view of the absence of primary legal sources and the scarcity of relevant secondary literature on the subject, any judicial engagement with the relationship between these two normative spheres is considered particularly valuable for the purposes of this inquiry.

Beyond the general body of case-law addressing themes such as the rights of peoples and minorities,[8] more concrete judicial consideration of the relationship between self-determination and constitutional law can be identified. From the perspective of international law, this relationship was explicitly examined in the International Court of Justice's (ICJ) Advisory Opinion on Kosovo.[9] From the constitutional law perspective, issues of self-determination have arisen notably in: (a) the case of *Texas v. White*, concerning the secession of Texas from the United States; (b) a series of cases brought before the Constitutional Court of the Socialist Federal Republic of Yugoslavia, in which constituent republics challenged the constitutionality of their secession; and (c) the landmark *Reference re Secession of Québec* decided by the Supreme Court of Canada.[10]

From the constitutional perspective, a potentially significant development was the action brought by the Spanish government in 2003 before the Spanish Constitutional Court against the Basque government, which had declared its intention to adopt a new and controversial statute of autonomy for the País Vasco. According to the Spanish central authorities, the plan effectively concealed a proposal for an unconstitutional amendment to the Spanish Constitution. The Constitutional Court, however, refrained from addressing the merits of the case and instead adopted a formalistic approach. It declared the action inadmissible on the ground that a declaration of unconstitutionality would have been premature, given that the proposed statute was classified merely as a preliminary legislative act rather than a formal resolution. Nonetheless, the provisions of the proposed statute (La Propuesta de Estatuto Político de la Comunidad de Euskadi, widely known as the Plan Ibarretxe) manifestly derogated from both the existing Estatuto de Autonomía del País Vasco and the Spanish Constitution, insofar as they envisaged the transfer of significant administrative and political powers from the central government to the Basque authorities (Acierno and Cruz 2005, 687–9).

In *Texas v. White*, the State of Texas filed for an injunction against the holders of federal bonds that had been sold by the Confederate government of Texas during the Civil War. The adjudication of the case raised significant jurisprudential questions concerning the legal status of Texas as a Confederate State and the constitutional implications of secession. The Supreme Court ruled that Texas's secession from the United States was illegitimate, emphasizing the United States' nature as "an indestructible Union." In the words of Chief Justice Chase:

> [T]he perpetuity and indissolubility of the Union by no means implies the loss of distinct and individual existence, or of the right of self-government by the States. On the contrary, it may be not unreasonably said that the preservation of the States and the maintenance of their governments are as much within the design and care of the Constitution as the preservation of the Union and the maintenance of the National government. The Constitution, in all its provisions, looks to an indestructible Union composed of indestructible States.[11]

According to Chase's reasoning, the American Constitution functions in a dual capacity: it protects the self-government of individual States while simultaneously guaranteeing the unity of the Federation. Chase's interpretation is distinctly contractarian, insofar as he considers the consent of peoples—or political communities—to be the sole source of political legitimacy.[12] He also acknowledges that his reading of the Constitution is deeply informed by the American Republican tradition.[13] Furthermore, the Court held that secession could only be lawfully achieved either through a constitutional process, involving the consent of the States, or effectively through revolution outside the constitutional framework.[14]

The Yugoslav judicial experience concerning constitutional law and self-determination began as a constitutional crisis and gradually escalated into a military and humanitarian crisis. During the early 1990s, the Constitutional Court of the Socialist Federal Republic of Yugoslavia adjudicated a series of cases addressing the constitutionality of secession by the constituent republics. The crisis was triggered in 1989 when the Slovenian legislature adopted several legislative acts amending the Republic's Constitution (Budding 2008, 109). One of these amendments declared that Slovenia was part of Yugoslavia but emphasized that this association was based on "the lasting, integral and inalienable right of the Slovene nation to self-determination, which also include[d] the right to secession and to association [with other nations]." Moreover, these amendments stipulated that Slovenia had the authority to determine the procedures through which it could exercise the right to secession (Budding 2008, 109).

The Slovenian incident prompted the Federal Parliament to request the Yugoslav Constitutional Court to rule on the constitutionality of these legislative acts. Although the Court acknowledged that all socialist republics possessed a right to self-determination, which included the right to secession, it held that the regulation of the procedures for exercising that right fell within the jurisdiction of the federal, not the republican, authorities (Budding 2008, 109). According to the Court, unilateral secession by Slovenia would be unconstitutional without the unanimous consent of all Yugoslav republics. Achieving such unanimity would have required the adoption of a constitutional amendment establishing a concrete framework for constitutional negotiations among the republics (Pavković and Radan 2007, 224–5). The Court ultimately found that certain aspects of the Slovenian legislative amendments were contrary to the Yugoslav Constitution, which explicitly provided that the borders of Yugoslavia could "not be altered without the consent of all Republics and Autonomous Provinces" (Budding 2008, 109).

The Supreme Court of Canada addressed a landmark constitutional case on self-determination in its 1998 *Reference re Secession of Québec*. The Court first noted the absence of a secondary rule of recognition under international law and proceeded to examine the issue within the constitutional framework. The federal government's formulation of the question presented explicitly raised the scenario of normative overlap between international and constitutional law:

> In the event of a conflict between domestic and international law on the right of the National Assembly, legislature or Government of Quebec to effect the secession of Quebec from Canada unilaterally, which would take precedence in Canada?

Regrettably, the Court declined to address this question directly, reasoning that "there [had been] no conflict between domestic and international law to be addressed in the context of [the] Reference." The Court concluded, after consulting the amicus curiae, that under international law there was no right to unilateral secession except in specific circumstances—namely, where a people was governed as part of a colonial empire, subjected to alien subjugation, domination, or exploitation, or possibly denied any meaningful exercise of its right to self-determination within the state of which it formed part. In all other circumstances, peoples were expected to pursue self-determination within the framework of their existing state (Turp 2003, 186).

As in *Texas v. White* and the Yugoslav constitutional experience, the Supreme Court of Canada gave primacy to the constitutional framework. It placed particular emphasis on a set of constitutional principles, including federalism, democracy, constitutionalism, the rule of law, and the protection of minorities.[15] The Court rejected the notion that Québec, relying solely on existing constitutional principles, possessed a unilateral right to secede from Canada. Nevertheless, it held that a clear majority vote in favor of secession could provide Québec with the necessary democratic legitimacy to initiate negotiations with the other participants of the federation toward a constitutional redefinition of its status.[16] In the event of a positive referendum outcome, the Court maintained that the other members of the federation would have a corresponding obligation to engage in such negotiations.

In the Court's view, the reconciliation of the legitimate interests of all parties within the federation could only be achieved at the political level, not through unilateral legal action. Much like the decision in *Texas v. White*, the Supreme Court of Canada remained faithful to the contractarian tradition. By emphasizing the continuous process of constitutional dialogue among the members of the federation, the Court effectively invoked the idea of a horizontal *contrat social* among the peoples of Canada as the underlying source of legitimacy for the federal constitutional order. As we will see in the following section, the constitutional reasoning articulated by the Supreme Court aligns closely with Edward McWhinney's Gründnorm thesis, which posits the existence of a revisable federal or social contract as the political raison d'être of federal states.

The absence of a rule of recognition and the resulting doctrinal confusion regarding the relationship between international self-determination and constitutional law also permeated the reasoning of the international judiciary. In its advisory opinion on Kosovo, the ICJ notably avoided addressing the issue of self-determination. The Court adopted a highly formalistic approach, declining to engage with the concept of remedial secession on the grounds that it lay "beyond the scope of the question posed by the General Assembly."[17] The ICJ reasoned that Kosovo's interim Constitutional Framework, being based on Security Council Resolution 1244, possessed an international legal character.[18] Perhaps the most intriguing aspect of the Court's reasoning was its argument that the authors of Kosovo's declaration of independence had not sought to act within the constitutional framework of the interim administration (i.e., as the Assembly of Kosovo), but rather had acted "in their capacity as representatives of the people of Kosovo."[19] Specifically, the Court held that "the authors of that declaration did not act, or intend to act, in the capacity of an institution created by and empowered to act within that legal order but, rather, set out to adopt a measure the significance and effects of which would lie outside that order."[20] Concerning the Serbian constitutional framework, the Court concluded that the constitutional laws of Serbia were not applicable to Kosovo, insofar as the object and purpose of Resolution 1244 had been to establish a temporary legal regime superseding the Serbian Constitution.[21]

The advisory opinion on Kosovo attracted extensive criticism from both the judiciary and international legal scholarship. A central theme among these critiques was the ICJ's reliance on perceived intent, namely its determination that Kosovo's provisional institutions of self-government intended to act outside the given constitutional legal framework.[22] Judge Bennouna, for instance, observed that "[i]n law, it is not merely because an institution has adopted an act exceeding its powers (ultra vires) that the legal bond between the institution and the act is broken. In such case, the institution must be considered to be in breach of the legal framework that justifies and legitimizes it."[23] Further criticism targeted the

Court's narrow interpretive approach, particularly its reluctance to address the normative content of the right to self-determination, the emerging concept of remedial secession, and its outdated application of the principle of "silence" in international law based on the Lotus doctrine. [24]

Legal controversies arose from the manner in which the ICJ chose to address the relationship between international and constitutional law, particularly with respect to Security Council Resolution 1244 and Kosovo's provisional constitutional framework. The primary ambiguity concerned whether the Court ought to have assessed the legality of the Declaration of Independence by reference to both legal frameworks. [25]

Judge Koroma strongly emphasized the territorial integrity of the Federal Republic of Yugoslavia, as affirmed by the Rambouillet Accords, distancing himself from the Court's majority. He contended that the international presence in Kosovo had not created a constitutional legal vacuum and argued that Kosovo was intended to enjoy substantial autonomy and self-government during the period of international civil administration, while remaining an integral part of the Federal Republic of Yugoslavia. [26]

Judge Yusuf, by contrast, drew upon the reasoning of the Supreme Court of Canada in its *Reference re Secession of Québec*. He distinguished between internal and external self-determination and endorsed the view that only in extreme circumstances—and as an *ultima ratio* after the exhaustion of all domestic remedies—might a people whose right to internal self-determination had been denied be entitled to claim remedial secession. [27] Yusuf explicitly classified the removal or denial of autonomy as a breach of the right to internal self-determination. [28] With regard to the relation between international and constitutional frameworks, he maintained that, although Kosovo's interim regime was established through international processes, it did not constitute a mere extension of the international legal mandate. Consequently, the unilateral declaration of independence could only be considered ultra vires in relation to Kosovo's domestic legal order. [29]

The ICJ's decision to pursue a formalistic approach left little room for meaningful judicial reflection on the deeper relationship between self-determination and constitutional law. Drawing from the few and often inconsistent judicial remarks, it becomes apparent that there was considerable confusion among the judges as to the precise role of Serbia's Constitution in the case. After reformulating the original question, the Court opted for a monistic perspective, effectively setting aside the constitutional status of Kosovo. It confined its focus to the legality of the Declaration of Independence under the framework of the interim administration established by Resolution 1244. As previously noted, the ICJ controversially applied a test of perceived intent, concluding that the authors of the declaration did not act within the interim constitutional framework, but rather "in their capacity as representatives of the people of Kosovo."[30]

Unlike the international legal treatment of the relationship between self-determination and constitutional law, the constitutional perspective appears more harmonized, consistently giving precedence to internal constitutional processes and principles. The judicial reasoning in the *Reference re Secession of Québec* reveals an explicit embrace of the contractarian political tradition, as well as a notably favorable reception of the emerging concept of remedial secession. This stance stands in sharp contrast to the traditional Kelsenian dichotomies, particularly the strict exclusion of politics and "value-judgments" from legal reasoning.

The constitutional—or federal—judge typically places strong emphasis on the importance of political consensus among the constituent states or republics, viewing it as essential to preserving the unity of the federation (as exemplified in *Texas v. White* and the *Reference re Secession of Québec*). Like the international judge, the constitutional judge is generally unable to pronounce definitively on the precise content of the post-colonial right to self-determination or on the normative relationship between international self-determination and constitutional law. Aware of the inherent indeterminacy of the post-colonial international right of peoples to self-determination, the constitutional judge, while acknowledging the possibility of *de facto* secession, tends to insist on the necessity of adhering to rigid constitutional processes as the legitimate avenue for the realization of self-determination within the constitutional framework.

## The Legal Theory

Self-determination is both a legal and political principle. If one adopts a strictly formal, legal positivist stance, the appropriate approach to distinguishing between the legal and political dimensions of self-determination would be to anchor the analysis in Kelsen's fundamental dichotomy between legal and political theory. According to legal positivism, jurisprudence emerges as a normative science, in contrast to political theory, which operates as a descriptive account of political relations. Within this framework, it is also crucial to distinguish political theory from politics. Hans Kelsen believed that any serious scientific endeavor must distance itself from politics because "scientific statements are statements about reality as opposed to value statements" inherent in political discourse (Kelsen 1971, 358).[31]

According to Kelsen, only ethics and jurisprudence can be regarded as genuine normative sciences. He maintained that any scientific engagement with politics should be strictly objective, requiring political scientists to examine political phenomena descriptively, without making or presupposing value judgments. Allen Buchanan, for example, a prominent figure in moral political theory, has adhered to this typology by avoiding value judgments and favoring a neutral perspective. He has proposed a structured approach to analyzing the issues that should be considered by those drafting a constitution that includes a right to secession. His work outlines alternative prototypes for such a right and offers reflections on their comparative advantages and disadvantages (Buchanan 1991, 129).

Kelsen's own position on self-determination has been encapsulated in his assertion that the political right to secede is more a statement of will than a right in the strict legal sense. He has argued that this distinction does not resolve the legal question, which would require an institutional act by a competent legal body (Groarke 2004, 98). Nonetheless, Kelsen has acknowledged the possibility of overlap between legal and political domains, emphasizing that, while the science of law must remain distinct from politics, the law-making process itself cannot be entirely separated from it (Kelsen 1971, 365). Within this context, Kelsen has identified three specific points of intersection between law and politics: the extent to which political structures and balances are reflected in national constitutions, the discretionary power exercised by the judiciary, and the role of international disputes. He has argued that national constitutions inherently incorporate both legal and political elements, asserting that no legal instrument exists without an extra-legal purpose, as law is always a means rather than an end when considered from a teleological perspective (Kelsen 1971, 372). From his standpoint, both the international right to self-determination and constitutional law belong fundamentally to the political domain—not only because of these intersections but also because they function as legal mechanisms aimed at achieving political objectives.

From a legal theory standpoint, there are profound doctrinal inconsistencies and theoretical gaps. These are often ascribed to the absence of a secondary rule of recognition—a law or principle guiding legal theorists toward reliable doctrinal inferences. In general, the predominant legal interpretation of the right has been profoundly ambiguous. Legal theory delineates two versions of the right: the so-called international right to self-determination and its constitutional counterpart. Concerning "constitutional self-determination," extant theories reveal the challenge in defining this right or principle and in explicating its connection to the international version. Additionally, the elusive rule of recognition has prompted international jurists to sidestep the Kelsenian legal–political divide, actively integrating elements from political theory to bridge doctrinal voids. Further complicating matters is the ongoing debate over what truly defines a "people" and, by extension, who can justly claim the right.

Shifting focus to international primary sources, common article 1(1) of both the UN Covenant on Civil and Political Rights and the UN Covenant on Economic, Social, and Cultural Rights asserts that "[a]ll peoples have the right to self-determination. By virtue of that right they freely determine their political status and freely pursue their economic, social, and cultural development." Echoing this sentiment, the Helsinki Final Act declares: "[b]y virtue of the principle of equal rights and self-determination of peoples, all peoples always have the right, in full freedom, to determine, when and as they wish, their internal and external political status, without external interference, and to pursue as they wish their political, economic, social, and cultural development."

In the post-colonial era, discussions surrounding the right to self-determination have predominantly shifted toward its internal dimension. Two primary viewpoints have emerged: a conservative-realist perspective that emphasizes state sovereignty and the principle of non-interference, and a liberal-contractarian approach that regards public participation as a fundamental element of any constitutional framework aligned with self-determination.

Jeremy Waldron, representing the conservative stance and drawing on the Helsinki Final Act, argues that self-determination, in its moderate form, simply entails that the people of a country have the right to establish their own constitutional and political arrangements free from external interference (Waldron 2010, 397). In contrast, Antonio Cassese articulates a more expansive interpretation, advocating for substantive public participation. For Cassese, the "free determination of political status" requires that peoples must have the ability to choose their legislators and political leaders without manipulation or undue influence from domestic authorities (Cassese 1995, 53). Cassese further appears to connect the international right to internal self-determination with a specific constitutional framework, particularly emphasizing the rule of law. He suggests that internal self-determination should be interpreted in conjunction with other provisions of the Covenant, especially Article 25, which guarantees the right to vote and civic participation, whether directly or through elected representatives (Cassese 1995, 53).

Edward McWhinney's theory closely aligns with Cassese's contractarian approach. McWhinney conceptualizes self-determination within a broader framework that links peoples' rights, pluralism, devolution, and constitutional amendments to Kelsen's Grundnorm. He views the Grundnorm as a political, extra-legal construct that remains subject to political revision, dependent on evolving societal conditions (McWhinney 2007, 12).

## The Political Theory Perspective

The discourse surrounding the right to external self-determination has attracted substantial consideration from political theorists, particularly those aligned with, or influenced by, moral theory. Moral theory predominantly engages in the articulation and examination of political procedures. Specifically, it focuses on a *modus operandi* rooted in, and stemming from, a political moral assertion. Within the realm of political self-determination, this moral assertion frequently resonates with the call for moral redress in response to prior deprivation or maltreatment. Moral theory postulates that a remedial right to secession inherently ties to the notion of political legitimacy, emerging when the bond between a populace and its governing body dissipates. This theory prominently resonates with contractarian principles.

Considering constitutional self-determination, and particularly the constitutional acknowledgment of secession, moral theory advances a constitutional framework that either endorses the constitutional recognition of secession or offers a rationale that explains the avoidance of codifying secessionist rights. The debate regarding whether integrating secession is morally commendable or whether it curtails or exacerbates secessionist aspirations has been intense among scholars. Cass Sunstein, a liberal proponent of the constitutionalist school, critiques constitutional secession, arguing that constitutionally recognizing a right to secession could undermine the democratic functions of a polity, as it perpetually becomes a strategic consideration in political deliberations (Sunstein 2001, 102). In contrast, Wayne Norman supports constitutional secession provisions in multinational states, arguing that secessionist politics are inevitable (Norman 2001, 98). For Norman, the constitutional enshrinement of secession aligns with the tenets of "multinational constitutionalism" because it offers "a better disincentive for secessionist politics than would constitutional silence on the issue" (Norman 2001, 229).

Allen Buchanan adopts a distinct position, deliberately avoiding discussion on the potential consequences of incorporating secession provisions into constitutional frameworks. In contrast to Norman, Buchanan argues that proposing a model constitutional law that accommodates secessionist claims is impractical, given the diverse historical, moral, and political contexts shaping constitutional traditions (Buchanan 1991, 129). Rather than endorsing a single constitutional model, Buchanan advocates for a structured framework to guide those drafting constitutions that include a right to secession. He suggests alternative models and evaluates their respective advantages and limitations (Buchanan 1991, 129). His approach appears to champion a neutral set of constitutional options, distinguishing between two primary models: a procedural model, which establishes formal constitutional steps for groups seeking secession, and a substantive model, which imposes specific justificatory requirements, thereby prioritizing state sovereignty over secession (Buchanan 1991, 132).

Excluding Buchanan's "more" value-neutral method, the majority of political theories gravitate back to the contractarian-realist binary. Contractarianism mirrors the moral theory of remedial secession, while the realist perspective overlooks the morality dimension and champions the constitutionalization (or not) of secession for stability's sake. The realist view interprets national constitutions as political tools, whereas the contractarian viewpoint posits that a moral secession right emerges when the social contract between the public and its government is violated. Both these schools have interwoven with legal theory, but contractarianism holds a more dominant position in both constitutional and international legal discourse.

At its core, contractarianism serves as a bridge between political and moral theories, grounded in the notion that political legitimacy derives from implicit social contracts between citizens and their rulers. This perspective holds that governance is legitimized through the consent of the governed, making it a foundational concept in both constitutional and international legal discourse. National constitutions function as crucial mediators between the populace and their government, a principle deeply embedded in fundamental assumptions of international law.

Political philosopher Michael Walzer articulates this idea by portraying the state as an inseparable fusion of people and governance, asserting rights to territorial integrity and political sovereignty in relation to other states. He contends that "[f]oreigners are in no position to deny the reality of that union [. . .]. Hence their conduct [. . .] is, or it ought to be, determined [. . .] by a morally necessary presumption: that there exists a certain 'fit' between the community and its government and that the state is 'legitimate'" (Walzer 1980, 212).

From the perspectives of political science and international relations, contractarianism serves as a crucial framework linking domestic and international politics. International relations theorist John Williams underscores this connection, emphasizing its role in shaping both state authority and international interactions (Williams 1998, 20). Contractarianism, while primarily a political ideology, has significantly influenced theories of constitutional and international self-determination. Michla Pomerance, an international legal theorist, praises contractarianism and liberal democracy, highlighting in her discussions on self-determination that democratic systems supported by representative governance and regular elections offer "the surest guarantee of genuine 'self-determination' for all the peoples encompassed within that government's jurisdiction" (Pomerance 1982, 38). She suggests that genuine democracy continuously affirms a right to self-determination, but in its absence "all rule is bound to be experienced as 'alien' sooner or later" (Pomerance, 38). For the West, Pomerance concludes, any other political organizations such as communist regimes are ipso facto alien and incompatible to the internal aspect of political self-determination (Pomerance, 39). In the same vein, Andras Sajo, a judge at the European Court of Human Rights and a notable constitutionalist, perceives a constitution as a multifaceted sociocultural entity, not merely a technical document (Sajó 2005, 243, 245). He proposes that national constitutions possess an element of public participation, a component that grants them legitimacy and a higher normative stature (Sajó, 250). Many legal scholars specializing in constitutional law and international self-determination theory resonate with contractarian philosophy in their academic pursuits, a convergence critiqued by the Critical Legal Studies movement (Carty 1991a).

However, not all scholars concur with Pomerance's liberal inclinations. Brad Roth decouples democracy from public engagement, arguing that constitutional frameworks "need not be democratic or liberal" (Roth 1999, 56). Similarly, Dominic McGoldrick adopts a diluted and non-liberal contractarian viewpoint, arguing that national constitutions inherently reflect public values (McGoldrick

2000, 14). This detachment of internal self-determination from liberal democracy and the assertion that constitutions inherently entail public values echo political realism.

Carl Schmitt, a renowned proponent of political realism, distinguishes legality from legitimacy and critiques parliamentary systems (Schmitt 2004, 4). Schmitt criticizes parliamentarism and Max Weber's famous existential parameter of political legitimacy, namely that people should believe in the law. Nevertheless, Schmitt acknowledges a minimal popular consent element in constitutional orders, arguing that the instinct for political existence should provide for a right to civil disobedience and resistance (Schmitt 2004, 87).

While political realism has woven its way through constitutional and international legal theories (a well-known example is the principle of effectiveness), the international legal mainstream remains predominantly inclined toward contractarianism and democratic ideals (Franck 2000). This leaning is evident in how legal scholarship and constitutional judiciaries have addressed post-colonial self-determination rights and their association with constitutional law. The growing acceptance of remedial secession, either as a forthcoming legal development or an 'emerging' right for oppressed groups, indicates the extensive overlap of moral theory into the international legal discourse on self-determination, now deviating considerably from traditional Kelsenian classifications.

## Challenging the Penumbra

It follows from the above that there is a conspicuous absence of a secondary rule of recognition related to the international right to self-determination and its particular connection to its constitutional counterpart right. The void created by the lack of *lex specialis* and *lex generalis* has prompted international legal scholars to lean heavily on arguments sourced from political theory, especially the contractarian tradition. It is suggested that political philosophy, notably social contract theories, has exerted significant influence on the international legal interpretation of self-determination and its interrelation with constitutional law. As a case in point, legal scholars often endorse the subsidiary use of remedial secession as a *de lege ferenda proposition* (Kingsbury 2001, 90). Remedial secession is part of a broader moral and political theory that argues national governments have a moral obligation to the populations they serve. The incorporation of remedial secession into legal doctrine is partly due to its deep connections with social contract theory.

Similarly, when integrating constitutional law into the international legal theory of self-determination, scholars like Antonio Cassese, Marc Weller, and Edward McWhinney have adopted frameworks from the contractarian tradition. Weller, in particular, views national constitutions as tangible expressions of the sovereign will of state populations (Weller 2008a, 31). His efforts to meld contractarianism with legal positivism and Kelsenian definitions have guided him to deduce that, from an international legal theory viewpoint, the constitutional nuances of self-determination can be categorized merely as domestic political constructs. These can either be freely adopted or disregarded during the routine diplomatic trajectory of international recognition (Weller 2008a, 46). In contrast, McWhinney's extra-legal Gründnorm theory seemingly aligns more closely with the Kelsenian demarcation between legal theory and politics. Yet, the strict nature of this dichotomy restricts legal scholars from addressing the existing gaps, thus rendering them unable to finalize conclusions about the relationship between the two normative frameworks.

In its current state, the law on self-determination has metamorphosed into a complex theoretical blend of legal and political methods, deviating significantly from Kelsen's vision of a pure normative science. Conflicting political traditions have added complexity to international legal theory. The stark ideological divide between contractarianism and political realism is clearly visible in international legal practices. For example, one could contrast Rosalyn Higgins' firm commitment to political realism and state sovereignty with Judge Dillard's strong assertion that it is the populace that should determine territorial destiny, not vice versa (Higgins 1994, 127).

Legal philosophers such as H.L.A. Hart have argued that a certain degree of doctrinal vagueness is not only tolerable but even justified by what he describes as the "problems of the penumbra"—those areas of uncertainty that fall "outside the hard core of standard instances or settled meaning" (Hart 2009, 31). In contrast, Thomas Franck questions this acceptance of ambiguity in legal doctrine. In the context of international self-determination, he suggests that the real issue lies not in inconsistent application, but in the doctrinal inconsistency itself. For Franck, the clarity of legal rules is essential, as it contributes to their transparency and thereby strengthens the likelihood of voluntary compliance by the international community (Franck 1992, 56).

Both Franck and Rosalyn Higgins note that the post–Cold War era has seen a marked rise in what Franck refers to as post-modern tribalism—an upsurge in secessionist claims unprecedented in scale (Franck 1993, 3–27; Higgins 1993). Franck traces the development of normative structures through their historical trajectories and cautions that legal doctrines, if left vague, are susceptible to manipulation and even what he terms "opportunistic creation" (Franck 1992, 5). The international right to self-determination, with its inherent ambiguity, seems to exemplify this troubling dynamic. As Sir Gerald Fitzmaurice aptly observed, "a legal principle, if it is truly one, must be capable of definition and circumscription, and of application in accordance with objective rather than merely subjective criteria" (in Pomerance 1982, 66).

The absence of a clear rule of recognition, along with the resultant doctrinal ambiguity regarding the content and scope of the right to self-determination and its relationship with constitutional law, has found its way into legal practice. In the Kosovo advisory opinion, the ICJ followed a conspicuously formalistic line, declining to address remedial secession by asserting it lay "beyond the scope of the question posed by the General Assembly."[32] The ICJ perceived that, rooted in Security Council Resolution 1244, Kosovo's interim Constitutional Framework bore international legal significance.[33] Notably, the judicial rationale intriguingly incorporated an implicit reference to the Lotus Principle, while emphasizing that the authors of the declaration of independence did not intend to operate within the constitutional framework of the interim administration for Kosovo (specifically as the Assembly of Kosovo), but rather "acted together in their capacity as representatives of the people of Kosovo."[34] The ICJ maintained that "the authors of that declaration did not act, or intend to act, in the capacity of an institution created by and empowered to act within that legal order but, rather, set out to adopt a measure the significance and effects of which would lie outside that order." [35] In the context of the Serbian constitutional order, the ICJ determined that the constitutional laws of Serbia were inapplicable, given that the primary objective and intent of the 1244 Security Council Resolution was to institute a transitory legal regime superseding the Serbian Constitution.[36]

The ICJ's decision to follow a formalistic and ad hoc approach on Kosovo did not allow space for meaningful judicial reflections on the content and scope of self-determination and the concept of remedial secession. Drawing from the few and erratic judicial comments, it appears that there has been much confusion among the judiciary as to the exact role of the Constitution of Serbia in the case. After having reformulated the initial question, the ICJ chose to apply a political realist approach and set aside the problem of Kosovo's constitutional status altogether. It then focused on the legality of secession with respect to the constitutional framework of the interim administration on Kosovo as set out in Council resolution 1244. As noted above, the ICJ applied a controversial measure of perceived intent and concluded that the authors of the declaration of independence did not seek to act within the interim constitutional framework but acted instead "in their capacity as representatives of the people of Kosovo."

Constitutional Courts have offered more tangible resolutions, predominantly aligning with the contractarian tradition. A consensus from a constitutional standpoint dictates that the international right to self-determination should comply with constitutional norms. Prominent constitutional cases concerning self-determination have consistently ruled that secession within federal structures cannot be legitimately executed outside the constitutional frameworks. After the American Civil War, the Supreme Court of the United States in *Texas v. White* decreed in 1869 that Texas' secession was illegal due to the United States' "indestructible Union" nature. The Supreme Court further mandated that for a US state to secede, all States must unanimously consent.

In the 1990s, the Constitutional Court of the Socialist Federal Republic of Yugoslavia addressed a series of cases regarding the constitutionality of the constituent republics" secession. Echoing the *Texas v. White*, the Yugoslav Constitutional Court stipulated that unilateral secession would be unconstitutional without an unanimous consent from all republics. Achieving this consensus would necessitate a constitutional amendment, thereafter laying the groundwork for constitutional negotiations amongst the republics (Pavković and Radan 2007, 224–5). Similarly, the Supreme Court of Canada, in the *Reference Re Secession of Québec* in 1998 acknowledged the *lacuna* in international law and determined that Québec and other Canadian provinces would be legally bound to collectively negotiate a constitutional remedy, should Québec's population express a clear secessionist intent, possibly through a referendum. Consequently, the constitutional perspective has showcased coherence by superimposing a constitutional lens on the international right to self-determination, favoring domestic constitutional processes. The constitutional discourse underscores a consensus-oriented element, resonating with McWhinney's social contract-Gründnorm hypothesis and Weller's proposition that constitutions epitomize popular will. The constitutional viewpoint, having achieved a notable degree of refinement, systematically invokes the social contract notion, enabling the constitutional judiciary to infer principles to navigate self-determination disputes.

One could draw the conclusion that there is a critical need for legal scholars to address the ambiguities surrounding self-determination. This requires a thorough reassessment of the right to self-determination. To date, legal positivism has been inadequate, failing to provide clear principles or rules that could offer definitive insights into the content of the right to self-determination or the normative interactions between international self-determination and constitutional law. This lack of clarity allows for subjective interpretations and enables political theories, subjective 'value judgments,' and contractarian elements to permeate and occupy these doctrinal gaps.

## Notes

1 One may refer, by way of example, to the constitutional recognition of the Basques and Catalans as distinct constitutional entities; the linguistic communities in Belgium; the recognition of the peoples of Sudan and the indigenous populations in Latin America; and the constitutional provisions concerning Quebec and other provinces within the Canadian Constitution.

2 For instance, Corsica has been designated as a collectivité territoriale under French law, pursuant to Article 72 of the Constitution de la République Française of October 4, 1958.

3 The demarcation of the Republics in the Yugoslav Constitution, for example, prompted the controversial application of the *uti possidetis juris* principle by the Badinter Commission on Yugoslavia. See Arbitration Commission 1992. For a discussion of the incorporation of the *uti possidetis* principle into the constitutional law of Latin American States, see Radan 2002, 89.

4 Such general proclamations are typically found in the preambles of most Socialist Constitutions.

5 A constitutional declaration of unity can be found in Article 2 of the 1978 Spanish Constitution, which states: "The Constitution is based on the indissoluble unity of the Spanish nation, the common and indivisible homeland of all Spaniards, and recognizes and guarantees the right to autonomy of the nationalities and regions which make it up, and the solidarity among all of them."

6 Article 39 of the Ethiopian Constitution stipulates that "[e]very Nation, Nationality and People in Ethiopia has an unconditional right to self-determination, *including the right to secession*." (Constitution of the Federal Democratic Republic of Ethiopia, August 21, 1995, emphasis added.)

7 "The powers not delegated to the United States by the Constitution, nor prohibited by it to the States, are reserved to the States respectively, or to the people" (U.S. Constitution, Amendment X).

8 Particularly relevant are: the *Exchange of Greek and Turkish Populations* (Lausanne Convention VI, January 30, 1923, Article 2), *Collection of Advisory Opinions*, 1925 P.C.I.J. (Ser. B) No. 10 (Feb. 21, 1925); *the Greco-Bulgarian "Communities," Collection of Advisory Opinions*, 1930 P.C.I.J. (Ser. B) No. 17 (July 31, 1930); *Legal Consequences for States of the Continued Presence of South Africa in Namibia (South West Africa) Notwithstanding Security Council Resolution 276* (1970), Advisory Opinion, 1971 I.C.J. 16 (June 21, 1971); *Legal Consequences of the Construction of a Wall in the Occupied Palestinian Territory*, Advisory Opinion, 2004 I.C.J. 136 (July 9, 2004); and *Western Sahara*, Advisory Opinion, 1975 I.C.J. 12 (Oct. 16, 1975).

9 *Accordance with International Law of the Unilateral Declaration of Independence in Respect of Kosovo*, Advisory Opinion, 2010 I.C.J. 141 (July 22, 2010).

10 *Reference Re Secession of Quebec*, [1998] 2 S.C.R. 217 (Can).

11 *Texas v. White*, 74 U.S. 700 (1868), Syllabus, para. 5.

12 "The people, in whatever territory dwelling, either temporarily or permanently, and whether organized under a regular government, or united by looser and less definite relations, constitute the state." *Texas v. White*, Majority Opinion, para. 16.

13 *Id.* At para. 17. *See* also Copeland 2009, 868–9.

14 This resembles the international principle of effectiveness. *See Texas v. White*, Majority Opinion, para. 6.

15 *Reference Re Secession of Quebec*, [1998] 2 S.C.R. 217 (Can), para. 49.

16 *Id.* para. 87.

17 Kosovo Advisory Opinion, para. 82.

18 *Id.* at para. 88–9.

19 *Id.* at para. 105.

20 *Id.*

21 *Id.* at para. 100.

22 *See* for instance the Declaration of Vice-President Tomka, Dissenting Opinion of Judge Bennouna, Dissenting Opinion of Judge Koroma and Separate Opinion of Judge *Sepúlveda-Amor.*

23 Dissenting Opinion of Judge Bennouna, para. 44.

24 *See* particularly the Declaration of Judge Simma.

25 *See* for instance Separate Opinion of Judge *Sepúlveda-Amor.*

26 Dissenting Opinion of Judge Koroma, para. 13.

27 Separate Opinion of Judge Yusuf, para. 15–16.

28 *Id.* at para. 13.

29 *Id.* at para. 20.

30 Kosovo Advisory Opinion, para. 105.

31 It is not the intention of the book to engage in the philosophical debate of positivism's value free thesis. It may be noted, however, that Leo Strauss articulated a famous polemic against positivism's fact-value distinction. According to Strauss: "[i]n about the last decade of the 19th century, social science positivism reached its final form by realizing or decreeing that there is a fundamental difference between facts and values, and that only factual judgments are within the competence of science: scientific social science is incompetent to pronounce value judgments, and must avoid value judgments altogether. . . . This means that the ground which is common to all social scientists, the ground on which they carry on their investigations and discussions, can only be reached through a process of emancipation from moral judgments, or of abstracting from moral judgments: moral obtuseness is the necessary condition for scientific analysis . . . The habit of looking at social or human phenomena without making value judgments has a corroding influence on any preferences. The more serious we are as social scientists, the more completely we develop within ourselves a state of indifference to any goal, or of aimlessness and drifting, a state which may be called nihilism" (Strauss 1959, 18–19).

32 Kosovo advisory opinion, para. 82.

33 *Id.*, para. 88–9.

34 *Id.*, para. 105.

35 *Id.*

36 *Id.* para. 100.

# 2

# Breaking Barriers

## Beyond Authority: Redefining Law's Epistemological Paradigm

We saw that the lack of a recognized rule of recognition has led many legal scholars, including Weller and McWhinney, to base their studies of the international and constitutional right to self-determination on social contract theory.[1] This raises an important question: Is this merely an ad hoc academic difficulty or does it reflect a deeper structural inadequacy within the discipline to address ambiguities?

I argue that the challenges are primarily due to the structural limitations of the discipline of law. From both legal and sociological perspectives, there is a prevailing view that law does not fall within the scope of social sciences. This perception stems from the discipline's distinct and narrow focus, which differentiates it from general and legal sociology, and its divergence from standard social science methodologies, particularly qualitative and quantitative research methods. The conception of law as a closed system of knowledge has been widely criticized, particularly for its detachment from broader sociopolitical contexts and its self-referential, autopoietic nature (Kedar 2006, 112; Willke 1991, 108–19). This restrictive view presents law as an epistemologically stagnant discipline—one that contributes little to our empirical understanding of the world and remains largely inaccessible to those outside its domain, with the exception of a few social scientists who examine legal professionals as a distinct social group (Samuel 2010, 295).

Geoffrey Samuel, drawing a parallel between traditional theology and legal reasoning, suggests that both fields operate within an authority paradigm that limits their potential to contribute meaningfully to epistemological debates in the social sciences (Samuel 2010, 169). He argues that overcoming this limitation requires legal theorists to adopt an external and interdisciplinary approach. This orientation becomes especially pertinent in comparative law, where the methodological focus often shifts away from appeals to authority and toward empirical and conceptual analysis more characteristic of scientific inquiry (Samuel 2010, 195). A similar position is taken by Pierre Bourdieu, who insists that a truly 'scientific' study of law must extend beyond jurisprudence to include a reflexive examination of the scholarly practices that constitute it. For Bourdieu, maintaining critical distance from the internal dynamics of the legal field is essential to uncovering the structural tension between formalism and instrumentalism. On this view, an authentic scientific engagement with law demands that legal scholars distance themselves from the normative commitments and professional allegiances that reinforce these opposing tendencies (Bourdieu 2001, 193).

The scientific authority of law is often said to rest on a quasi-logical foundation, one that privileges internal coherence and causal structure. This foundation gives rise to what has been described as a closed logical system (Samuel 2010, 197). Within such a system, deductive reasoning proceeds from a set of commonly accepted legal axioms, thereby grounding the perceived 'scientific' status of the legal syllogism (Samuel 2010, 197). From this perspective, however, it becomes apparent that legal reasoning, while quasi-logical, does not fully qualify as scientific in the strict sense.

Neil MacCormick draws a clear distinction between general logic and the more context-sensitive logic specific to legal reasoning (MacCormick 1978, 40). He maintains that the process of logical justification in law is shaped by the normative framework of the legal system as a whole, rather than by a body of descriptive or explanatory theory (MacCormick 1978, 103). Confronting the limitations of inductive reasoning, MacCormick points to situations in which rules fall short—either due to ambiguities within the rules themselves, contested classifications of relevant facts, or disagreement over the legal grounds of a given claim or decision (MacCormick 1978, 100). In such cases, he proposes turning to what he terms "second-order justification," typically involving the appeal to a more general principle that can be applied to the case at hand (MacCormick 1978, 101). Although this second-order mode of justification bears a resemblance to induction, it does not amount to induction in the conventional sense. It relies on the presumption that unresolved legal questions can be brought into principled coherence through the application of overarching norms—a presumption that cannot always be sustained. MacCormick's account of legal induction, in this light, is ultimately grounded in two key pillars: a commitment to consequentialist reasoning and a drive for systemic consistency and coherence (MacCormick 1978, 107).

Beyond the quasi-logical character of legal reasoning, the complexities of language and the plurality of legal methodologies—from functional to hermeneutical and dialectical—contribute to a multifaceted model of reasoning that resists empirical validation (Samuel 2010, 198). The legal syllogism, far from being a purely deductive structure, is enriched by these diverse elements. It accommodates multiple conceptions of logic and incorporates principles such as systematization, democracy, legal certainty, and the rule of law (Samuel 2010, 198). These features introduce a form of dialectical instrumentalism, which challenges legal theorists to navigate the multiple, and at times divergent, rules within legal systems—rules that, as MacCormick emphasizes, "should [also] make sense when taken together" (MacCormick 1978, 152; see also McCrudden 2010). This intricate configuration marks a clear departure from strictly logical reasoning and compels a return to the foundational questions: should a logic of coherence be prioritized, even if it comes at the cost of rigorous logical rationality? And what standards might enable a meaningful evaluation of such rationality?

Historically, Gottfried Wilhelm Leibniz regarded the precision of Roman jurisprudence as exemplary, drawing parallels between its structure and the geometric method (Oeser 2003, 29). Friedrich Carl von Savigny similarly considered Roman law a model of juridical method, marked by an advanced synthesis of deductive and inductive reasoning. He emphasized how Roman jurists managed to interweave theory and practice: they were seen to grasp each principle alongside its practical application, and to identify in each case the rule that governed it. Their facility in moving between the general and the particular was viewed as a sign of intellectual mastery (Oeser 2003, 129). For Savigny, such qualities underscored the importance of judicial objectivity and the logical application of law through disciplined reasoning (Oeser 2003, 155).

In modern civilian legal thought, this emphasis on formal rationality has evolved from a conception of judgment as *ars judicandi*—the art of judging—toward *mos geometricus*, a method informed by logical formalism (Samuel 2010, 175). Hans Kelsen contributed to this shift by insisting that law, as a normative system, must be clarified and connected through logical means, thus reinforcing its alignment with 'objective' rationality (Oeser 2003, 7; Kelsen 1973, 245). Without such standards of reasoning, legal theory risks devolving into speculative abstraction.

In legal theory, Max Weber was among the first to distinguish between logically formal rationality and mere formal rationality. The former refers to a system in which legal reasoning operates through internally coherent, rule-based logic grounded in the legal order itself. The latter, by contrast, designates a framework that emphasizes the deductive application of established norms without necessarily engaging with their substantive coherence or moral grounding (Trubek 1994, 227). Expanding on Weber's distinction, Jürgen Habermas characterizes law as formally rational insofar as it is organized through analytically precise concepts, deductive rigor, and rule-oriented reasoning (in Teubner 1994, 429). However, Habermas is critical of this model. He argues that such formal rationality tends to become superficial, eroding the internal precision it initially promises. In his view, this reductionism allows legal systems to be instrumentalized—used as mechanisms of systemic self-preservation—while avoiding normative scrutiny by the broader social world, or what he refers to as the "lifeworld" (in Raes 1994, 395). This instrumentalization, he contends, not only undermines the legitimacy of legal integration but also stifles the development of communicative rationality. Over time, an excessive reliance on procedural formality risks producing social disengagement and a fragmented collective consciousness (Raes 1994, 395).

## Arguing for an Open-System Approach to Legal Reasoning

The central question posed is: should the law be guided by more than just a superficial demand for coherence? A primary assertion of this book is in the affirmative. In the realm of legal syllogism—encompassing interpretation, systematization, functionalism, and the invocation of abstract principles—the rules of logic stand out as the pivotal constant. These rules can steer legal syllogism toward rational, or syllogistically sound, conclusions. True syllogistic credibility of law can only be reclaimed by moving beyond the authority paradigm, the closed logic of law, and the constraints of legal formalism and coherence. A self-contained and autonomous legal system cannot be inherently logical. Rather than veering away from logic, legal theorists should lean into classical interpretations of logic to evade mere formal rationality—which may or may not align with logical rationality—and to sidestep instrumentalist perspectives. Law is seen to possess a teleology, being both "natural, in the sense that it has to be found out and is not made by any arbitrary act of will and rational because it is not solely a fact of observation" (Ritchie 1945, 12). The scientific examination of law does not necessarily require stepping outside of it, contrary to the assertions of Bourdieu and Samuel.

Laws of thought and the so-called canons of reasoning (Jevons 1948, 117) function in harmony with natural cognitive processes, standing distinct from societal structures. The question of whether such cognitive laws can be applied to societal contexts, in the same manner they are in natural sciences, sparked a heated debate, with Hume famously introducing the fact-value or is-ought dichotomy. While delving deeply into this debate is beyond the scope of this book, it is worth noting that even 'classical logicians' like John Stuart Mill believed the mathematical inexactness of humanities and social sciences was not synonymous with unscientific thinking. For Mill, "whenever it is sufficient to know how the great majority of the human race or of some nation or class of persons will think, feel, and act, these propositions are equivalent to universal ones. For the purposes of political and social science this is sufficient" (Mill 1950, 313). Similarly, in his *Novum Organum*, Francis Bacon argued that his approach addresses both ethical and factual issues (J. Cohen 1989, 8). Logic is often called the art of reasoning, exploring how we think and the rules for doing it effectively (Mill 1950, 7). This encompasses the formulation of clear definitions, the art of scientific elucidation, classification, varied inferences, syllogism creation, analogy usage, hypothesis formulation, and scrutiny of logical fallacies such as contradiction and non-sequiturs, among others.

It is also essential to differentiate between propositional and syllogistic (term) logic due to their fundamental divergence. In propositional logic, the validity of the premises implies that if the premises are accurate, the conclusion must inevitably follow. From a propositional standpoint, the actual truth or falsehood of the premises is irrelevant to the argument's validity. An argument can be structurally valid yet fundamentally flawed. Conversely, syllogistic logic is term-based. While often sidelined by mathematicians and formal logicians for not meeting the exacting standards of precise sciences, syllogistic logic proves invaluable for inexact sciences—especially those reliant on natural language arguments like law. This is attributed to its capacity to dissect a natural language assertion, diving deep into a sentence to analyze the interrelation of its components. Syllogistic logic scrutinizes the compatibility of a syllogism's constituent terms from a logical perspective, ensuring they function coherently and logically. Here is an example of syllogistic logic: "All days when it is raining are days where the sidewalks are wet; today is a day when it is raining; so, today is a day when the sidewalks are wet." The subject term (S) is "today," the predicate term (P) is "the days with wet sidewalks," whereas the middle term (M) is "rainy days." In formal terms this goes: "All M are P (major premise); all S are M (minor premise); so, all S are P (the conclusion)."

A syllogism is a more fundamental, primitive and direct type of logic that enables us to look at how things and properties are related to one another. There is an added value to this type of logic from the scope of the inexact sciences because the syllogism essentially 'pierces' the procedural character of logical validation and enables the theorist to make substantial evaluations by entering 'inside' the various sentences and their properties. There are also other types of logic such as modal and probability logic, the examination of which, however, is outside the scope of this book. This chapter focuses on the cognitive operations of inductive and deductive reasoning, both of which underpin the structure of the legal syllogism.

Inductive reasoning—often described as the logic of science (Minto 1915)—involves the process of identifying and substantiating general propositions based on particular instances (Mill 1950, 171). It traditionally proceeds from specific observations to broader generalizations, allowing the thinker to move from the known to the unknown. Through this process, one derives universal principles from individual cases, making induction a central method of discovery in both scientific and legal contexts (Jevons 1948, 202; Joseph 1916, 554–65). It is widely regarded as the only logical method by which broad axioms and foundational principles can be formulated. As such, it remains essential to the advancement of knowledge, particularly in disciplines that rely on the articulation of general laws from empirical data (Buchdahl 1951, 16; Mill 1950, 170).

Deduction, on the other hand, embodies logical derivations from the general to the specific, applying overarching principles and axioms to distinct instances. As Mill characterizes it, deduction is the act of interpreting general propositions (Mill 1950, 135). Deductive reasoning "consists in combining two or more propositions synthetically, and thus arriving at a conclusion which is a proposition of truth of less generality than the premises, that is to say, it applies to fewer individual instances than the separate premises from which it was inferred" (Jevons 1948, 210). Deduction adds nothing new but rather organizes or synthesizes pre-existing knowledge. When viewed through the lens of strict mathematical reasoning, deduction is definitive, always guiding us to certain conclusions. This contrasts with induction, which is inherently open-ended due to its inherent leap of probability (J. Cohen 1989, 102).

In real-world scenarios, it is rare for someone to categorize their reasoning as being exclusively inductive or deductive. Typically, both methods intertwine. However, Mill contested a prevailing misapprehension of his era, which suggested that all inference was purely deductive. He introduced the striking logical argument that "all inference is at bottom Inductive [and] that Deduction is only a partial and accidental stage in a process the whole of which may be called Induction" (Minto 1915, 262; Mill 1950, 170). Mill's rationale hinged on the idea that "Induction is a generalization from observed particulars, while Deduction is merely the extension of the generalization to a new case, a new particular" (Minto 1915, 262–3). This perspective on induction as not just deriving general conclusions from specific examples, but as a broader act of direct generalization from particulars, has been also described as expansion (Buchdahl 1951, 16). According to this refined definition, induction includes all forms of rational abstract thinking that contribute something new to existing knowledge (Buchdahl 1951, 16). In certain situations, even a single instance might suffice for a complete inductive inference (Joseph 1916, 400).

While there appears to be no extensive study on the intersection of law and logic, modern logicians like Jonathan Cohen echo the traditional views of Bacon and Mill regarding the scope and application of logic in non-natural or 'inexact' disciplines. Cohen underscores the importance of inductive logic within the Anglo-American, common law tradition. He argues that through induction, a presumption against legal change emerges, and general legal statements "about a particular kind of issue [are] supported by argument from certain past judicial decisions within the pertinent jurisdiction" (J. Cohen 1989, 2). Reversely, the application of established precedent is a deductive process, which according to Cass Sunstein, necessitates the application of analogy, namely an appraisal and deliberation on the differences and similarities between different cases (Sunstein 1996, 77).

In his discussion of *Justice and the Scientific Method*, Clarence Morris draws attention to Benjamin Cardozo's treatment of legal induction, which he connects to the concept of legitimate expectations. Cardozo is portrayed as emphasizing the judicial practice of reasoning from precedent, suggesting that when judges are faced with a range of decisions concerning related issues, they tend to identify an underlying principle that both unifies past judgments and guides their application to new cases. This principle, he argued, naturally extends itself in a coherent and logical manner. Such continuity, in Cardozo's view, grants the principle a kind of normative primacy, grounded in its orderly development over time. He further maintained that adherence to precedent must be the general rule if the legal system is to inspire confidence in its impartiality and consistency. In the absence of alternative criteria, Cardozo saw formal legal reasoning as the primary instrument through which courts could avoid arbitrariness and ensure that justice is administered in a manner that is both predictable and impartial—qualities he regarded as fundamental to the very idea of law (Morris 1960, 940–1).

In the field of international law, inductive reasoning plays a central role, particularly in the formulation of general principles of law and in the development of customary international law. In such contexts, jurists often begin with specific legal concepts drawn from domestic systems—such as *bona fide* or *res judicata*—and gradually abstract from them to formulate principles of broader, often universal, applicability. Georg Schwarzenberger, one of the few theorists to examine the function of induction in international legal reasoning, describes this process as one in which particular principles are successively subsumed under increasingly general categories, until they are ultimately unified under one or several overarching legal concepts (Schwarzenberger 1965, 74). He further notes that this inductive movement may be reversed through deductive reasoning, allowing for specific rules to be derived from higher-order abstractions (Schwarzenberger 1965, 74). In the case of customary international law, for example, legal scholars and practitioners identify consistent patterns of state practice. When such patterns are accompanied by *opinio juris sive necessitatis*—the belief that the practice is legally obligatory—they become recognized as one of the principal formal sources of international law.

Both Max Weber and Jürgen Habermas have argued that, with the exception of the common law tradition, legal academic reasoning tends to rely predominantly on deductive syllogisms, whereby general legal norms are systematically applied to particular cases. This tendency is reinforced by theories such as Hans Kelsen's Gründnorm and H.L.A. Hart's Rule of Recognition, both of which presuppose a hierarchical structure of legal concepts from which clear deductive inferences can be drawn (Kelsen 1971, 221).

In contrast, Georg Schwarzenberger offers a sustained critique of this deductive paradigm in his *Inductive Approach to International Law*, advocating instead for an inductive methodology. He expresses concern over what he views as the inherently eclectic and unreliable outcomes often produced by deductive legal reasoning (Schwarzenberger 1965, 90). In his view, the derivation and application of lower-order principles from abstract norms can be marred by subjectivity and logical inconsistency, frequently resting on speculative reasoning and arbitrary selection from both natural and positive law (Schwarzenberger 1965, 13). Schwarzenberger attributes part of this instability to the ambiguous boundary between *lex lata* (the law as it is) and *lex ferenda* (the law as it ought to be), which he sees as undermining the certainty of international legal deduction (Schwarzenberger 1965, 47, 65). His skepticism extends to natural law approaches as well; he cautions that the process described as "law-finding" within naturalist frameworks often conceals a more discretionary process of "law-making" (Schwarzenberger 1965, 12).

Against this backdrop, Schwarzenberger defends the inductive method as a more empirically grounded alternative. He argues that it offers a safeguard against the subjectivism, speculative tendencies, and opportunistic distortions that can afflict deductive reasoning. According to him, only through inductive verification—grounded in the "law-creating processes" and "law-determining agencies" outlined in Article 38 of the Statute of the International Court of Justice—can legal propositions avoid remaining mere hypotheses, whether derived from deduction, speculation, or intuition (Schwarzenberger 1965, 6, 129). However, despite his strong praise for inductive reasoning, Schwarzenberger does not advocate for its unrestricted application in international legal theory. He holds all logical methods, including induction, to standards of consistency, systemic coherence, and the conventional verification process of "the three law-creating processes of international law" which fundamentally revolve around the principle of state consent (Schwarzenberger 1965, 50, 19). He contends, for example, that unless a "legal principle bears the hall-mark of one of the three law-creating processes of international law, it may not be used for purposes of deducing from it legal rules and obligations" (Schwarzenberger 1965, 50). Schwarzenberger also applies Popper's falsification principle to inductive outcomes, suggesting that even if an inductive conclusion passes the consent verification test, it remains tentative "until falsified by more convincing subsequent evidence" (Schwarzenberger 1965, 96).

In a notable exchange, Dr. C. Wilfred Jenks challenged Georg Schwarzenberger's inductive theory by invoking one of Schwarzenberger's own premises—namely, the centrality of state consent. Jenks contended that both deductive and inductive reasoning must receive validation from "law-determining" bodies operating through "law-creating" processes in order to be recognized as legitimate methods of legal reasoning (Schwarzenberger 1965, 132). In response, Schwarzenberger dismissed this claim as fundamentally misguided. He argued that requiring endorsement for a logical method as a condition of its applicability is both illogical and self-defeating. In his words, such a demand "would not mean to reduce inductive reasoning ad absurdum, but to jettison altogether reason and common sense" (Schwarzenberger 1965, 132).

Yet this position is internally inconsistent. While Schwarzenberger subjects both inductive and deductive legal reasoning to the authority of state consent—treating recognition by legal institutions as a form of inductive verification—he simultaneously insists that this overarching validation process need not itself be sanctioned, on the grounds that it belongs to a separate cognitive category. Taken to its logical conclusion, this argument suggests that logic and rationality, though grounded in universal cognitive norms, are ultimately contingent upon recognition by states, and yet remain somehow epistemically autonomous. Such a stance risks endorsing the validity of even logically inconsistent arguments, provided they have been ratified through consensual legal processes.

This tension reveals a deeper conceptual difficulty. If the very standards of logical validity in international law are subordinated to the principle of state consent, then the rational foundations of the discipline become precarious. What results is a form of legal positivism stripped of its normative coherence, where even contradiction may be elevated to legal validity through institutional endorsement. Such a position is not only philosophically problematic but also undermines the credibility of international legal reasoning as a rational enterprise. Returning to the initial question about the scientific nature of international legal reasoning: adopting either MacCormick's closed logic or Schwarzenberger's inductive method suggests a negative answer, as both approaches prioritize authority over pure logic. A fundamental problem with Schwarzenberger's approach is his assumption that reason requires external validation, despite being a natural cognitive process independent of societal constructs (Jevons 1948, 1). Schwarzenberger overlooks this crucial detail, basing his inductive theory on an extreme anthropomorphism that views states as advanced, rational entities capable of thought and reasoning. Any argument that the logic of international legal reasoning depends on state approval is inherently flawed. Rationality is autonomous and does not rely on external confirmation. Both induction and deduction are natural human reasoning mechanisms used to discover truth. Therefore, it is the language of validity, not approval, that should describe these methods.

## The Rationality Crisis

The present chapter aims to elucidate the complexities of defining self-determination, its scope, and its interplay with constitutional law. I suggest that these complexities stem from both the misuse of inductive reasoning and the pervasive influence of the authority paradigm, which dominates international legal thought by prioritizing state consent in the application of inductive reasoning. We will analyze the dominant international legal interpretations of self-determination and constitutional law, explain why constitutional law has been comparatively more successful at bridging the gap between these two concepts, and discuss the problems arising from the incorrect application of inductive reasoning in international law and the extensive influence of the authority paradigm, which causes a rationality crisis. The rationality crisis extends beyond mere logical inconsistencies; it has significant sociological implications that affect the coherence and understanding in the legal discourse surrounding international and constitutional self-determination. Drawing on Jürgen Habermas' concept of legitimacy and Émile Durkheim's theory of *anomie*, this section argues for a rational revisiting of international legal thinking. To restore its credibility and logical integrity, international legal discourse must adhere to logical rules.

Habermas describes a rationality crisis as a situation where a system's sustainability and cohesion are endangered by conflicting demands. When a system is overwhelmed by more issues than it can address, inherent contradictions arise. These contradictions demand, for the system's survival, a change in the system's structure, or relinquishing elements previously considered integral to its fabric (Habermas 1988, 27). Though Habermas primarily envisioned this concept in the contexts of administration and economics (Habermas 1988, 46), it is proposed here that the idea can also be applied more generally, to situations marked by systemic illogicality.

Habermas argues that even when a discipline has clear gaps in rationality and internal inconsistencies, its scientific credibility can still remain intact. This is because the discipline can function based on a partial understanding of the system and its problems, even if there is not a comprehensive, discursive justification (Habermas 1988, 84). In fact, the prestige of science can coexist with both widespread critique of biases and a new form of specialized, esoteric knowledge (Habermas 1988, 84). This dynamic is evident in the inconsistent theoretical approaches to international and constitutional self-determination. Here, divergent and sometimes opposing perspectives on these rights are masked as 'valid debates' over their meaning and interpretation.

Oren Perez, in his examination of law's contradictions and the formalization of inconsistencies, suggests that these incoherencies do not always signify injustice or randomness. Instead, they can represent a structured openness to varied needs (Perez 2006, 129). When these inconsistencies are perceived as temporary and confined, they are not inherently problematic. Perez believes that for this type of "legitimizing" incoherence to work effectively, three conditions must be met: a diverse and dispersed group of legal observers, viewing the inconsistency as a short-lived occurrence, and ensuring that such inconsistencies are only a minor part of the broader legal framework (Perez 2006, 129).

A crisis in rationality is not always manageable, however. When there is a lack of rationality, it can sometimes lead to a crisis in legitimacy. Habermas believes that there is often a balancing act at play: an ample supply of legitimacy can make up for lapses in rationality, just as increasing organizational rationality can offset shortcomings in legitimacy (Habermas 1988, 93).

The subsequent section delves deeper into how the complex relationship between international rights to self-determination and constitutional law can bring about such a crisis in legitimacy. Paired with the rationality deficit, this leads to a shaking of the foundations of international legal theory. This issue manifests as a challenge to the credibility of international legal scholarship and the international courts and forums that grapple with these inefficiencies. A significant consequence of this systemic issue is a stark mismatch between established norms and the real needs and just expectations of society's members (Habermas 1988, 48). This imbalance can lead to a societal crisis, paving the way for anomic behavior by groups and individuals whose rights remain ambiguous.

Habermas believes that law operates with its own inherent rationality, which is fundamentally a formal logic akin to Weber's ideas. It is structured around analytical thinking, strict deductive reasoning, and rule-based logic (Teubner 1994, 429). In his critique on rationality crises, Habermas delves into how this formal logic interacts with factual truth and the validity of norms. He argues that normative validity is deeply intertwined with empirical truth. However, the true validity of a norm can only be understood by referencing a "rationally motivated agreement" (Habermas 1988, 105). Merely adhering to procedural and decision-making methods is not enough. That is because these methods are anchored in a limited view of rationality that only allows for deductive reasoning (Habermas 1988, 105). Habermas points out that the legal system's procedural nature restricts the quest for genuine truth and reason to simple consistency checks, due to the lack of inductive arguments, which can bring forth new insights and truths. Yet, the real advancement of knowledge requires substantial argumentation—logical reasoning that goes beyond mere deduction (Habermas 1988, 107).

In Habermas' context, there is a significant crisis in rationality when it comes to how international law approaches the relationship between self-determination and constitutional law. The foundation of international legal doctrine leans heavily on a procedural understanding, primarily governed by the principle of state consent. This framework typically permits strict deductive reasoning and occasionally incorporates a superficial form of inductive reasoning, primarily for affirming the system's foundational beliefs. However, this kind of inductive reasoning, as represented by Schwarzenberger, seems more aimed at reinforcing the dominance of state consent in the legal process rather than genuinely expanding legal knowledge. This section aims to step back from this narrow approach and apply more comprehensive logical rules. The goal is to highlight how the dominant principle of state consent influences, and consequently skews, the international legal dialogue on self-determination and constitutional law. But to dive into this analysis, one must first grasp the mechanics and intentions behind logical syllogisms, which are a form of mediate inference.

Inference is a broader idea than the syllogism. At its core, inference is the logical act of deducing implications from a given statement. It is about drawing conclusions, either general or specific, based on prior knowledge or accepted facts. Essentially, if you start with a certain proposition (or propositions) known as the premise(s), through inference, you arrive at a new proposition called the conclusion (Minto 1915, 146). Inference aims to validate a statement based on certain facts or statements that supposedly lead to it (Mill 1950, 109). John Stuart Mill explained this as reasoning in its broadest sense, stating that when you infer or derive belief in a statement because of another statement, you are engaging in reasoning (Mill 1950, 109). Inferences can be immediate or mediate. With immediate inference, you draw a conclusion straight from a single proposition. Mediate inference, on the other hand, involves multiple propositions to arrive at a conclusion (Minto 1915, 102).

A syllogism is a specific type of mediate inference, where a middle term is essential to make the connection. Derived from the Greek words *σύν* and *λόγος*, meaning "together" and "thought," a syllogism involves combining two propositions to form a third, known as the conclusion. As Jevons puts it, if we cannot directly compare two things, we often use a third, middle term, to make the comparison (Jevons 1948, 126). This middle term is unique because it does not appear in the final conclusion, and the syllogism can either hold up (be valid) or not (be invalid). A syllogism is seen as valid if the derived proposition or conclusion is of equal or lesser generality than the initial propositions. Essentially, a syllogism is a tool for deductive reasoning or perfect induction, aiming to confirm that the conclusion aligns with the initial premises.

Logician William Minto pointed out that syllogisms are particularly helpful in handling arguments that are not fully articulated or are elliptical in nature, often called enthymemes. In such arguments, one premise is stated openly while the other remains implied or understood. The syllogism's practical role, then, is to bring these concealed premises to light, making their implications crystal clear and contesting what might otherwise go unquestioned.

By fundamental syllogistic principles, a syllogism always comprises three terms. Taking the international legal arguments by Weller and McWhinney on the connection between self-determination and constitutional law, and breaking them down into a syllogism, we get:

P1: In federal or polyethnic states, the international right to self-determination (S) is [affected/defined by all] serious disruptions of constitutional rights (M).
P2: In federal or polyethnic states, [all] serious disruptions of constitutional rights (M) are violations of social contracts (P).
C: In federal or polyethnic states, the international right to self-determination (S) is [affected/defined by] violations of social contracts (P).

In the realm of informal logic, the syllogism stands as procedurally valid. Both Weller and McWhinney apply the structure "All S is M; all M is P; hence, all S is P." This means, if every S is an M and each M is a P, then all S must be P. Both theorists employ the social contract idea to define their middle term (M), though they differ in crafting their arguments.

For McWhinney, while he does not explicitly mention the social contract, its presence is implied through his reference to the "power-sharing arrangement" among the Serbs, Croats, and Slovenes (McWhinney 2007, 11). Also, seemingly following the orthodox Kelsenian dichotomies and classifications, his syllogism operates outside the international law framework, instead situating itself within foundational norms and political theory. Even if the syllogism appears valid on the surface, McWhinney does not endorse the conclusion due to the operation of the authority paradigm, arguing that the syllogism is extra-legal and thus inadmissible from the scope of international legal theory (McWhinney 2007, 12).

Weller, conversely, directly engages with the social contract idea (M. Weller 2008, 31). He positions the authority paradigm at the syllogism's conclusion, leading to this assertion: the right of self-determination for peoples in federal or multiethnic states can be influenced by constitutional arrangements (termed "constitutional self-determination"). Yet, he argues, this "constitutional self-determination" is not an independent right. Instead, it is a supporting ground for entities seeking to secede. Weller believes that while international law might acknowledge constitutional law, constitutional self-determination is a conservative doctrine that does not "purport to broaden the scope of the right to self-determination is international law" (M. Weller 2008, 40).

It is worthwhile here to consider the constitutional viewpoint. The Supreme Court of Canada, for instance, implicitly acknowledged the existence of a horizontal social contract among the peoples of Canada and placed particular emphasis on the "continuous process" of constitutional discussion among the members of the Federation (Oliver 2000, 81). Even though the prevailing constitutional legal syllogism also draws upon the social contract, its conclusions are 'more' sound since they are not exposed to the authority paradigm, namely state consent.

Weller's and McWhinney's arguments highlight the distinction between logical validity and legal admissibility in international legal theory. Specifically, a logically valid point can be (a) either accepted or rejected legally if it is extra-legal (i.e., outside the realm of existing law); (b) either tenable or untenable, if it contravenes law; and (c) either endorsed or dismissed, if it is rejected or modified according to the authority paradigm of international law.

In international legal theory, we often encounter enthymemes—syllogisms with assumed and suppressed minor premises—and invalid syllogisms, which are deductions that break basic logical or reasoning rules (Jevons 1948, 127). For example, in their indirect discussions on constitutional self-determination, both James Crawford and Antonio Cassese suggest that constitutional guidelines may potentially set boundaries on the international right to either internal or external self-determination (Cassese 1995, 265; Crawford 2006,

**Table 2.1** Validity and Approval in Law, Logic, and Politics

| Law/Politics | Law | Logic | Authority Paradigm |
|---|---|---|---|
| Admissible | Tenable | Valid | Approved |
| Inadmissible | Untenable | Invalid | Unapproved |

145). The suppressed minor premise is that there is an international right to external self-determination that can be constitutionally suppressed. While their syllogism holds up logically, with the conclusion fitting the given premises, both their implied premise and the resultant conclusion are legally flawed because international law does not recognize a post-colonial right to secession that can be limited in this way.

Theorists like Javaid Rehman and Markuu Suksi posit that the international right to self-determination finds expression within constitutional frameworks. Their argumentative style is immediate, as they do not use a mediating element (middle term) to connect international self-determination with constitutional law. Both believe that international self-determination acknowledges constitutional stipulations regarding the definition of peoples, autonomy, and federal structures. Rehman emphasizes the intertwined nature of these two legal realms, stating that "constitutional arrangements can substantially influence international law" (Rehman 2000, 286). He further suggests that the international right to self-determination takes concrete form within constitutional structures. Markku Suksi takes a more assertive stance. He believes that while international law does not explicitly grant a right to autonomy, establishing autonomous regions at the national level can indicate an acknowledgment of the right to self-determination. Moreover, Suksi believes that a country might be legally bound "not to worsen or abolish" its national laws on self-determination without the approval of the affected peoples (Suksi 1998, 164).

Rehman and Suksi both argue that there is a mutual interplay, reliance, and even synergy between self-determination and constitutional law. They suggest that international self-determination is realized through constitutional stipulations, and altering constitutional frameworks regarding autonomy might breach the international rights to self-determination of the impacted peoples. However, both these conclusions are flawed both legally and logically. Here is why: Rehman and Suksi employ what is known as immediate inference, drawing conclusions about the relationship between self-determination and constitutional law without introducing a connecting or middle term. Traditional deductive reasoning is syllogistic, requiring three terms and two premises to validate a conclusion. Though there are exceptions where a conclusion can be deduced just by combining two propositions without a mediating term, this only holds when there is an evident relationship between the two terms or propositions. For immediate inference to be applicable, the terms or propositions in question must be directly relatable or comparable.

To compare two different entities, either qualitatively or quantitatively, there must be a relationship between them. John Stuart Mill defines "relation" as a characteristic attributed to an object, involving other entities beyond just itself and the observer (Mill 1950, 53). This relational attribute can be described in various ways: one thing resembling another, one thing differing from another, one being near or far from another, one preceding or following another, and so forth. Unique relational attributes, like likeness or unlikeness, causality, sequence, and simultaneity, are considered distinct in their own right (Mill 1950, 55). For Mill, the foundation of any relationship or comparison is rooted in the Aristotelian idea of "*fundamentum relationis*" (Mill 1950, 53). This concept suggests that when two entities are deemed related, their relationship hinges on an underlying quality, fact, or phenomenon present in both, consistently or under specific conditions. Taking the debtor-creditor relationship as an example, Mill explains that the basis of their relation lies in the thoughts, emotions, and intentions (either actual or potential) of the involved parties or other related individuals (Mill 1950, 54). Resemblance itself is an emotional response, a conscious recognition by the observer. All notions of likeness, difference, and similarity are, at their core, perceptions of relational resemblance or feelings. At times, the similarity between two relationships is termed an analogy (Mill 1950, 56). This perception of resemblance can vary in intensity, ranging from indistinguishable (or identical) to just faintly similar. The question is whether there is a shared attribute between the right to self-determination and constitutional law. This could be a relationship based on similarity, cause and effect, sequencing, or any other foundational relation (*fundamentum relationis*) from which an analogy or comparison can be drawn. But, are there commonalities or foundational relations between these two notions?

Upon reflection, one sees that self-determination and constitutional law are not tangible facts or physical entities for comparison. They are legal ideas; concepts; norms; human artifacts. Applying concepts like similarity, causality, or sequencing to these abstract ideas is not straightforward without a deeper phenomenological examination. While one might simplistically argue that they are linguistically related because both pertain to the rights or principles guiding the self-determination of peoples, this linguistic connection does not constitute a foundational relationship 'inherent' in their nature. One could counter by suggesting a potential normative hierarchy or order between them, especially if one adopts a monistic perspective where international self-determination denominates the constitutional right. Yet, this does not align with the arguments of Rehman and Suksi, who suggest that international self-determination is realized through constitutional measures. Hence, even if these concepts were comparable directly, the conclusions drawn would remain flawed.

While there are compelling empirical signs that self-determination and constitutional law intersect—both addressing similar patterns of political rights and the rightful expectations of people concerning self-governance, autonomy, non-discrimination, political participation, and access to governmental frameworks—a mere 'intuition' of this overlap is not sufficient for a concrete conclusion. The international right to self-determination and constitutional law, being distinct concepts, cannot be directly compared. Using immediate inference to delineate their relationship is not valid since there is no evident foundational relationship, a *fundamentum relationis*, to rely on. Instead, to build a cogent argument, it is crucial to use a middle term for crafting a valid deductive syllogism.

In such a syllogism, three elements are essential: the ideas of self-determination and constitutional law, and a third, the middle term. For Weller, this bridging concept is an expansive view of the social contract. McWhinney, similarly, sees this middle term as the social contract, but conceives it in the form of the foundational norm or Gründnorm. Even though neither Weller nor McWhinney directly invoke this concept, it emerges from their view of national constitutions as the adaptable, institutional manifestations of a people's will (M. Weller 2008, 31; McWhinney 2007, 12). The prevailing inclination to root the middle term in the social contract theory is understandable given that both international legal and political theories, especially the liberal tradition, spring from a shared philosophical ancestry (Carty 1991a). But is the social contract theory truly a fitting definition for the middle term?

For a syllogism to be sound, its middle term must be unambiguous (Jevons 1948, 127). Furthermore, all three terms in the syllogism should have clear and singular meanings to prevent equivocation—a significant semi-logical fallacy, often called the fallacy of the ambiguous middle when found in the middle term (Jevons 1948, 171). The social contract concept, unfortunately, is inherently vague and fluid. While it serves as a political metaphor representing the adaptable political equilibrium among diverse groups in federal contexts—and the implied understanding that this equilibrium would persist unless renegotiated—it is not solid enough.

For clarity and accuracy, all terms in a syllogism should be clearly and properly defined (Minto 1915, 84). A concept is considered scientifically sound when it is unambiguously outlined. As noted by logician H. W. B. Joseph, a "definition should not be expressed in obscure or figurative language" (Joseph 1916, 114). While metaphors like 'social contract' or 'implicit agreement' can guide toward a certain comprehension of a topic, they do not convey direct understanding. They may suggest or lead up to a right understanding of a subject, "but do not directly express it" (Joseph 1916, 115). In reality, this challenge of ambiguity and equivocation seems to plague many international legal syllogisms regarding self-determination and constitutional law. This doctrinal muddle, seen in the frequent swapping of terms like 'right to' and 'principle of' regarding self-determination, underscores the pressing need for sharper and more consistent definitions.

From our exploration in the first chapter, it is evident that there is no established legal rule or principle elucidating the connection between the international right to self-determination and constitutional law. Even with this legal void, international legal theorists have formulated theories, but these are riddled with logical inconsistencies. This arises from the absence of a middle term in international legal doctrines, crucial for constructing valid deductive syllogisms. Invalid syllogisms; logical fallacies; phenomena of equivocation; enthymematic syllogisms with suppressed, untenable premises and the submission of inductive and deductive reasoning to the distorting effect of the authority paradigm have produced an obscure legal discourse on the relation between self-determination and constitutional law. This discourse is a far cry from rationality and in fact manifests a deep-seated rationality crisis, echoing Habermas' sentiments. Nonetheless, theories should coherently align general and specific statements without contradiction (Oeser 2003, 45). They should aim to be as objective, methodical, and precise as possible. Only through rigorous definition and clarification of terms and concepts can valid deductive syllogisms be constructed.

Legal principles are constructed from concepts, which are inherently abstract. Rather than pointing to a singular, specific object, they encompass a multitude of similar entities (Oeser 2003, 64). Logic's role lies in assisting theorists to dispel ambiguity, refine these abstract notions, clearly define terms, and organize them coherently (Minto 1915, 48). While the syllogistic method is inherently synthetic or deductive, inspecting individual terms and concepts calls for a process of analysis, which is inherently inductive (Jevons 1948, 207). To address the prevailing rationality crisis, international legal experts need to move beyond the authority paradigm. They must revisit the foundational premises governing the international legal perspective on the connection between self-determination and constitutional law. To discover the pivotal middle term, they need to lean on inductive reasoning.

According to Mill, induction revolves around observation and elucidation (Minto 1915, 15). Jevons perceives it as a knowledge-acquiring discovery method, wherein overarching conclusions emerge from aggregating and scrutinizing specific instances (Jevons 1948, 202–3). However, induction in non-exact sciences or disciplines is not solely formal, numerical. As will be further explained in the following sections, it resonates with Aristotle's perspective on induction (*ἐπαγωγή*), which embeds an element of insight.

## The Legitimation and Anomic Crisis

This section aims to demonstrate how the rationality crisis in international law not only persists but also evolves into a crisis of legitimation and *anomie*.

Habermas' concept of legitimation is distinct from the traditional political notion of state legitimacy. State legitimacy typically addresses philosophical and political questions about the basis and necessity of a state's legal order. It seeks to understand why and how citizens acknowledge, or should acknowledge, the supreme authority of the state (P. Groarke 2004, 31–127). It further probes whether the relationship between citizens and governing bodies is defined by coercive or consensual norms, and if the criteria for legitimacy include specific constitutional frameworks, democracy, the rule of law, and other related principles (Roth 1999, 37–73).

Habermas' notion of legitimation stands distinct from this traditional political understanding. Habermas' concept carries a systemic implication. In the face of a legitimation crisis, the legitimizing apparatus struggles to sustain the necessary degree of loyalty from the masses, especially when implementing economic system directives (Habermas 1988, 46). Though Habermas primarily emphasizes the economic facets, I suggest that his theoretical framework is versatile, rendering it applicable across diverse scenarios. He notably ties the idea of legitimation deficits to the administrative inability "to maintain or establish effective normative structures to the extent required" (Habermas 1988, 47). Expanding upon the term "administration," it can be inferred to include various authoritative bodies, extending beyond just governmental agencies to encompass the judiciary, academia, international legal entities, and other analogous institutions.

In Habermasean terms, a legitimation crisis occurs when a system experiences alterations that its current legitimation capacity cannot accommodate (Habermas 1988, 48). When there is a deficit in rationality, the system's need for legitimation or systemic justification escalates (Habermas 1988, 58). However, if there is a rationality surplus, it can offset the need for immediate legitimation and vice versa (Habermas 1988, 93). For Habermas, a system should strive to make itself as independent as possible from the need for constant legitimation (Habermas 1988, 69). In international law, this is accomplished through the "mediatisation" of law, a mechanism that insulates the system from continuous scrutiny, thereby providing a degree of functional autonomy (Raes 1994, 395). This autonomy is achieved by imposing a form of strategic, procedural rationality. However, this often leads to the "colonization" of the lifeworld, creating social forms that are alienated and pathological (Raes 1994, 395).

Although law as a medium is significantly detached from permanent questioning, "law as an institution requires a legitimation of legal norms and procedures by reference to valid authority and consensual rightness of decisions" (Raes 1994, 395). Sometimes, a legitimation crisis can be managed by absorbing it into a broader imperative of system maintenance (Habermas 1988, 58). However, this is not always effective, particularly when the legitimation issues cannot be ignored without jeopardizing the satisfaction of legitimate societal needs (Habermas 1988, 58). In such cases, significant revisions to the normative structures may become essential. In other words, a legitimation crisis becomes acute when neither a surplus of rationality nor systemic imperatives for maintenance can adequately address the issue. When this happens, substantial changes are often required to bring the system's normative structures in line with the demands for legitimation (Teubner 1994, 443).

In the context of international law, a rationality crisis evolves into a legitimation crisis when judicial bodies and the legal academia fail to provide satisfactory solutions to legal problems based on justifications that meet three criteria: (a) they go beyond the specifics of an individual case, (b) they are inherent to the legal system, and (c) they are logically structured, adhering to specialized rules of deductive reasoning (Trubek 1994, 227). The absence of these elements fosters what is referred to as "modern state interventionism" (Teubner 1994, 443). Here, interventionism can be interpreted broadly to encompass not just state or governmental actions but also judicial and academic forms of intervention.

The advisory opinion on Kosovo serves as an illustrative example of both a rationality and a legitimation crisis in Habermasean terms. In this case, the ICJ resorted to judicial interventionism because it was unable to construct a valid, and therefore legitimate, deductive syllogism. The court failed to offer a form of legal justification that could generalize beyond the unique situation of Kosovo to address the broader issues of self-determination and remedial secession. In other words, the ICJ could not produce a universally applicable legal rationale, thus failing to meet the criteria that would avert a legitimation crisis. This shortfall not only undermines the authority of the court but also poses broader questions about the legitimacy of the international legal system in handling complex issues like self-determination.

The ICJ's advisory opinion on the legality of unilateral declarations of independence reveals a rationality deficit in the judicial syllogism. The Court indicated that there is no general rule in international law—either in treaty or customary law—that forbids declarations of independence. It stated, "[i]n no case [. . .] does the practice of States as a whole suggest that the act of promulgating the declaration was regarded as contrary to international law" (para. 79).

Judges Yusuf and Simma took issue with the Court's reasoning, arguing that relying on the Lotus Principle is outdated and that silence in international law should be interpreted more expansively. Judge Simma, specifically, criticized the Court's formalistic approach. According to him, the Lotus Principle means that "restrictions on the independence of States cannot be presumed because of the consensual nature of the international legal order" (Declaration of Judge Simma, para. 2). He took issue with the Court's equation of "the absence of a prohibition with the existence of a permissive rule," pointing out "the possibility that international law can be neutral or deliberately silent on the international lawfulness of certain acts" (Declaration of Judge Simma, para. 3).

Judge Yusuf, in his Separate Opinion, diverged from the ICJ's formalistic approach by suggesting that the legality of a declaration of independence is not the focal point. According to him, "since a declaration of independence is not per se regulated by international law, there is no point assessing its legality, as such, under international law" (Separate opinion of Judge Yusuf, para. 5). However, he goes further to state that what matters is "what the declaration of independence implies and the claim it expresses to establish a new State" (para. 5). Judge Yusuf's nuanced approach looks at the larger context, noting that certain claims to statehood are encouraged in international law, particularly in cases involving decolonization or alien subjugation. He specifically refers to Southern Rhodesia and Katanga in the 1960s to illustrate claims that are discouraged by international law (para. 5). This reflects an embrace of the concept of remedial secession, which suggests that international law should support a claim to external self-determination under exceptional conditions such as discrimination or persecution targeted against a racially or ethnically distinct group (paras. 11, 16). Judges Sepúlveda-Amor and Trindade also agreed with Judge Yusuf's perspective, particularly on the point that the Court should have explored the concept of remedial secession (Separate Opinion of Judge Sepúlveda-Amor, para. 35).

In analyzing the ICJ's judicial syllogism on the legality of unilateral declarations of independence, it is clear that the problem is not solely a matter of interpreting the silence in international law, as guided by the Lotus Principle. Instead, the issue is a logical fallacy called equivocation, which occurs when a word or phrase is used in two different ways within the same argument. The syllogism presented by the ICJ can be broken down as follows:

P1: All that is not forbidden to states is allowable (for states).
P2: All declarations of independence are not forbidden to states.
C: All declarations of independence are allowable (for non-state actors).

The court's conclusion is flawed not because it overreaches the scope of its premises, but because it does not logically follow from them. The error arises from a logical fallacy known as equivocation, where the same term is used inconsistently, leading to a misleading argument. In this case, the term "what is allowable" is ambiguous; it refers to "states" in the first premise and to "non-state actors" in the conclusion. This inconsistency is similar to saying, "an elephant has a trunk; a car has a trunk; therefore, an elephant must be a car," which is clearly fallacious.

Additionally, the focus of judicial critique on the interpretation of silence in international law obscures this logical flaw. The Court seemingly intended to use inductive reasoning to establish whether there exists a negative custom or prohibitive law regarding declarations of independence. However, the Court stopped short, focusing only on the absence of state practice (or silence) without addressing the *opinio juris* aspect that is crucial for the formation of customary international law. This is insufficient because the mere absence of state action does not necessarily equal lack of a prohibitive rule. Had the Court examined the missing element of *opinio juris*, it might have reached a different conclusion. Therefore, the Court's conclusion is not only logically flawed but also lacks a comprehensive legal foundation, as the lack of state practice alone is insufficient to definitively conclude the presence or absence of customary international law and does not constitute a formal source of international law. This contributes to what is described as a rationality crisis and arguably a legitimation crisis in international law.

The Court's handling of Kosovo's constitutional status further muddles the already complex relationship between international and constitutional law. Specifically, the issue lies in reconciling Kosovo's provisional constitutional framework with the Yugoslav Constitution it replaced. The Court argued that:

> resolution 1244 (1999) and UNMIK regulation 1999/1 [. . .] had the effect of superseding the legal order in force at that time in the territory of Kosovo and setting up an international territorial administration. For that reason, the establishment of civil and security presences in Kosovo deployed on the basis of resolution 1244 (1999) must be understood as an exceptional measure relating to civil, political and security aspects and aimed at addressing the crisis existing in that territory in 1999. (Kosovo advisory opinion, para. 97)

However, Security Council Resolution 1244 reaffirms the territorial integrity and sovereignty of the Federal Republic of Yugoslavia, while simultaneously authorizing the establishment of an international civil presence in Kosovo. This interim administration was mandated to facilitate substantial autonomy for the people of Kosovo within the framework of Yugoslav sovereignty. Its purpose was to provide transitional governance, oversee the development of provisional democratic self-governing institutions, and ensure conditions conducive to a peaceful and normal life for all inhabitants of Kosovo. The Security Council Resolution 1244 makes explicit that the establishment of an international civil presence in Kosovo was intended as a temporary measure. It did not aim to abrogate the constitutional order of the Federal Republic of Yugoslavia on a permanent basis. Therefore, even accepting the view expressed in the Kosovo Advisory Opinion—namely, that the declaration of independence was not issued by the Provisional Institutions of Self-Government and fell outside the legal framework established for Kosovo during the interim administration (para. 103)—it would be inaccurate to assert that Kosovo existed in a legal vacuum. This is particularly evident given that the constitutional order of Yugoslavia was never formally or definitively dismantled. As Judge Tomka observes in his Declaration, the United Nations, in establishing an interim administration, effectively assumed responsibility for the governance of a territory that remained, in legal terms, part of Yugoslavia (Declaration of Judge Tomka, para. 24).

The Kosovo advisory opinion, therefore, appears to be flawed due to an irrational line of reasoning underpinned by an invalid deductive syllogism—a lapse that significantly influenced the opinion's conclusion. Beyond this issue of rationality, the Court also fell short in addressing the legal question at hand through the application of impartial legal criteria that would be relevant beyond the specific case. Instead, the Court introduced a novel criterion based on perceived intent, opting for a makeshift legal solution tailored to the case. This approach can be seen as judicial interventionism, especially when viewed through a Habermasean lens.

As mentioned above, the existence of rationality deficits underscores the need for legitimation, which means that a legal system must provide a compelling justification for any deviations, exceptions, or ad hoc solutions that cannot be explained within its existing normative framework or by invoking a general principle like a state of emergency. In the case of the Kosovo advisory opinion, this rationality deficit is neither offset nor rectified by a surplus of legitimation. Rather, it metastasizes into a crisis of legitimacy precisely because the Court's ad hoc opinion regarding Kosovo cannot be justified by existing international legal standards or any legitimate exception. The Court's ad hoc solution for Kosovo "cannot be met by the existing supply of legitimation" (Habermas 1988, 48)

In his Declaration, Judge Tomka explicitly criticized what he viewed as a lack of legal legitimacy and an unwarranted exercise of judicial interventionism by the International Court of Justice. He observed that, as of February 17, 2008, the legal regime governing the United Nations' administration of Kosovo had not undergone any formal change. What had shifted, in his view, were the political circumstances and factual realities on the ground. Judge Tomka argued that the majority of the Court allowed these political developments to influence their legal reasoning, thereby departing from the principle of judicial restraint and failing to adhere strictly to the applicable legal framework (Declaration of Judge Tomka, para. 35).

Both the judiciary and academic circles grapple with gaps in rationality, particularly concerning the legal theory of self-determination. This confusion often gets a pass under the guise of academic pluralism, which not only tolerates but also perpetuates these inconsistencies and gaps in legitimacy. The challenges faced by legal scholars and the judiciary in logically formulating arguments about issues like remedial secession or the relationship between international self-determination and constitutional law eventually contribute to a wider cultural crisis. This crisis manifests as international *anomie*, or a state of normlessness.

According to Habermas, a cultural crisis occurs when there is a disconnect between the bureaucratic and professional systems and the actual needs and expectations of society's members (Habermas 1988, 48). This becomes a foundational, systemic contradiction when the core principles of a system perpetually pit individuals and groups against each other with mutually exclusive claims and intentions. Such systems are desperately in need of ideological backing and legitimacy to mask this inherent asymmetry and conflict (Habermas 1988, 27). The core contradiction—essentially, the incompatibility of different groups' expectations—needs to be suppressed and hidden. Only when this systemic imbalance comes into the open, in the form of direct confrontations and conflicts, is it fully recognized and acknowledged.

In the realm of self-determination, there is a glaring mismatch between the legal framework and the legitimate expectations of peoples. Both the academic community and international courts have struggled to clarify the relationship between self-determination and constitutional law, leaving a cloud of uncertainty and skepticism. This makes people question whether international law can even address issues like post-colonial claims to self-determination. Meanwhile, discussions about remedial secession are gaining traction as a prospective approach in international law. This heightens public expectations and gives the impression that there are formal legal pathways available, even though the international judiciary has not officially confirmed or refuted this in cases like the Kosovo advisory opinion. This leads to a cultural crisis: there is a disconnect between academic and judicial discussions about self-determination and what the public actually expects, or claims, as their right. Despite plenty of rhetorical declarations, there is a lack of concrete guidelines—either as legal rules or established theories—that can be used to assess the legitimacy of these diverse claims and expectations.

This legal ambiguity appears to be intentional, serving to obscure a fundamental contradiction in international self-determination theory: the sweeping assertion that all peoples possess the right to self-determination. This broad claim raises collective expectations that ultimately prove incompatible with two crucial elements: firstly, the foundational legal principle of state sovereignty, and secondly, the divergent interests and expectations of other communities.

The concept of *anomie*, a state of normlessness and de-regulation, becomes crucial in this context, causing what can be termed an anomic crisis. Émile

Durkheim introduced this concept in his seminal work, *Suicide*, to describe situations where there is a large gap between societal standards and people's expectations. Though Durkheim initially linked *anomie* to industrialization, the theory is widely applicable to various social, legal, and political arenas, making it particularly relevant for legal theory:

> At the very moment when traditional rules have lost their authority, the richer prize offered these appetites stimulates them and makes them more exigent and impatient of control. The state of de-regulation or anomy is thus further heightened by passions being less disciplined, precisely when they need more disciplining. But then their very demands make fulfillment impossible. Overweening ambition always exceeds the results obtained, great as they may be, since there is no warning to pause here. Nothing gives satisfaction and all this agitation is uninterruptedly maintained without appeasement. Above all, since this race for an unattainable goal can give no other pleasure but that of the race itself, if it is one, once it is interrupted the participants are left empty-handed. At the same time the struggle grows more violent and painful, both from being less controlled and because competition is greater. (Durkheim 1951, 253)

According to Durkheim, *anomie* arises as a "pathological mental state" in individuals who are not adequately regulated by societal norms, leading to a "malady of infinite aspiration" (Downes and Rock 2007, 91). He argues that healthy societies naturally impose limits on individual ambitions. These limits are typically accepted by the public based on the authority they respect and deem fair (Agnew 1997, 29). When people reject these societal boundaries, it is often because they either find them unfair or lack respect for the authority that imposed them (Agnew 1997, 35). Without effective or rational societal limitations, people chase unrealistic and unattainable goals, causing social deviance. Durkheim maintains that this deviance is, in essence, a symptom of the absence of a functioning society (Agnew 1997, 31). Therefore, when societal norms and limitations fail to align with public aspirations, the resulting *anomie* exacerbates the crisis, extending it from a cultural to an anomic stage.

Robert Merton expanded on Émile Durkheim's concept of *anomie*, introducing his "strain theory," a cornerstone in contemporary sociology. For Merton *anomie* is a "breakdown in the cultural structure," particularly manifesting when there is a significant disconnect between society's goals and the ability of group members to achieve those goals within socially acceptable means (Schacht 1994, 101). In Merton's framework, societal structures consist of two key elements: firstly, a set of culturally defined goals and group interests that serve as the "frame of aspirational reference," and secondly, socially acceptable ways, essentially, the rulebook, of achieving those goals (Merton 1996, 78). Groups generally try to align their collective ambitions and cultural aims with these socially acceptable pathways. However, when a society's prescribed solution to a problem is abstract or impractical, people often opt for more concrete or feasible solutions, regardless of whether these solutions are considered legitimate. Merton argues that if this divergence between goals and means continues to grow, societal cohesion starts to weaken, resulting in a state of *anomie* (Merton 1996, 80).

Merton's theory of *anomie* is categorized within social strain theories, and it differs significantly from Durkheim's original conception. Unlike Durkheim, who saw *anomie* as resulting from a lack of social regulation, Merton suggests that *anomie* arises precisely because of society's presence. Specifically, society encourages expectations that cannot be met through socially accepted means (Agnew 1997, 37).

In the context of international law, this tension between societal goals and legitimate methods of achieving them is pervasive. Merton observes that the emphasis on national power is often incompatible with the inadequate organization of legitimate ways—defined and accepted internationally—to reach this goal. This misalignment leads to the undermining of international law. Tactics such as "undeclared warfare" or the bombing of civilian populations may be rationalized, much like individual acts of illegitimacy can arise under similar societal conditions (Merton 1996, 84). In Merton's view, the issue of *anomie* does not lie in the aspirations of particular groups or individuals but in the social system itself. *Anomie* is seen as a "condition of the social surround," a product of systemic issues, rather than the failings or limitations of specific individuals or groups (Schacht 1994, 102). This shifts the focus to the structural elements of society that create conditions conducive to *anomie*, underscoring the need for systemic solutions.

Social anomic theorists have delved into the ideas of reference groups and relative deprivation to explain human behavior and social dynamics. According to reference group theories, people are consistently mindful of what others are doing and thinking. This sense of other-awareness necessitates that individuals "take the role of the other" to understand both the world and themselves from the viewpoint of others (A. Cohen 1997, 53). Consequently, people are significantly influenced by their association, or lack thereof, with specific groups, which serve as their "points of reference and comparison" (Passas 1997, 64). These reference points are crucial as they shape individuals' goals and standards. In this framework, the concept of relative deprivation is of particular importance. This sentiment of deprivation arises when people compare themselves to these reference groups and find themselves lacking in some way. As one description of relative deprivation outlines:

> [W]e can roughly say that A is relatively deprived of X when (i) he does not have X, (ii) he sees some other person or persons, which may include himself at some previous or expected time, as having X (whether or not this is or will be in fact the case), (iii) he wants X, and (iv) he sees it as feasible that he should have X. (Passas 1997, 66)

Therefore, reference group theories and the notion of relative deprivation offer a lens through which to understand how individuals' perceptions of their social standing can influence their actions and possibly contribute to a state of *anomie* or social strain. People experience a sense of relative deprivation by making comparisons between themselves and others who possess certain benefits or advantages that they lack.

It is important to differentiate between relative deprivation and inequality; the two are not synonymous. Inequality refers to an objective difference in access to resources or opportunities, and it may or may not result in a subjective feeling of relative deprivation (Passas 1997, 67). In other words, inequality can exist without necessarily inducing feelings of deprivation, discontent, or injustice. On the other hand, relative deprivation is specifically tied to the subjective experience and emotional response to perceived inequality.

The theories of reference groups and relative deprivation can be extended to the realm of international legal theory, particularly in relation to the concept of self-determination. Legal doctrines such as the right of all peoples to self-determination, remedial secession, and "constitutional self-determination" elevate the expectations and standards for various peoples or groups. According to the *anomie* theory, "feelings of relative deprivation are encouraged by any social process that diminishes barriers to comparison and emulation between the advantaged and the less advantaged" (Passas 1997, 73). In systems or ideologies that advocate for egalitarianism, relative deprivation is exacerbated, potentially leading to states of *anomie* and deviant behaviors among the less advantaged. This is because egalitarian theories generally make no distinctions among individuals or groups, engendering the belief that "everyone can make it." This, in turn, broadens the scope for comparisons with virtually any other individual or group in the society, thereby increasing the potential for feelings of relative deprivation (Passas 1997, 70). Moreover, when these elevated expectations are not met by corresponding achievements, the sense of relative deprivation is likely to intensify (Passas 1997, 77). Essentially, the gap between what is aspired to and what is actually achievable grows, exacerbating feelings of deprivation and discontent. This can have significant implications for how legal doctrines like self-determination are perceived and engaged with, potentially leading to destabilization or conflict if not adequately addressed.

According to Merton's theory on *anomie*, a state of normlessness can manifest not just in the absence of regulation but also when there is a lack of consensus on what is considered legitimate norms or when social relations are fraught with uncertainty and insecurity (Schacht 1994, 105). The domain of international and constitutional law surrounding the concept of self-determination fits into this latter scenario. The ambiguities related to the concept of self-determination—including its post-colonial interpretations, the notion of 'constitutional self-determination,' and the legally contested idea of remedial secession—generate significant uncertainty. This undermines the legitimacy and attainability of claims to self-determination, particularly those emanating from post-colonial contexts.

The egalitarian language used in discussing self-determination enlarges the sphere of reference groups, increasing the potential for comparisons. This discrepancy between popular expectations and the actual state of legal norms or theories creates a situation of de-regulation. It also amplifies the likelihood of deviant, violent, and anomic behaviors among groups or peoples who believe they have a legitimate right to remedial secession or other forms of self-determination. These groups, by comparing themselves to reference groups that have successfully achieved self-determination, are likely to experience feelings of relative deprivation. According to strain theory, these feelings increase the propensity to engage in anomic behavior as a means to pursue what they perceive as their rightful claim to self-determination, be it remedial secession, international, or constitutional in nature.

The *anomie* theory, applicable to both individuals and collectives, holds particular relevance to the right to self-determination, especially when considered alongside the social theory on collective identity. The latter suggests that "most human action is oriented to the achievement, preservation, or demonstration of an identity" (A. Cohen 1997, 56). When lawful means to achieve or communicate this identity are lacking or ineffective, alternative methods are pursued, leading to a state of *anomie*.

In summary, the issue of self-determination is currently mired in a rationality crisis compounded by significant legitimacy and anomic problems. Confusion surrounding the legal norms and principles of international and constitutional self-determination, as well as evolving interpretations and approaches to remedial secession, has led to a gap between what is legally structured and what is popularly expected or deemed legitimate. According to the Habermasean theory of legitimation, such crises of legitimacy and *anomie* cannot be sustained indefinitely. If these legitimation deficits cannot be reconciled with either a surplus of rationality or some imperative for system maintenance (like a state of emergency), then substantial changes must occur. Therefore, the inconsistencies and ambiguities in international law concerning self-determination are not just academic concerns but pressing issues that risk creating long-term instability if not adequately addressed.

## Toward the Logical Reconstruction of the International Legal Syllogism: Developing a Middle Term by Means of an Expanded Induction

The previous sections have shown that the failure to adequately articulate the relationship between self-determination and constitutional law transcends academic discussion. It signals a deeper issue of logical consistency both in scholarly and judicial circles. While it is impractical to address all the logical shortcomings concerning self-determination, this work aims to closely scrutinize and reconstruct a specific aspect: the syllogism that connects international self-determination to constitutional law. By doing so, it seeks to fill both a legal and rational gap, offering a heuristic framework that might be applicable to other legal issues as well.

As mentioned earlier, the relationship between international self-determination and constitutional law cannot be straightforwardly inferred because the two concepts are not directly relatable. To arrive at a valid conclusion, we need to construct a more nuanced argument, known as a mediate inference or syllogism. Currently, this syllogism is incomplete because it lacks a 'middle term' to connect the two main concepts.

Weller and McWhinney have proposed using the social contract as this middle term, but from the standpoint of syllogistic logic, we explained that this is not a satisfactory solution. Furthermore, both of their theories—and the syllogisms that result—are shaped by an overriding focus on the authority paradigm. McWhinney's syllogism operates outside international legal reasoning, namely at the level of Gründnorm and Realpolitik, and is thus incapable of producing any valid legal conclusions. Weller, on the other hand, completes the syllogism within the international legal realm but embraces the authority paradigm and readjusts his legal conclusion accordingly.

However, syllogistic reasoning is a natural cognitive process that is not tied to any authority-driven framework. Finding the right middle term, the connecting concept between international self-determination and constitutional law, is neither readily apparent nor easily inferred from existing legal doctrine. Furthermore, it cannot be simply assumed based on the philosophical leanings of international law toward the liberal tradition. To reconstruct this legal syllogism logically, we must define the middle term through a process of expanded induction, namely induction unrestrained from the authority paradigm.

According to Erhard Oeser's theory of evolutionary self-construction, induction is not just a matter of listing examples; it is a creative process essential for building "universal law hypotheses" and formulating new concepts. Oeser refers to this form of induction as "super induction," and he argues that it enables us to make the jump from specific observations to broader legal principles. This process is closely tied to the abstraction involved in forming new concepts (Oeser 2003, 48). Albeit unconsciously, induction already operates as a necessary heuristic process in legal reasoning and produces legally tenable conclusions. Legal analogies and the process of juridical analysis, namely the "decomposition of the existent . . . legal material into its basic elements," are by definition inductive (Oeser 2003, 161; Noyes 1940, 511).

The use of inductive reasoning is grounded in the fundamental assumption that nature is characterized by inherent patterns, relationships, and causal sequences. Within this context, Aristotelian induction, or *ἐπαγωγή*, offers a comprehensive model of inductive logic that proves particularly well-suited to the qualitative dimensions of the social sciences and the humanities. While enumerative induction remains fully applicable to their quantitative methodologies, it is the conceptual analysis and qualitative inquiry that align more naturally with the Aristotelian account. This stands in marked contrast to traditional logicians such as John Stuart Mill, who explicitly exclude intuition or insight from the realm of logic, relegating them to psychology or metaphysics. For Mill, logic is concerned strictly with inference, not with intuitive truths (Mill 1950, 8–10).

Aristotle, by contrast, treats intuition as integral to the inductive process. The term ἐπαγωγή (*epagoge*), derived from the verb ἐπάγω (*epago*), carries connotations of being led or moved—of bringing or applying something forward, even of causing or impelling (L. Groarke 2009, 121). It signifies a kind of mental movement that originates externally and proceeds from particular instances to universal understanding. In his *Metaphysics*, Aristotle attributes to Socrates the initial application of induction through ἔλεγχος (*elenchus*, a form of dialectical refutation) and ἀπορία (*aporia*, a state of puzzlement). These elements, which constitute what is often referred to as Socratic irony, aim not merely at contradiction but at inducing intellectual clarity in the audience (L. Groarke 2009, 122).

In his *An Aristotelian Account of Induction*, Louis Groarke elaborates that Aristotelian induction is best understood as an act of insight—a process of intellectual discernment rather than mere accumulation of data. The goal is not only to verify propositions but to uncover the underlying reasons that render them intelligible. Induction in this Aristotelian sense becomes a cognitive tool for deeper comprehension of the nature of things (L. Groarke 2009, 123). To illustrate this model, Groarke refers to the classic inductive example: observing that Swan A is white, Swan B is white, Swan C is white, and so on, before inferring that all swans are white. Whereas standard induction ends with a generalization not formally provable, the Aristotelian approach presses further, asking whether whiteness is essential to the nature of swans. It calls for an inquiry into the metaphysical properties of both swans and whiteness. This moment of synthesis—often described as a flash of insight—is where the essential characteristics of the phenomenon are grasped (L. Groarke 2009, 137). It is, in effect, an *aha!* moment, a creative leap in understanding in which the underlying causes of phenomena are intuitively apprehended (L. Groarke 2009, 123).

Groarke describes this as the initial stage of Aristotelian induction, where ἐπαγωγή is understood as a capacity for precise mental insight. It enables the acquisition of concepts, definitions, universals, logical and metaphysical principles, foundational natural facts, and even moral truths (L. Groarke 2009, 123). Thus, Aristotelian induction is not merely a method for drawing generalizations from empirical observations; it is also a profound epistemological tool for intellectual discovery and the formation of knowledge.

For Aristotle, induction functions as the means by which first principles and axioms are established, enabling access to the essence of things. Although conceptual understanding begins with sensory experience, the foundational principles of knowledge arise from *nous*, or intellectual insight (L. Groarke 2009, 174). The initial stage of this process is not considered an inference in the strict sense, nor an argument or a proof. Rather, it is described as a cognitive movement that leads the mind to apprehend a connection between terms, whose necessity is grasped immediately and without recourse to discursive reasoning (L. Groarke 2009, 174). Often referred to as "intuitive induction," this phase is grounded in rational insight—precisely the kind of cognitive act dismissed by John Stuart Mill and other modern logicians, who exclude it from the domain of logic and reduce it to the psychological or metaphysical. Louis Groarke challenges this exclusion, arguing that Mill and his successors fail to recognize the indispensable creative dimension of Aristotelian *ἐπαγωγή*, which, in his account, is neither a subjective psychological state nor a speculative metaphysical gesture, but a legitimate leap from particulars to universals (L. Groarke 2009, 123).

Even accepting, for the sake of argument, Mill's critique that Aristotelian induction rests on psychological grounds, Edmund Husserl's phenomenology offers a powerful rejoinder. Husserl maintains that intuition, even if mentally constituted, can produce genuine, objective knowledge. For him, intuition brings the knower into direct contact with "the thing itself," establishing a foundation of self-evidence upon which both scientific axioms and formal logic must ultimately rely (Husserl 1970a, 128). In this way, Husserl implicitly affirms the Aristotelian account of induction, particularly in its emphasis on insight as the first step in the formation of knowledge.

This perspective also undermines Georg Schwarzenberger's claim that intuition and phenomenology are merely hypothetical unless validated by international legal processes. If Husserl is correct, then the epistemic value of intuition does not depend on legal recognition to be valid. Rather, it serves as the condition for the possibility of objective knowledge, including within legal reasoning.

Consequently, any attempt to reconstruct the international legal syllogism concerning self-determination and constitutional law must transcend such misunderstandings. It must instead begin with an unencumbered inductive inquiry aimed at identifying the middle term—that is, the mediating concept which enables the transition from general legal principles to specific normative conclusions. Aristotelian induction, particularly as refined by Husserl's phenomenological insights, offers a method for achieving this task. It calls for *a prior* engagement with the phenomenology of rights—through a process of abstraction, insight, and conceptual analysis—which then enables the systematic evaluation of empirical data pertaining to self-determination and constitutional law. Through this dialectic, one can discern and define the essential characteristics of the middle term, thereby grounding legal conclusions in a more rigorous and philosophically sound framework. It has been suggested that applying the scientific method to law first requires restoring and systematizing the relationship between legal concepts and their originating data (Noyes 1940, 511). This indicates that all legal concepts must be (re)connected to a tangible material reality, specifically the societal actions, events, or relationships these concepts are intended to regulate or address, as revealed through phenomenology or naive realism (Noyes 1940, 511, 518). The prevailing view of law as a self-contained, norm-creating system (the authority paradigm) hinders a thorough phenomenological examination and a proper investigation into the fundamental properties of legal concepts. However, as deficits in rationality and legitimacy continue to escalate, along with increasing social *anomie*, there is a growing urgency to challenge the authority paradigm. This necessitates adhering to logical rules and rigorously testing the rationality of international legal reasoning.

## Note

1 A revised version of this section, as well as arguments and ideas from this chapter appear in Baka 2022.

# 3

# The Rational

## Reconstructing the Middle Term: Induction, Essence, and the Right to Self-Determination

In reconsidering the international legal syllogism concerning the relationship between the right to self-determination and constitutional law, it becomes evident that the crucial middle term, namely the conceptual bridge linking major and minor premises, cannot be derived from legal theory alone. Although the notion of the social contract is frequently invoked, it proves inadequate in this context. Operating primarily as a political metaphor, it lacks the precision required of a logical middle term and fails to meet the standards of the authority paradigm that governs international legal reasoning. Conclusions drawn from such a construct would neither be authorized nor validated within this framework.

As concluded in the preceding chapter, the middle term must instead be identified through a rational process rooted in induction. Aristotelian induction, or *ἐπαγωγή*, offers a comprehensive methodology for this. Unlike enumerative induction, which depends on the accumulation of empirical instances, Aristotelian induction involves a phenomenological reduction aimed at uncovering the essence of the concept under investigation. Departing from the formal logic associated with Mill and other modern logicians, Aristotelian induction incorporates intuition or insight—an essential cognitive function for re-establishing the intrinsic connection between legal entities and their foundational origins. This phenomenological exercise is particularly crucial in light of the significant conceptual confusion surrounding the definition and scope of the international right to self-determination. This chapter undertakes the first stage of Aristotelian induction—the moment of insight—revealing that legal rights are constituted not solely by observable characteristics but by an underlying essence and a set of essential properties.

The chapter begins with a critical examination of the dominant analytic conception of legal rights. It argues that contemporary jurisprudence and mainstream legal thought, shaped predominantly by legal positivism and the Anglo-Saxon analytical tradition, tend to interpret legal rights through an interactionist lens, rooted in the right–obligation duality. This approach, closely aligned with logical positivism and the Wittgensteinian view that meaning arises through social use, frames rights within a contextual and consensual paradigm. However, this analysis contends that such a framework leaves a surplus of meaning unexamined—a dimension of legal rights that cannot be exhaustively accounted for within the boundaries of sociolinguistic practice.

This surplus points to the essence of legal rights. Drawing on Aristotle's theory of induction and the metaphysics of essences, the chapter posits that this essence—*τὸ τί ἦν εἶναι*, or 'what it was to be'—constitutes a necessary property of legal rights. It represents a state of being that persists independently of shifting contextual or consensual meanings. To further explore this dimension, the chapter addresses the limitations of the Wittgensteinian framework and returns to the philosophical foundations of legal rights by integrating Aristotelian induction with Husserl's transcendental phenomenology. The objective is to challenge prevailing logical and semantic assumptions embedded in mainstream legal theory and to initiate a rational-phenomenological reconsideration of the general theory of legal rights. In doing so, the analysis seeks to recover the semantic and conceptual content left unresolved by the Wittgensteinian model.

The inductive identification of the middle term, particularly as it pertains to the right to self-determination, requires a process of abstraction and insight into the phenomenological structure of legal rights. This process necessitates a Husserlian-style *epoché*—the suspension of all contextual and intentional structures, including concepts such as constitution, constitutional self-determination, internal and external self-determination, remedial secession, and the doctrinal distinction between legal rights and legal principles. At the end of this phenomenological reduction, the analysis concludes that the core of legal rights is rooted in a fundamental desire to preserve tranquility—understood as a natural mode of being. This metaphysical insight forms the epistemological foundation for a renewed understanding of legal rights and offers the necessary basis for reconstructing the international legal syllogism through Aristotelian induction.

# The Theory of Rights: A Critical Review of Logical and Semantic Presumptions

## Rights against Others: Claimability as a Necessary Condition

The philosophical and theoretical foundations of legal rights are typically sought in legal positivist, moral-deontological, or natural law traditions, and only rarely in the logical realm. Moreover, mainstream legal thought tends to approach legal rights in an actively positive manner, that is, by focusing on what rights encompass or on the extent of their inclusivity, while relegating their negative aspect to the realm of obligations imposed on others.

Legal rights are often conceptualized through geometrical or metaphorical frameworks, depicting them as structures with a core and a periphery, or likening them to solar systems whose orbits house claims, legal advantages, liberties, powers, and immunities, while external to them lies an indefinite matrix of duties, disabilities, and liabilities, following Hohfeld's famous classification (Hohfeld 1913, 16; Martin 1993, 88–9). The persistent reliance on geometrical and metaphorical imagery exposes the scholarly difficulty in directly defining the concept of a legal right. Indeed, as Schlag notes, legal rights have been variously treated "as concepts, as argumentative trumps, as factors of production, as preconditions to bargaining, as bearer-enabling entitlements, as bearer-disabling entitlements, as totems, as sources of social solidarity, as legitimation devices, and so on" (Schlag 1996, 263). The geometrical understanding of legal rights reflects a characteristic feature of the analytic aesthetic, wherein "law is spatialized" and subdivided into "various subparts" (Schlag 1996, 271). Within this framework, rights are conceptualized through the imagery and metaphors of property (Schlag 1996, 277). The underlying logic of this spatial compartmentalization lies in the core purpose of the analytic aesthetic itself: the production of a well-ordered juridical system, in which legal concepts are properly structured and clearly delimited (Schlag 1996, 274).

The property analogy further implies that rights are conceived as possessed, as individual territories not to be trespassed upon by others. Austin famously described rights as "residing with persons," where the right-bearer is regarded as the owner of the right, exercising "complete dominion and control within the scope of his right" (Schlag 1996, 279). It is precisely this form of territorialization that the solar system metaphor seeks to capture, enabling rights to be conceptualized through property-related images (Schlag 1996, 281). The roots of this conceptualization can be traced back to Roman law, where *dominium* and *ius* were used during the later Empire in ways strikingly similar to the modern use of the term right (Tuck 1979, 13). The property analogy was subsequently appropriated by Hugo Grotius in *Mare Liberum*, wherein *dominium* was analogically extended to natural rights (Tuck 1979, 62). It is particularly noteworthy that the French term for self-determination, *l'auto-détermination*, is often used interchangeably with *l'auto-disposition*, a term evoking the freedom to dispose of oneself, which highlights the material extension of the property analogy at both the individual and collective selves.

Interestingly, in mainstream international legal discourse, the analytic aesthetic often coexists with what Schlag terms the instrumentalist aesthetic. Unlike the analytic commitment to order and stability, the instrumentalist aesthetic privileges the rhetoric of legal progress and reform. In this vision, rights are depicted as sources, instruments, or ends of societal change—or indeed as embodying all three at once (Schlag 1996, 285). The instrumentalist aesthetic grounds its operations and its broader ideological justifications in the purported absence of objectivity and *a priori* constraints on legal reasoning. As Judge Richard Posner famously argued, "there is no such thing as 'legal reasoning.' The justification (akin to scientific verification) of legal decisions—the demonstration that a decision is correct—often is impossible. No bounds can be fixed *a priori* on what shall be allowed to count as an argument in law" (Schlag 1996, 298).

Both the property analogy associated with the analytic aesthetic and the absence of objectivity and *a priori* constraints characteristic of the instrumentalist aesthetic presuppose the existence of a social context. To possess a right is to possess it in relation to others, while the lack of syllogistic constraints suggests that doctrinal solutions must be determined contextually rather than deduced formally. The significance of social context has been emphasized by leading legal positivists such as Hans Kelsen and H. L. A. Hart.

Kelsen, following Austin, emphasized the primary importance of the concept of duty in relation to that of right (Kelsen 1971, 358). In his view, to be the bearer of a right is either to have a right to act in a certain manner or to have a right that imposes an obligation on another to act accordingly (Kelsen 1971, 277). He further explained that stating someone has a right to behave in a particular way may simply mean that the individual has no duty to behave otherwise (Kelsen 1971, 277–8). Freedom, on Kelsen's account, can only be conceptualized as the negation of duty and, consequently, as the absence of external social constraints.

This conceptualization implies that others—including the state—are under an obligation not to interfere with the various expressions of individual freedom (Kelsen 1971, 278). Kelsen's philosophy regarding rights and freedom found expression in mainstream legal doctrine through the classical distinction between positive and negative rights. According to this traditional dichotomy, positive rights correlate with duties imposed upon the state to take affirmative action, whereas negative rights correspond to a general obligation of noninterference, binding both the state and its citizens (Feinberg 1993, 71; Gewirth 1996, 31).

The symmetry between rights and duties, often referred to as the "doctrine of the logical correlativity of rights and duties" (Feinberg 1994, 119), has emerged as a major axiom within legal positivism and, in particular, within the formalist school of thought (Lyons 1998, 276). This doctrine aligns with the predominance in analytic legal philosophy of the concept of claimability, which holds that legal rights are conceived as discrete and atomic spheres of claims asserted against others. It has often been asserted that for legal rights to exist, they must be claimed (Golding 2007, 324), and that their characteristic use is precisely "to be claimed, demanded, affirmed, [and] insisted upon" (Feinberg 1994, 128).

Within this framework, Wesley Hohfeld's classic theory stands as perhaps the landmark theoretical analysis of legal rights. Hohfeld distinguished and classified eight fundamental legal concepts, which are regarded as the "lowest common denominators of the law" (Smith 1993, 54). According to his theory, these basic concepts form the essential units of legal analysis and can be arranged both antithetically and correlatively, providing a systematic framework for understanding the structure of legal rights. From Hohfeld's classification, it follows that legal rights may be conceptualized as rights-claims in the strict sense, privileges (or liberties), powers, or immunities. Each of these categories presumes that legal concepts are understood relationally: possessing a right implies that another is under an obligation; enjoying a privilege implies the absence of a right against the holder; exercising a legal power presupposes that another is liable to that authority; and holding an immunity implies that the power of a law is disabled with respect to the individual (Martin 1993, 29–32; Smith 1993, 54–5). This logical geometry of legal rights reflects what has been described as the mainstream, confrontational view of the function of rights (Wellman 1997, 8). It suggests that legal relations are defined by structured oppositions and mutual positioning. Furthermore, this geometry has been enriched by a broader theory of obligatoriness or bindingness, whose intellectual roots can be traced back to classical sources in jurisprudence such as the philosophies of Thomas

Hobbes, Jeremy Bentham, and John Austin (Wellman 1997, 49). According to this mainstream account, a legal duty is considered genuine only when it is backed by legal punishment for disobedience (Wellman 1997, 49).

Although Hohfeld's model originally proposed a two-term relational structure—linking two parties through rights and duties—it has often been reinterpreted as a three-term relation, according to which the existence of legal rights presupposes not only two parties but also a judicial institution to enforce or recognize the claim (Wellman 1997, 8). Alongside this primary understanding, a secondary approach to the logical structure of legal rights has emerged, particularly visible in the writings of H. L. A. Hart and other subsequent theorists. This secondary view maintains that legal rights do not merely consist of interlocking legal relations but also embody a central concept of liberty, surrounded by a protective perimeter of duties (Wellman 1997, 7). The central notion of liberty is frequently referred to as the 'core' of legal rights.

Hart suggested that Hohfeld's fourfold classification could be unified under a broader genus, namely, the basic idea of legal advantage (Hart 1982, 165). He further indicated that this basic notion could be traced in the writings of Jeremy Bentham. In Hart's formulation, the concept of core-liberty does not reject the traditional correlativity between rights and obligations. Rather, it implies a perimeter of duties that limit, but do not directly correspond to, the exercise of human freedom. To illustrate this point, Hart offered the example of scratching one's head. He observed that although the 'right' to scratch one's head does not, in a strict sense, correlate with an obligation imposed on others not to interfere, there nevertheless exists an aggregate of institutionalized obligations—such as duties prohibiting assault or trespassing—which indirectly protect the act (Hart 1982, 171). Thus, Hart's conceptualization of the legal right as a core unilateral liberty does not entirely eliminate the relational and contextual dimensions of rights; rather, it presupposes the existence of an institutionalized perimeter of legal obligations (Hart 1982, 171–4).

It has been suggested that the primary purpose of Hohfeld's logical structure was to resolve what has been termed the "modal ambiguity in the language of rights" (Wellman 1997, 64). Indeed, one of the central aims of analytic philosophy has long been the facilitation of deductive logic and the promotion of clarity and precision in meaning (Gorman 2003, 111). From the perspective of analytic thought—and as follows from Hart's analysis of legal rights—the doctrine of right–duty symmetry, along with the recourse to the perimeter of legal rights (i.e., the network of corresponding duties), serves to enable the deduction of the meaning, content, and scope of legal rights. Conversely, any deviation from the standard model of deductive reasoning, especially when it purports to generate new knowledge, is generally regarded as failing to provide genuine knowledge at all (Gorman 2003, 108). Yet, a significant critique of Hohfeld's structure has been the argument that his analysis presupposes a "sufficient prior grasp" of the meaning of the terms right and duty (Gorman 2003, 139). Given that, within the mainstream analysis of legal rights, the most basic and semantically irreducible building blocks are precisely the correlatives of right and duty—and bearing in mind that Hart's core-right concept ultimately aligns with the notion of rights as liberties or legal advantages, without abandoning the necessity of right–duty correlativity for attributing meaning to legal rights—the deductive tools employed in legal reasoning do not suffice to provide a deeper understanding of these fundamental terms. Such understanding, as it seems, necessarily requires induction.

However, the mainstream tradition in legal thought remains notably averse to inductive reasoning processes, such as the use of analogies. Inductive reasoning is seen as unpredictable and, to a large extent, a creative operation, one that cannot be empirically verified and thus should be employed only with great caution, if at all (Kelsen 1973, 249–51). It is therefore unsurprising that mainstream international legal reasoning, being firmly grounded in the principles of legal certainty and state consent, remains inherently resistant to inductive analyses, which are perceived as introducing an undesirable degree of uncertainty. Nonetheless, it has been widely acknowledged—by the majority of logicians, and most notably by John Stuart Mill—that it is impossible to reason by deduction alone; no thinker can entirely escape the operations of induction.

## Claimability as a Necessary Condition Due to the *a Priori* Rejection of Objective Rationality: The Inevitable Recourse to the Exclusivity of Social Meaning and Wittgenstein's Language-Games

In legal rights theory, the prevailing inductive approach appears to be formally inductive rather than Aristotelian, as it is based entirely on the observation of social data. This standard methodology can be summarized in the view that, in order to induce legal meaning, one must avoid resorting to inner or metaphysical considerations—such as those engaged through Aristotelian induction—and should instead anchor the entire field of legal semantics to paradigms of social experience and, in the context of international law, to state practice. In this regard, Jean D'Aspremont has observed the modernist decline—and, indeed, the near-total abandonment—of Aristotelian induction, which he describes as a mining activity aimed at extracting pre-existing meaning (D'Aspremont 2012, 577). He highlights the semantic instability that inevitably follows from this methodological shift. According to D'Aspremont, because legal knowledge, like all knowledge, can be produced only empirically, it is through social experience and discourse that concepts, meanings, and ultimately realities are generated—or, more precisely, constructed (D'Aspremont 2012, 582, 591). However, the assertion that all knowledge is socially constructed leads D'Aspremont to recognize that the absence of empirical objectivism (D'Aspremont 2012, 591) spawns a profound semantic instability. He identifies two primary causes for this instability: first, the economizing function of words, which inevitably reduces the richness of meaning (D'Aspremont 2012, 590); and second, the unavoidable struggles for interpretative authority and persuasiveness among international legal scholars (D'Aspremont 2012, 576).

Both modernist and postmodernist discourses, in different ways, embrace this dismissal of objective rationality and metaphysics in legal theory. This critical stance has been further developed within the tradition of Critical Legal Studies, notably by scholars such as Duncan Kennedy and Martti Koskenniemi. In a closely related vein, Duncan Kennedy has argued that, since legal rules are not physical objects, their application must inevitably be understood as a socially subjective process (D. Kennedy 1998, 255). He suggests that this process may, over time, achieve a degree of automaticity if the application of facts to rules becomes so routinized that it leads to an agreement on an interpretive formula (D. Kennedy 1998, 255). Nevertheless, Kennedy maintains that no rational, objective, or correct application of legal rules can ever be definitively demonstrated, since the notion of correctness, as commonly employed in mathematics, science, or logic, is simply inapplicable in the legal domain (D. Kennedy 1998, 255).

Martti Koskenniemi's postmodern critique in *From Apology to Utopia* centers on an unfolding oxymoron within international legal reasoning: the simultaneous political demand for objective normativity and the reliance on subjectivism and social context—namely, state practice—for the production of international legal meaning (Koskenniemi 1989). This circular relation is what Koskenniemi describes as the helpless doctrinal trajectory that moves from political apology to the utopia of logical and metaphysical objectivity. He remarks that, in order to demonstrate the reality of international law, the modern lawyer must show that the law is at once normative and concrete: that it binds a state regardless of its behavior, will, or interests, yet that its content can still be verified by reference to precisely those factors (Koskenniemi 1989, 17).

To expose the futility of this circularity, and particularly to support his nihilistic rejection of objective rationality, Koskenniemi draws upon the deconstructivist method, employing in particular Jacques Derrida's concepts of *différance* and the dangerous supplement (Koskenniemi 1989, 6–15, 530–2). He cites Derrida's assertion that "there is no outside-text" (*il n'y a pas de hors-texte*), where Derrida insists that reading cannot legitimately transgress itself toward a metaphysical, historical, or psycho-biographical referent external to language, nor toward a signified meaning existing independently of the text (Koskenniemi 1989, 531). Koskenniemi embraces Derrida's claim that no true, extra-textual meaning exists, since no metaphysical or objective referent can be identified to anchor such meaning. In Derrida's critique of Rousseau's *Confessions*, Rousseau is portrayed as treating writing as a semantically impoverished and parasitic substitute, a tool used merely to restore the "truer" and more authentic act of living speech (Derrida 1997, 142). For Derrida, this hierarchy attaches a greater semantic value to presence over absence. However, Derrida argues that both presence and absence depend upon the same singular operation of *différance.*

According to Derrida, *différance* produces what it simultaneously forbids; it enables the very oppositions it also renders impossible (Derrida 1997, 143). Presence, he argues, presupposes and relies upon absence, just as absence presupposes and relies upon presence. Neither can exist autonomously or independently, even though they are structurally opposed. Even speech, often associated with presence, does not, for Derrida, constitute a self-sufficient foundation. It too must be understood as a supplement—an addition that presupposes another absence. Derrida explains that the supplement acts only to replace; it insinuates itself where there is a void, filling it only by marking a prior lack. As such, it functions as a compensatory and vicarious addition, always standing in for what is absent, such that the sign itself is already a supplement of the thing it purports to signify (Derrida 1997, 145).

Derrida further equates presence, which he regards as itself a sign and thus a *suppléant,* with essence, thereby rejecting the possibility of *a priori* or inner, objective meaning. He asserts that the supplement is dangerous to Reason because it always remains merely a representation or an image of the thing-itself, never the thing-itself (Derrida 1997, 149). For Derrida, there can be no self-sufficiency or transgression in meaning because Nature itself generates the original insufficiency: there is a lack in Nature and, precisely because of this lack, something additional is produced (Derrida 1997, 149). Reason, in this framework, is not incapable of grasping insufficiency; rather, it is constituted by it.

It becomes clear that Derrida's deconstruction operates not simply as a mode of critical analysis but as a radical form of rational demolition. His theory tends toward nihilism, as it undermines the very possibility of objective knowledge and casts doubt upon all forms of logical inference, treating empirical data itself as unstable supplements. In many ways, Derrida introduces a radicalized form of Nietzschean skepticism into semiotics. Yet his theory risks self-negation, for while it rejects the objectivity of Reason, it simultaneously relies upon Reason to articulate and advance the very notion of *différance*. For if *différance* already exists, Derrida's method seems to presuppose its extraction, suggesting that it has essence. If, alternatively, *différance* is a product of the mind's interpretation of empirical representations, then Derrida's intellectual operation rests upon a form of inductive reasoning that would necessarily require some degree of stability and objective authority. Finally, if *différance* itself is understood as a supplement, it shares the same instability and precariousness attributed to every other sign in Derrida's deconstructivist theory. It might not be an exaggeration to include Derrida alongside Paul Ricoeur's "philosophers of suspicion"—Nietzsche, Marx, and Freud—who all posed the problem of "the lie of consciousness" and "consciousness as a lie" (Ricoeur 1989, 97).

No coherent theory can be truly founded on Derrida's deconstruction, for deconstruction systematically negates the very possibility of systematizing an objective—even a critical—theory of knowledge. At most, what might be described as theory within a deconstructive framework could only mimic Derrida's method, without, if it remains true to itself, reaching rational conclusions. Deconstruction as a method annihilates the possibility of rationality itself, for it destabilizes all premises and thus invalidates the syllogistic process, even where it might seek nihilistic conclusions. Koskenniemi appears fully aware of this tension and offers his own apologia for not being a genuine deconstructivist. In a footnote early in *From Apology to Utopia*, he acknowledges the risk that the attempt to identify a "center" or "deep structure" within legal discourse might replicate what Derrida identified as a metaphysics of presence. Koskenniemi notes that such an effort might involve a "groundless belief" in the explicated structure as a transcendental signifier—a foundational concept whose meaning would not derive from further reference to another structure, but rather from reference to itself (Koskenniemi 1989, 10). Yet he insists that this is not his claim. Instead, he maintains that while the routine of legal argumentation does seem to display a reasonably evident center of assumptions and a limited range of operations from which consequences are drawn, this structure is historically contingent and thus lacks the overriding force necessary to contain all argument within itself.

In his review article of Koskenniemi's *From Apology to Utopia*, Anthony Carty emphasizes that by employing the *langue-parole* phraseology of Claude Lévi-Strauss, Koskenniemi is more of a structuralist rather than a post-structuralist (Carty 1991, 163). Carty notes that such an approach is necessarily self-contradictory and leads Koskenniemi to the artificial imposition of divisive dilemmas so that the author can be truthful to his post-structuralist proclamations (Carty 1991, 165). Koskenniemi ultimately exposes the (political rather than methodological) reasons why he is averse to rationality: "[a]ppealing to principles which would pre-exist human society and be discoverable only through faith or *recta ratio* was to appeal to abstract and unverifiable maxims which only camouflaged the subjective preferences of the speaker. It was premised on utopian ideals which were *constantly used as apologies for tyranny*" (Carty 2012, 859).

Since, within both mainstream and critical legal theory, legal meaning cannot be produced through purely rational methods, the only remaining alternative appears to be social conventionality. Both Koskenniemi and D'Aspremont echo a line of thought already developed by Jürgen Habermas when they argue that it remains possible to limit the spectrum of subjectivism and the inevitable cacophony of international legal reasoning by securing a minimal consensus on a common professional vocabulary among scholars and jurists. For D'Aspremont, given that legal meaning is not metaphysical, it cannot be extracted in the traditional sense; nevertheless, it is still possible to understand the social criteria governing its application (D'Aspremont 2012, 582).

One of Koskenniemi's stated ambitions has been to describe the language of international law, to expose its inherent limitations, and to provide resources for the emancipatory use of international law's professional vocabulary (Koskenniemi 1989, 589). In order to avoid the obvious self-contradiction that would arise from admitting that international law possesses an essential structure, Koskenniemi emphasizes that he is not offering a description of an international legal grammar, but rather of the social and cultural context within which native speakers of international law operate (Koskenniemi 1989, 589). However, both

Habermas's theory of emancipatory communication and the critical suggestion that a common vocabulary might emerge dialogically to contain the cacophony of international legal discourse presuppose essential possibilities of empathy, communication, mutual understanding, and agreement. These, however, are precisely the 'metaphysical' qualities—the Aristotelian *essence*—that Derrida's deconstructive project explicitly rejects.

The conditions necessary for empathy and transcendental intersubjectivity, that is, the essential possibility of sharing a common understanding of concepts and things, have been major themes of phenomenology. Edmund Husserl addressed these in his *Ideas* (Husserl 1931), and they were substantially expanded by thinkers such as Edith Stein, Max Scheler, Emmanuel Levinas, and Alfred Schütz. Following Husserl, Schütz observed that although mutual understanding through empathy does not always occur in fact among ego-subjects, it remains always possible in principle. It follows, according to Schütz, that factually separated worlds of experience can be joined together through interconnections of actual experience, forming a single intersubjective world (Schütz 1966, 52).

Although both Koskenniemi and D'Aspremont reject the objectivity of Reason,[1] it is hardly surprising that the operation of intuition nevertheless transgresses their arguments. As the necessary and natural first stage of induction, intuition cannot be fully contained; rather, it inevitably manifests itself in various forms. Beyond the theme of transcendental intersubjectivity, D'Aspremont, while affirming the exclusivity of social meaning, acknowledges that behind the paroles there exists a given (social) phenomenology of things and circumstances. He notes that "[w]ords express concepts that, by definition, have an economizing function, for they refer to a given state of affairs" (D'Aspremont 2012, 589). Koskenniemi proceeds with greater caution, suggesting that "[w]ords are only raw material that the language-speaker uses in order to formulate sentences and grasp meanings transmitted as part of the social life" (Koskenniemi 1989, 566). Yet, despite his critical distance, he repeatedly invokes a notion of shared intuition among legal scholars, a notion that ultimately leads him to conclude that the grammar of international law—though socially, and not rationally, defined—may still be subject to distinctions between appropriate and inappropriate use.[2]

While the poststructuralist critique of logic within the Critical Legal Studies movement led many scholars to embrace Habermasian approaches to communicative action and rational discourse, a different trajectory emerged within legal formalism. For formalist thinkers and those committed to normative ideals of legal reasoning, the adoption of Derrida's deconstructive methodology, and even the therapeutic recourse to Habermas' neo-Marxist theory of communication, remained out of the question. Instead, the philosophical grounds for rejecting Reason within the mainstream were sought and found in logical positivism, particularly in Ludwig Wittgenstein's semantics and theory of language.

Contextual meaning and social use constitute the foundations of Wittgenstein's language-game theory, a framework that has exerted considerable influence on legal positivist thinking (Kelsen 1971, 277–8; Lefebvre 2011, 99). Early Wittgenstein's approach marked a decisive break from his mentor Bertrand Russell, who had maintained that language and meaning could not be studied apart from the empirical world as a detached logical syntax (Russell 1995, 341). By contrast, late Wittgenstein held that meaning (Bedeutung) is produced through participation in language-games. Even fundamental terms such as "true" and "false," as well as ethical and evaluative expressions like "good" and "bad," were, in his view, to be explained (erklärt) through linguistic examples rather than through appeals to metaphysical entities (Wittgenstein 1974, 77; Wittgenstein 2009, 36). Wittgenstein famously stated that "[t]he use of a word in the language is its meaning" and that "meaning is the role of the word in the calculus [of language]" (Wittgenstein 1974, 60, 63). In this respect, he appeared to equate meaning with use and community agreement. According to the logic of the language-game theory, since language functions as a medium of communication, an *a priori* human agreement is necessarily presupposed for the establishment of both definitions and judgments (Wittgenstein 1974, 59–60). Thus, meaning is both generated and verified through communitarian consensus (Wittgenstein 2009, 30, 88). In line with this logic, Wittgenstein suggested that meaning specification and ascertainment occur exclusively through contextual and consensual poles. For instance, he observed that a sentence such as "this is here" would only make sense to someone who considers the special circumstances under which such a phrase is typically used (Wittgenstein 2009, 48). Wittgenstein's strong emphasis on context and social consensus forms part of the broader project associated with logical positivism—an enterprise fundamentally aimed at avoiding "imputing inappropriate metaphysical overtones to [. . .] concepts" (Bix 1993, 52).

*A contrario*, Wittgenstein's logic of language implies that the absence of context and social use deprives words—and even entire sentences—of their concrete meaning, rendering them entirely nonsensical (Wittgenstein 2009, 81). His ultimate point appears to be that no essential or acontextual meaning exists. Consequently, any attempt to examine the meaning of a word solely through intellectual reflection, independently of context and social practice, inevitably leads to seeking meaning within the realms of subjectivity and the psychological (Conant 1998, 239). Wittgenstein uses terms such as "nonsense," "nonsensical," and "unintelligible" to describe words and statements that fall outside any concrete linguistic context (Conant 1998, 229). Although he does not deny that words may possess an abstract or ideal meaning, he argues that such meaning can be grammatically and semantically asserted only through actual use. Moreover, as one commentator has observed, if there is a necessary connection between "our" words and "what we mean," this necessity does not arise from universals, propositions, or rules, but rather from the "form of life" that allows certain syntactical stretches of language to function as assertions (cited in Conant 1998, 229). Wittgenstein's theory of meaning can thus be seen as an expansion of Ludwig Gottlob Frege's well-known three principles: first, always sharply separate the psychological from the logical, and the subjective from the objective; second, never inquire about the meaning of a word in isolation, but only within the context of a proposition; and third, never lose sight of the distinction between concept and object (Conant 1998, 231).

## The Operation of Communitarian Semiotics in the Theory of Legal Rights and the Semantic Incredibility of the Social Contract

In legal theory, the foregoing reflections translate into the assertion that, because language is thoroughly indeterminate, "no rule can determine the scope of its own application" (D. Kennedy 1998, 560), and that "formal law-ascertainment derive[s] from social practice" (D'Aspremont 2011, 15). The theoretical and philosophical foundations of legal positivism thus incorporate the Wittgensteinian poles of consensus and context. Indeed, within the legal mainstream, social context has traditionally been regarded as pivotal for the formulation and ascertainment of legal meaning. A characteristic example is H. L. A. Hart's social thesis and his broader theory on legal determinacy, which introduced the well-known concept of the penumbra—a legitimate zone of legal indeterminacy encompassing issues that fall "outside the hard core of standard instances or settled meaning" (Hart 2007, 35). For Hart, the limitation of the penumbra and the determination of legal meaning are ultimately realized in judicial practice. According to Hart's theory, the penumbra reflects what he described as the "open texture" of legal language. The open texture implies that legal rules possess a core (or plain) meaning alongside an inevitable zone of vagueness. This vagueness is not seen as a defect but rather as an advantageous feature, since it is impossible for legal drafters to foresee all possible scenarios to which a rule might later be applied (Bix 1993, 8).

It is important to emphasize that Hart's notion of core or plain meaning does not entail essentialism. Even in so-called "plain" cases, context and consensus remain decisive, for in such instances "the general terms seem to need no interpretation . . . the recognition of instances seems unproblematic or 'automatic' . . . there is a general agreement in judgments as to the applicability of the classifying terms" (cited in Bix 1993, 7). Thus, the distinction between "easy" and "hard" cases does not rest on the inherent clarity of legal terms, but rather on the density of judicial consensus concerning a particular legal issue (Bix 1993, 37).

The concept of open texture practically signifies that, due to the inherent unpredictability of rule application, legal rules will always be susceptible to the penumbra. Consequently, no clear and *a priori* definition of individual legal terms can ever be conclusively possible (Bix 1993, 30). Hart's social, or conventionality, thesis suggests that the grounding of legal rules and, consequently, the formulation of law-ascertainment criteria, should be sought within "the practice of law-applying authorities" (D'Aspremont 2011, 51). However, as D'Aspremont observes, the transformation of the social thesis into a communitarian-semantic thesis does not fully eliminate the problem of the penumbra (D'Aspremont 2011, 55). According to D'Aspremont's reading of Hart, the primary function of the social thesis is to prepare the ground for the development of socially agreed law-ascertaining criteria, which in Hart's framework are embodied in the rule of recognition (D'Aspremont 2011, 195).[3] Because it is social consensus that defines the content and semantic boundaries of legal meaning, it follows, according to D'Aspremont, that a minimal agreement on concrete linguistic indicators becomes crucial. He thus advocates the establishment of a *de minimis* legal grammar that could standardize the mechanics of legal reasoning (D'Aspremont 2011, 30, 34).

Nonetheless, a significant problem arises from this approach. Although linguistic standardization might facilitate instances of deductive legal reasoning, legal induction, such as the application of new legal analogies, cannot, by its nature, be fully anticipated. Therefore, even the most narrowly tailored and sophisticated legal vocabulary would be unable to address the inherent unpredictability that inductive reasoning introduces into legal interpretation.

Hans Kelsen offers a differentiated semantic approach, although he remains broadly within the Wittgensteinian confines of contextual assertion and logical positivism. According to Kelsen's pure theory of law, emphasis must be placed on the rational construction of legal systems, particularly on the "structural relationships of legal norms within [them]" (Golding 2007, 185). This generates a distinct model of systemic interpretation that prioritizes the position of individual rules within an organized hierarchy of norms. Furthermore, Kelsen recognizes a "certain discretionary range" within which judges are permitted to "'concretize[]' a general norm to [. . .] a particular case" (Griffin 2008, 140).

As previously discussed, Wittgenstein's contextual and consensual logic of language excludes any concept of *a priori*, inner, or essential meaning, relegating such notions to the realm of psychology. From the standpoint of analytical legal theory, therefore, any general theory of legal rights that seeks to transcend contextual and ad hoc considerations is condemned to be characterized as acontextual—and thus nonsensical.

Both Hans Kelsen and H. L. A. Hart embrace social meaning and the right–duty correlation theories as the foundations of legal rights (Griffin 2008, 108–9). Within the mainstream legal tradition, it is generally held that no truth-value can exist outside communitarian semantics. One of the classical objections posed by positivist critics to natural rights theories lies precisely in their perceived "mystification." Jonathan Gorman, for instance, finds it difficult to assent to "the metaphysical independence of rights" (Gorman 2003, 140)—that is, to the idea that rights exist by virtue of a natural order rather than through social convention. For Jeremy Bentham and subsequent legal positivists, who reject inner meaning and Aristotelian essentialism as mystical approaches to law, it remains inconceivable to accept the existence of inherent, primordial rights, namely rights that would exist independently of social membership, rooted solely in human nature. Bentham's famous characterization of natural rights as "simple nonsense—nonsense upon stilts" (in Buchheit 1978, 56) strikingly echoes Wittgenstein's critique of acontextual meaning. Moreover, within positivist legal thought, human rights are frequently understood as setting limits to the sovereignty of states (Buchheit 1978, 56). Yet this premise itself presupposes that it is the social and antagonistic environment that confers concrete meaning upon international legal rights. As previously discussed, claimability is widely regarded as a necessary existence condition for legal rights:

there cannot be a right without specifiable duty-bearers (Raz 2010, 328). Rights are conceptualized as entitlements—claims asserted on behalf of someone and directed against an entity responsible for reciprocal action to ensure the exercise of that right (Adelman 1994, 167).

Some theorists go even further, treating legal rights as "endorsed claims" that cannot be considered eternal or inalienable precisely because they are not prior to, nor independent of, social structures (Kamenka 1988, 127). James Crawford imports this claimability condition into the debate on self-determination, asserting that the right to self-determination must, by definition, be understood as a collective right asserted against a State (Crawford 1988, 164). He also appears to view with sympathy the concern raised by scholars such as Christian Tomuschat, who argue that extending the principle of self-determination to the postcolonial context risks unnecessarily internationalizing "the relation between the whole population of a state and its government" (Crawford 1988, 164). Another prominent semantic approach to self-determination, which is seemingly milder but does not dispose of the relational condition and the right–duty correlativity, is the view that the principle of self-determination entails a presumption of non-interference or non-domination (Waldron 2010, 397; Young 2001, 36, 38–9).

The semantic insistence on social conventionality also sheds light on the international legal inclination toward the social contract theory, and in particular the selection of the social contract as the logical connector between the international right to self-determination and constitutional law. It now appears clear—and indeed could have been anticipated—that legal scholars would seek to resolve lacunae and legal ambiguities by resorting to interpretations grounded in the social semantic thesis.

Even from a Wittgensteinian perspective, however, social contract theories reveal a serious defect: the absence of genuine context and authentic inter-subjectivity. As discussed previously, the social contract remains fundamentally a political metaphor, capable only of describing political conditions that might exist within hypothetical social environments. This social simulation can at best produce presumptive social agreements on meaning. Such presumptions are particularly problematic, as they lack the element of actual inter-subjective participation. This shortcoming raises significant concerns regarding semantic credibility, not to mention political legitimacy. In the absence of a rational foundation for social discourse, political assent can easily be manipulated and social consensus manufactured—often under the legitimizing rhetoric of democracy (Carty 2007, 198–9). As Anthony Carty points out, "[i]f there is no acceptance that there can be rationally objective ways of resolving differences of opinion about what is good or bad, it is inevitable that an anarchy of affirmations will, in fact, be resolved through the pressure, if necessary violent, of a preponderance of voices" (Carty 2007, 198). Even the presumably emancipatory effects attributed to Habermas' theory of communicative reason do not appeal to a concept of 'objective' rationality. As a result, although such a framework may seem to promote fairness in communication, it ultimately cannot preclude the risks of discursive coercion and semantic domination.

A fundamental flaw of contractarianism lies in its treatment of the individual. It tends to disregard the individual as an ethical monad and substitutes the phenomenology of intersubjectivity with an implied social consent and the abstract, industrialized notion of the public. The credibility of socially implied agreements is thereby undermined, as they fail to account for actuality, immediacy, and the phenomenology of mutual recognition among members of a society (Carty 2007, 221–45). In a similar vein, Johann Gottlieb Fichte provided one of the earliest and most significant critiques of contractarianism. Although he did not reject the social contract theory outright, Fichte argued that it rests on the political assumption of communitarian consent and fails to address the ontological conditions necessary for intersubjectivity, such as equality and mutual recognition (Brinkmann 2002, 5–7; Williams 2002, 47–8). It has been almost axiomatically asserted that, when stripped of its idealist constructions and social presumptions, the social contract tradition ultimately reveals two psychological conditions—security and self-preservation—as the fundamental human motives for the abandonment of the state of nature and the establishment of society (Vater 2006, 197).

Human and legal rights theorists often employ similar language when discussing the character of individual and collective rights. The prevailing argument is that the purpose of self-determination and collective rights is the protection of collective interests (Green 1994, 103; Réaume 1994, 119). However, beyond the frameworks of right–duty correlation and contractarian approaches to legal rights, there is a growing body of scholarly and judicial rhetoric that treats certain rights and freedoms—such as the right to life and human dignity—as more "basic," more "fundamental," and more "essential" than others. As John Finnis observes, such rhetoric cannot be adequately explained from the perspective of social conventionality alone (Finnis 2011, 205).

## A Critique of the Social Semantic Thesis from the Perspective of Critical Hermeneutics and Transcendental Phenomenology

As discussed above, both legal positivism and the Critical Legal Studies movement reject the authority of Reason, albeit on different grounds. Legal positivism is generally premised upon Wittgenstein's theory of social semantics, while Critical Legal Studies draws upon Derrida's concepts of *différance* and the dangerous supplement. Yet both premises can be challenged from the perspective of critical hermeneutics and phenomenology.

From a phenomenological standpoint, language is conceived not simply as a set of communicative acts anchored in social practice, but as "a certain system for representation of states of affairs" (Lohmar 2012, 379). Furthermore, in the phenomenological view, concepts and knowledge do not inherently possess a linguistic character from the outset (Lohmar 2012, 378). Paul Ricoeur, one of the principal figures in critical phenomenology and hermeneutics, explicitly challenges the contextual and consensual presuppositions underlying Wittgensteinian philosophy. According to Ricoeur, even analytic philosophy inevitably relies on a notion of *a priori*, for the very act of distinguishing what is sensible from what is nonsensical presupposes the existence of "a priori criteria of meaning, prior to any consideration of content" (Ricoeur 2013, 104). The task of hermeneutics, Ricoeur contends, is precisely to expose and reflect upon these hidden meanings and presuppositions that underlie our understanding of the world and the body of knowledge built upon that understanding (Ricoeur 2013, 99).

Regarding the contextual limitations imposed by Wittgenstein's logic of language, Ricoeur introduces the notion of the "autonomy" of the text. For Ricoeur, once produced, a text detaches itself from the author's intentions, the sociological conditions surrounding its production, and its original audience. This autonomy enables any text—or even any word—to be decontextualized and subsequently recontextualized in different frameworks and structures (Ricoeur 2013, 96). Thus, the Wittgensteinian model of language fails to exhaust the possibilities of meaning. As Ricoeur observes, "meaning is a reservoir of meaning ready to be used again in other structures" (Ricoeur 2013, 96). This dynamic potential for reinterpretation is what he describes as bricolage: a process wherein "the structure saves the event [and] the debris plays the role of a preconstraint, of a message already transmitted" (Ricoeur 1989, 45). It is precisely this surplus of meaning that provides the semantic basis for cultural enrichment, the continuity of tradition, and the very possibility of interpretation.

In his analysis of the presuppositions underlying structural analysis, Paul Ricoeur argues that the principal problem with attempts to limit meaning within language is that language, under such a view, is reduced solely to the object of empirical investigation (Ricoeur 1989, 79). Ricoeur highlights not only the "primacy of observation" but also the "subordination of inductive operations to deduction and the calculus" as key features of this restrictive approach (Ricoeur 1989, 79). From the structuralist perspective, Ricoeur observes, language appears to move in two directions: one ideal, involving the intention to say something, and one real, involving the act of saying something about the world (Ricoeur 1989, 82). These dual dimensions—immanence and transcendence—challenge the assertion that language can be understood purely through empirical analysis (Ricoeur 1989, 82). Although Ricoeur aligns more closely with critical theory than with Husserlian phenomenology, particularly insofar as his critical hermeneutics seeks to expose relations of force concealed within relations of meaning (Ricoeur 1989, 257), he nonetheless remains an ardent defender of phenomenology as a method of interpretation.

Ricoeur's position thus underscores the existence of a surplus of meaning that analytic philosophy and Wittgensteinian logic cannot adequately account for. This surplus belongs to the realm of the *a priori*, to essences and essential being. The hostility of analytic traditions toward essentialism is hardly surprising. Essences, being empirically inaccessible, are often dismissed as speculative constructions, psychological projections, or, in the dismissive language of analytic thought, "metaphysical ghosts" (Husserl 1931, 82). Yet, as Husserl contends, not all knowledge is grounded in empirical experience. Direct experience, he argues, provides only singular elements and not generalities (Husserl 1931, 85). Fundamental principles—such as the very rules of logic—must be grounded in what is given through immediate intuition, rather than derived solely from experiential data (Husserl 1931, 81).

Phenomenological intuition does not reside within the domain of psychology. In his *Ideas*, Edmund Husserl draws a clear distinction between psychology and phenomenology. Psychology, he asserts, is a science of experience—a science concerned with facts and realities—whereas pure phenomenology is not a science of facts but rather a science of essential Being, an eidetic science that aims exclusively at establishing "knowledge of essences (Wesenserkenntnisse)" rather than knowledge of empirical facts (Husserl 1931, 44). Although Husserl acknowledges that the essential and the eidetic are independent of the empirical sciences, he nevertheless maintains that "[no] fully developed science of fact could subsist unmixed with eidetic knowledge" (Husserl 1931, 35).

Phenomenological intuition, or essential insight, is neither psychological nor a product of imagination (Husserl 1931, 92). Rather, intuition serves as "a source of authority (Rechtsquelle) for knowledge" (Husserl 1931, 92). Addressing the criticism that intuition might differ among individuals, Husserl affirms that "what is perceivable by one Ego must in principle be conceivable by every Ego" (Husserl 1931, 150). Although he recognizes that, as a matter of fact, not every person stands in a relation of absolute empathy with others, he insists that there exist "essential possibilities for the setting up of [such] an understanding" (Husserl 1931, 150).

Any individual intuition grounded in empirical data can be transformed into essential insight (Husserl 1931, 54). Through the mental process of phenomenological reduction, it becomes possible to discern transcendently what is immanent: a world of essences and essential connections (Husserl 1931, 285). Even axiological considerations can be traced back to certain *protodoxa*—that is, *a priori* posited meanings and primary beliefs (Husserl 1931, 285). The task of phenomenology, therefore, is the reductive unraveling of the essence of concepts, the fixation of meanings, and the clarification of "the essentiality of the elementary concepts present in them" (Husserl 1931, 387). As a phenomenological enterprise, intuition differs radically from the formal understanding of induction. Husserl emphasizes that phenomenological intuition is not a mere logical transition from particular instances to general conclusions (Husserl 1970, 79). In his view, "[t]he content of [. . .] insight is not inferred from singulars," for while "[a]ll knowledge 'begins' with experience," it does not "arise" from experience (Husserl 1931, 85).

Husserl's theory of meaning should not be mistaken for a Platonism. Although it aspires to grasp essences, it always begins with experience, which through phenomenological reduction leads to an immediate, perceivable givenness. Husserl distinguishes between intentional experience (*noesis*)—that is, consciousness as an intentional act directed toward something—and the object and content of experience, the "perceived as such" (*noema*) (Husserl 1931, 257–60). The *noema* constitutes an objectivity that belongs to consciousness itself (Husserl 1931, 359).

In Husserl's framework, meaning (*Sinn*) can be doxically posited, as occurs in the formation of judgments. These posited meanings (*Sätze*) reveal doxic or value-laden presumptions, often articulated predicatively in terms of pleasure, demand, wish, preference, and similar modalities (Husserl 1931, 369). Max Scheler advances Husserl's categories of meaning further by proposing a logique du cœur—an "emotional apriorism"—applicable to values as well (Scheler 1961, xvii). According to Scheler, human emotions and senses can link individuals to a "value-charged" reality, revealing immediate access to axiological structures (Scheler 1961, xvii).

All of the foregoing considerations bear significant implications for the discipline of law. According to Husserl, the phenomenological method is applicable not only to theoretical sciences but also to normative sciences (Husserl 1970, 23). One of the few legal theorists to introduce the phenomenological method into legal theory was Adolf Reinach, who, following Husserl, argued that law is characterized by essential and objective structures. Reinach went so far as to claim that "structures which are generally described as specifically legal have an existence, as much as numbers, trees, or houses; that this existence [Sein] is independent of whether it is perceived by men or not and that it is in particular independent of any positive law. It is not only wrong but ultimately senseless to describe legal structures as creations of positive law" (in Friedmann 1973, 347). In his phenomenological analysis, Reinach placed particular emphasis on distinguishing between the legal *a priori* and natural law (Friedmann 1973, 348).

Conversely, Paul Amselek, another prominent theorist of the application of phenomenology to law, criticized Reinach's position and pessimistically concluded that neither Husserl's nor Scheler's aprioristic phenomenology could lead to definite axiological conclusions, while Heidegger's existential approach to law, he argued, remained adrift, given its dependence on the absurdity of the human condition (Amselek 1973, 376–80). However, Amselek appears to misinterpret both Husserl and, particularly, Scheler. His polemic against *a priori* values rests on the warning that it is impossible to discover authentic values by relying on what he terms a "confused or tangled intuition"—an intuition based on direct observation that then seeks to strip away factualities through phenomenological reduction (Amselek 1973, 378). Yet Scheler did not claim that one could perceive the essence of values simply through phenomenological reduction. Rather, he suggested that the world of facts and human reality themselves disclose axiological and value-laden structures. The phenomenological method, properly understood, is not a butcher-like process that seeks to eliminate facts in order to construct a purely Platonic realm of essences; on the contrary, since facts always remain the origin and source of essences, the connection between them is never severed. Phenomenological intuition does not commence from normative or value assumptions to be progressively stripped down to pure essence. Instead, it exposes essential structures after a naïve intuitive engagement with facts and empirical realities.

Regarding the problem of "confused or entangled intuition," Husserl himself acknowledges that the apprehension of essences admits different grades and layers of givenness, intuitability, and clarity (Husserl 1931, 194). There are higher and lower levels of intuitive apprehension, but this stratification does not undermine the validity of the phenomenological method. As for the issue of communicating such insights persuasively to others, Husserl is notably explicit. While recognizing the risk of being accused of elitism, he maintains that "insights can be tested and confirmed only by persons well-trained in the ability to engage in pure description in the unnatural attitude of reflection, trained in short to allow phenomenological relations to work upon them in full purity" (Husserl 1970, 91).

Phenomenological intuition, therefore, stands as a valid method of apprehension and reasoning in law and the philosophy of legal rights. In this spirit, the following and final section of the third chapter will proceed with a basic phenomenological reading of legal rights, grounded in Aristotelian philosophy, Husserl's concept of intuition, and the phenomenological *a priori*. As previously explained, this undertaking forms part of a broader inductive project, which seeks to replace the social contract concept as the middle term of the international legal syllogism concerning the relationship between self-determination and constitutional law. Methodologically, this project requires the suspension of all positivist semantic assumptions, including the social thesis and the right–duty correlation doctrine.

## The Phenomenology of the Right as Essence and Temporality

The critical examination of the semantic presuppositions underlying mainstream legal theory reveals a surplus of meaning in the concept of legal rights—one that cannot be adequately accounted for within either an analytical or formally inductive framework. This surplus coincides with the phenomenological concept of essence or essential being. However, because both formal logic and

Wittgensteinian communitarian semantics exclude intuition as a valid method of reasoning, formal induction proves insufficient for establishing the philosophical and legal foundations of a comprehensive general theory concerning the essence of legal rights.

Moreover, formal induction is inherently problematic for international law and legal theory. As previously argued, symbolic or mathematical logic is ill-suited to inexact sciences. These disciplines require alternative logical tools and methods because their purpose is not to express the world in strictly quantitative terms, but rather to address relational structures between concepts, to formulate definitions, to generate analogies, and to make substantive claims about the nature of things. These operations fall within the domain of informal or syllogistic logic, namely the logic appropriate to natural language arguments.

To grasp the essence of legal rights, one requires a method of inductive reasoning that integrates both intuition and phenomenological insight. As previously discussed, Aristotelian induction offers such a method. For Aristotle, knowledge of essences and the apprehension of first principles cannot be attained through deduction alone. In the *Posterior Analytics*, Aristotle underscores the necessity of intuition within inductive reasoning. He explains that among the intellectual faculties employed in the pursuit of truth, only scientific knowledge (*epistēmē*) and intuition (*nous*) are inherently true, whereas other faculties—such as opinion or discursive reasoning—are susceptible to error. Since first principles are more certain than demonstrations, and since demonstrations presuppose reason, it follows that the first principles themselves cannot be known scientifically. Hence, if scientific knowledge itself rests upon something more primary, and if no other faculty is more infallible than scientific knowledge except intuition, then it must be intuition that apprehends first principles. (Aristotle, Posterior Analytics 1960, 261)

In the *Topica*, Aristotle not only outlines a method of reasoning but also introduces a phenomenological theory of meaning, suggesting that arguments can be traced back to certain primary convictions and theoretical premises. Arguments, Aristotle proposes, arise from propositions, and he introduces the term 'problems' to refer to the subject matter of each argument. Every particular proposition or problem, he suggests, contains both an essence and other parts. The essential part he terms *τὸ τί ἦν εἶναι* (the "what it was to be" or, in simpler terms, the "definition"), whereas the remaining elements he designates as "properties." For Aristotle, "[a] definition is a phrase indicating the essence of something" (Aristotle, *Topica* 1960, 278–9). Thus, Aristotelian logic dictates that all meanings inherently encompass an essence, which should be captured within their definition.

For the reasons explained above, neither the mainstream nor the Critical Legal Studies approaches have so far adequately addressed the essence of legal rights. As Grzegorczyk observes, "[l]aw without objective foundation [. . .] appears arbitrary" (Grzegorczyk 1991, 122–3). Despite frequent references to the 'core' of legal rights within international legal discourse, what is intuitively invoked under this term falls short of true essentialism. Hart's concept of core-advantage or core-liberty, for instance, is not of essentialist quality. Rather, it remains confined within the consensual and contextual framework of Wittgenstein's logic of language, thereby presupposing a perimeter of duties for the articulation of rights. Similarly, mainstream rhetoric about the core and periphery of legal rights does not point toward an essentialist structure of legal concepts. Instead, it serves to describe the density of legal consensus surrounding particular legal matters.

For the Critical Legal Studies tradition, the situation is even more radical. Even where there appears to be prima facie semantic stability, international law remains fundamentally indeterminate. As Koskenniemi notes, this indeterminacy persists because international law is built upon contradictory premises and attempts to regulate a future in which even individual actors' preferences are unsettled (Koskenniemi 1989, 590).

As noted above, the most elaborate mainstream attempt to conceptualize human rights has been, following Hohfeld's analysis, to define them as conflicting individual interests. This approach reflects the liberal-contractarian tradition, according to which individuals enter into societies through the exercise of reasonable reciprocity, a process that leads to a just and symmetrical limitation of interests. According to John Rawls, individuals necessarily possess interests, without which they would be "either inert and passive, or likely to be swayed by unreasonable and sometimes blind passions and impulses" (Rawls 1999, 44). Among the most prominent of these interests are the protection of political independence, the safeguarding of free culture and civil liberties, the maintenance of security, the preservation of territory, and the promotion of the well-being of citizens. On this basis, people are said to accept legal norms insofar as they perceive those norms to be advantageous for themselves and for those they care about; over time, Rawls suggests, they tend to internalize such norms as ideals of conduct (Rawls 1999, 34). He characterizes this psychological process as "moral learning" (Rawls 1999, 44).

The chapter now turns to a phenomenological examination of the conceptualization of legal rights as interests, a conceptualization firmly anchored in the liberal mainstream *noesis*. According to this noematic model, legal rights are construed as interests 'against'—that is, they presuppose that the nature of human relations is fundamentally hostile and that the phenomenology of inter-subjectivity is rooted in emotions of suspicion and distrust. Under this model, the phenomenology of legal rights as interests is a phenomenology of constant claim and defense. It suggests that legal rights consist either in: (a) positive expectations for action—namely, positive entitlements to something and against others—or (b) negative entitlements. Negative entitlements can be further understood as phenomenological intentionalities directed toward a particular threshold of maintenance, beyond which there arises a negative expectation not to be deprived, oppressed, harmed, or deteriorated.

Both positive and negative conceptualizations presuppose that a certain state of affairs, a mode of being, a status, a situation, an institution, or a threshold is considered either acquired or legitimately claimed, essentially conceived, to borrow the analytic metaphor, as the 'property' of the subject of the right (SR). In both cases, the right, whether positive or negative, presupposes an alterity toward which the SR directs its intentionality as a form of defensive consciousness (Wall 2002, 53). Within this framework, the external otherness fulfills two roles: (a) it refers to the source-subject who nominally provides a particular structural benefit and bears the objective task of safeguarding the interests of the SR and (b) it encompasses the totality of other individuals regarded as potential violators of the SR's rights and legitimate interests.

The phenomenology of claim and defense aligns with Alexandre Kojève's *Phenomenology of the Right* (Kojève 2000). Kojève characterizes his phenomenology as descriptive behaviorism, suggesting that when dealing with a human phenomenon, it is often preferable not to begin by analyzing its internal content through introspection, but first to examine its external form using a behaviorist method (Kojève 2000, 35). Following this behaviorist model, Kojève describes legal rights as a three-partite relation involving: (a) individuals A and B, whose interaction gives rise to (b) the intervention of C, a third, disinterested, and impartial party tasked with annulling the illegal action of either A or B (Kojève 2000, 40).

Kojève appears to embrace the contextuality of meaning, asserting that "to have a right to" essentially means to have a right to some externalized, effective behavior—behavior that produces an objective or externally noticeable result (Kojève 2000, 36). Thus, for Kojève, rights cannot merely be moral or psychological expectations; they must be tied to observable outcomes. He distinguishes three possible juridical scenarios: (a) having a right, (b) not having a right, and (c) having a duty to do or omit something (Kojève 2000, 35). Through this categorization, he asserts a strong correlativity between rights and duties, maintaining that the presence of a duty necessarily implies the existence of a right, although the reverse is not always the case (Kojève 2000, 36). According to Kojève's phenomenology, having a right to an externalized result constitutes an adequate condition for the existence of a juridical situation (Kojève 2000, 36). Although Kojève does not employ Husserl's eidetic phenomenology of essences, he nonetheless speaks of the essence of rights. For Kojève, this essence is Justice—or rather, the Idea of Justice—as it manifests itself through the phenomenon of law, arising "in the event of an interaction between two human beings" (Kojève 2000, 39).

Kojève's descriptive phenomenology, while innovative in certain respects, is neither eidetic nor truly phenomenological in the Husserlian sense. Although Kojève moves away from the natural attitude characteristic of everyday perception, he does not abandon mainstream legal assumptions such as the right–duty symmetry, the contextuality of legal meaning, and the liberal conceptualization of rights as a form of defensive consciousness directed against others—a view itself permeated with negative assumptions about human nature. Moreover, Kojève situates the essence of law and legal rights within the domain of ideas and morality, asserting that Justice, or the Idea of Justice, constitutes the essence of law as a social phenomenon. However, in deriving Justice from the phenomenon of law and treating it as an idea, Kojève ultimately engages in a reduction that falls short of an eidetic phenomenological inquiry. Rather than reaching out to the essential structure of Justice through objective phenomenological analysis, being a Hegelian, he reintroduces an idealist abstraction. In doing so, Kojève contravenes one of the most fundamental principles of Husserlian phenomenology: the inseparability of fact and essence (Husserl 1931, 52–4).

In contrast to Kojève's approach, Husserl maintains that essences possess the character of immanence, essential necessity, and essential universality (Husserl 1931, 53). An essence is neither a subjective projection nor a mere ideal; it constitutes an objective eidos that exists beyond spatio-temporal determinations (Husserl 1931, 52). Husserl explains that an essence assumes concrete form and is posited as "having spatio-temporal existence, as something existing in this time-spot, having this particular duration of its own and a real content which in its essence could just as well have been present in any other time-spot" (Husserl 1931, 52). What belongs to the essence of one individual, moreover, can also belong to another (Husserl 1931, 53). By contrast, the conceptualization of the right as an "interest against" cannot achieve such universality, for it presupposes a collective and homogeneous state of defensive being for all individuals, as well as a morally negative predisposition toward others. Kojève's descriptive behaviorism, in this respect, does not reach the essential structure of legal rights. Rather, it remains at the level of immediate apprehension—a level that, in Husserlian phenomenology, belongs to a superficial stratum within a much richer set of strata, substrata, and sub-substrata of apprehension and phenomenological clearness (Husserl 1931, 192–201). Despite this phenomenological gradualism, Husserl insists that "for every essence . . . there exists, so to speak, an absolute nearness, in which its givenness is in respect of this graded series absolute, i.e., pure self-givenness" (Husserl 1931, 194).

A pure phenomenology of legal rights presupposes the bracketing and suspension of all structural and semantic assumptions, in accordance with Husserl's method of *epoché*. By "structural assumptions," I refer to constructs such as internal and external self-determination; secession; remedial secession; *de jure* and *de facto* secession; the distinction between international and constitutional self-determination; the Gründnorm; and the political concept of the social contract. By 'semantic assumptions,' I mean Hart's notion of the open texture of legal language and the associated concept of the penumbra; the analytical polarity of right and obligation; the consensual, contextual, and conventional nature of meaning; the liberal conceptualization of legal rights as interests against others; and, accordingly, the presupposition of a defensive mass consciousness directed at the protection and advancement of individual spheres of interest. What remains after this suspension is the phenomenological residuum: the essence of legal rights. This essence is not normative or minimalist in the sense understood by mainstream legal theory. It is neither a semantic compromise—resulting from the reduction of values to a single common denominator—nor a reflection of minimum needs that must be met, or minimum claims that must correlate with minimum obligations. The essence of legal rights exists independently of the two Wittgensteinian poles of context and consent: that is, independently of juridical or state consensus, and irrespective of whether there is an ad hoc conflict of rights among individuals.

From the standpoint of Husserl's pure phenomenology, the essence of legal rights does not assume any particular predisposition—neither positive nor negative—toward others. Consequently, it does not depend on a phenomenology of duties. Nor is the essence of legal rights metaphysical or mystical, nor is it derived from abstract ideas of justice in the idealist sense. As previously noted, intuition, also the first step in Aristotelian induction, is a natural mental process that cannot be fully controlled. A particularly revealing manifestation of this intuitive operation appears in what has been termed the "possession paradox," according to which "'having' a right is . . . of the most value when one does not 'have' the object of the right—that is, when one is denied direct or objective enjoyment of that right" (Adelman 1994, 165). This paradox highlights the essential role of temporality in the discourse on legal rights.

Legal rights, in their essence, emerge as institutionalized intentionalities—legal promises—toward restitution, triggered precisely when what is perceived as normalcy or the natural order of things is disturbed. Michel Villey articulates this point when he observes that, for Aristotle, the proliferation of crimes such as adultery, robbery, or hostage-taking within cities necessitates the invention of penalties and criminal procedures, all aimed at restoring a natural order that has either been disturbed or never fully attained. Public authority thus intervenes, exercising legislative power from which positive law is derived (Villey 1991, 9).

Ordinarily, the conditions of disturbance and restitution are institutionalized and incorporated into legal norms. Although it might initially appear that restitution necessarily requires Kojève's three-partite phenomenology, this is not a strict precondition. Theoretically, restitution could also be actualized within a two-partite phenomenology of social relations. Kojève's three-partite model assumes, *ab initio*, a situation of inequality or a hiatus in communication—or at least a presumption of such inequality—between the two immediate parties. When such a hiatus arises, the mediation of a third party becomes necessary for asserting the disturbance and proposing concrete modes of restitution. Moreover, the three-partite model presupposes a phenomenology of authority and acceptance, whereby the two immediate parties develop a psychology of trust toward the mediator. This structure, offering practicality and rapidity by detouring the difficulties of direct communication, has been gradually institutionalized over time through the establishment of mediators, arbitrators, courts, and tribunals.

It appears that what lies at the core of legal rights is not merely a demand or expectation for 'protection against' disturbances. Rather, it is a psychology of perseverance: a striving to maintain the natural mode of being and the natural order of things. The pursuit of the natural mode of being thus constitutes the fundamental purpose of legal rights, which are, based on an intersubjectivity of mutual recognition. The persistence, repetition, or seriousness of particular patterns of disturbance has given rise to the discourse on rights and has led to the institutionalization of mechanisms for restitution. Legal rights are structured attempts to organize—and inevitably fragment—the various forms of natural being that are threatened or compromised by acts of disturbance.

This brings forth the important question of what constitutes the 'natural mode of being' and what counts as 'disturbance.' Disturbance can take multiple forms. When generated by social interactions, it may manifest externally through acts such as physical assault, expulsion, forced relocation, deprivation, or psychological aggression in the form of threats, blackmail, or insults. Disturbance may also have internal manifestations, including emotional pressures and feelings of unfairness arising from perceived inequalities in social treatment. Likewise, when disturbance stems from natural circumstances, it may be externally manifested in events such as natural disasters, the destruction or inaccessibility of natural resources, famine, infectious diseases, sickness, or death. Internal manifestations in this context may include fear, weakness, and despair.

The natural mode of being, as outlined above, appears to possess an essence of its own. It corresponds to a psychological state of tranquility—or *ataraxia*—which may be understood as freedom from fear, worry, or distress.[4] This ideal condition enables individuals to express their identity, engage in meaningful interaction, preserve their habitual practices, and pursue their activities without interference. While *ataraxia* represents an ideal state, the human inclination to value and preserve it—alongside a corresponding aversion to disturbance, distress, and anxiety—is both concrete and existential. This inclination belongs to the essence of humanity itself.

The essence of legal rights (*τὸ τί ἦν εἶναι*) resides, then, in the natural and intuitive desire to bridge—either preemptively or therapeutically—the psychological distance between: (a) *ataraxia*, and (b) the disordered psychological state that results from an act or event of disturbance. In this view, the purpose of restitution is to restore this disrupted balance. Restitution, as both moral and social reaction, aims to re-establish *ataraxia* as the natural mode of being. Within this framework, what H.L.A. Hart describes as "the right as liberty", illustrated by his oft-cited example of the right to scratch one's head, should not be understood as freedom in the liberal sense of legitimately and unrestrainedly doing as one wishes. That framing already implies that such freedom requires thematization and protection against others, lest it be violated. Rather, such a right is better conceived as an unmarked expression of the natural mode of being—one that has either not yet been disturbed or has not been disturbed with sufficient gravity to warrant institutionalization.

The *τὸ τί ἦν εἶναι* of legal rights—as the normative coverage of the psychological distance from disturbance to tranquility—eventually takes legal form as a right to a concrete something. This transformation is driven by the empirical accumulation of data concerning recurrent patterns of disturbance, the severity of which acquires socially recognized psychological impact upon individuals and collectivities. That social recognition, in turn, leads to the institutionalization of legal rights, and inevitably, the institutionalization of a defensive predisposition toward others. Moreover, the severity of psychological impact resulting from a particular disturbance often gives rise to a discourse of hierarchy within legal rights. The 'core' of a legal right can thus be interpreted as that part of the natural being which is preemptively safeguarded from possible disturbance. It is worth noting that disturbance need not arise only through action; it may also result from omission or from the unexpected cessation of an established social practice, as encapsulated in the doctrine of legitimate expectations. The relation between the gravity of a disturbance and its psychological impact upon the natural mode of being is directly proportional. Consequently, the demand for restitution is similarly proportional to the gravity of the disturbance, and the adequacy of restitution is assessed according to whether it effectively restores *ataraxia* and the integrity of the natural mode of being.

Although *ataraxia* constitutes an essential quality of the natural mode of being, this mode is also characterized by other properties that are dynamic rather than static. What counts as 'normalcy' or the 'natural mode of being' is shaped and influenced by historical, sociopolitical, and cultural context: this is the domain in which the natural mode of being takes concrete and situated form. Within the phenomenology of legal rights, the element of time and temporality plays a particularly significant role. Temporality discloses that legal rights do not function as constant claims against others, precisely because *ataraxia* and the natural mode of being more generally, is grounded in a phenomenology of intersubjective recognition that does not presuppose suspicion or fear. When an act of disturbance occurs, *ataraxia* gives way to a disordered psychological state.

Legal rights, in this framework, are activated in response to that disturbance and are directed toward restitution. Once the natural mode of being is restored, legal rights once again become latent. Thus, in the natural condition, legal rights remain dormant; they are not continuous or ongoing claims but rather emerge only in response to specific disruptions.

It becomes apparent, then, that legal theories premised on "continuous rights" imply a state of constant alertness, fear, and defensive posturing—one fundamentally incompatible with the phenomenology of *ataraxia*.

Well before Heidegger's *Sein und Zeit* (Heidegger 1962), Aristotle had already explored the relationship between substance (*οὐσία*), being, and time. He argued that the temporal dimension is crucial because it distinguishes among: (a) actual being, (b) becoming, and (c) not-being yet possessing all the necessary conditions for becoming. To articulate this dynamic relation, Aristotle employed the concepts of actuality (*ἐν ἐνεργείᾳ*) and potentiality (*ἐν δυνάμει*) (Aristotle, The Metaphysics 1998, 266–8). His conception of actuality and potentiality was not merely speculative, but emerged inductively through analogical extensions of empirical paradigms, such as "the engaged builder / the apt-to-build, the waking / the sleeping, the engaged observer / the sighted animal with closed eyes, the thing carved from matter / the matter, and the processed / the unprocessed" (Aristotle 1998, 267). In each pair, Aristotle observed that the first term expresses an actuality, whereas the second embodies a potentiality in being. For Aristotle, potentiality denotes a capacity "to initiate processes in other things or to have processes initiated in [things] themselves by others" (Aristotle 1998, 266). Becoming, then, refers to a transitional mode of being—a condition that has not yet reached completion but is oriented toward a telos. As he explains, becoming does not possess a purpose in itself, whereas processes that contain their own ends (*ἐντελέχεια*) qualify as actions (Aristotle 1998, 268).

Furthermore, he also contends that actuality is ontologically prior to potentiality: "a potential builder is possessing a potentiality to build . . . [a] potential see-er is possessing a potentiality to see, and . . . [something] potentially visible is possessing a potentiality to be seen" (Aristotle 1998, 273). From these analogies, Aristotle inductively concludes that actuality is logically and ontologically prior to potentiality, and that "knowledge of the former is prior to that of the latter." What exists by necessity—such as first principles—exists in actuality and not in potentiality. Moreover, "anything with potentiality to initiate process in some particular way also has the potentiality not to initiate it in just that way" (Aristotle 1998, 273). Finally, Aristotle argues that in the domain of ethical or axiological evaluation, actuality is superior to potentiality, since what is actually good excludes the simultaneous existence of evil, whereas potentiality allows for the coexistence of both (Aristotle 1998).

From Aristotle's theory of actual and potential being, it follows that legal rights—conceived phenomenologically—are inert potentialities that may be actualized in response to internal or external acts or events of disturbance. In this respect, legal rights do not, in themselves, predispose their holders either for or against others as potential violators. Such predisposition only emerges when the potentiality of fear or defensive consciousness is externally triggered. There is, of course, a human potentiality for experiencing fear and developing defensive or even antagonistic orientations, but this capacity requires activation by an external cause. Moreover, because legal rights are not autonomous actions but rather psychological potentialities that may become actualities, they do not contain their own telos. The purpose of legal rights is not intrinsic but defined by the act or event of disturbance, which functions as their mobilizer. Since actuality is ontologically prior to potentiality, it must be the case—by necessity—that the very conceptualization of legal rights as potentialities was originally triggered by actual disturbances. Legal rights, then, are historically reactive and temporally situated phenomena that derive their form and necessity from the actual conditions they are meant to address.

## Notes

1 I keep referring to the objectivity of Reason as a natural mental process independent of human conventions, in order to distinguish it from whatever 'internal rationalities' have been instrumentally constructed and operate within the discipline of international law.

2 Koskenniemi employs the term "intuition" systematically throughout his book in order to justify his conclusion and this shared understanding among international lawyers. The author's view is that he uses the term in order to escape a direct reference to logic, reason, and the essential possibilities of communication and understanding (empathy).

3 A somewhat similar view has been previously put forward by Joseph Raz, who argued that the purpose of law is "to provide publicly ascertainable standards by

which members of the society are held to be bound so that they cannot excuse non-conformity by challenging the justification of the standard" (Raz 2009, 125).

4 *Ataraxia* is originally an Epicurean concept. It means serenity and freedom from distress and fears and, according to Epicurus, is the only true source of human happiness (Epicurus 1926, 52). A similar concept is introduced in the Tao Te Ching (道德經) of Lao Tzu.

# 4

# The Psychological

## Deprivation as a Collective Identity Distress Factor

It has been suggested that the middle term of the international legal syllogism concerning the relationship between self-determination and constitutional law cannot be deduced merely from legal theory. Instead, this requires a rational approach, specifically through an Aristotelian-type induction (*ἐπαγωγή*). This form of induction is a comprehensive mechanism of reasoning that extends beyond simple enumeration of instances, encompassing both observation and intuitive insight. Such intuition is crucial for re-establishing the connection between legal entities and "the data from which [. . .] they were originally derived" (Noyes 1940, 511).

At this stage, while I have started engaging in an 'unhindered' induction, I shift the focus away from abstract legal concepts such as legal rights, national constitutions, international treaties, and the theoretical ambiguity surrounding the designation of peoples as holders of collective rights. Instead, I propose that international jurists and legal theorists concentrate on the concrete material reality of acts of deprivation that impact collective identities, which in turn 'resurrect' the right of peoples to self-determination from a state of potentiality to one of actuality and actionable claim. The subsequent two chapters will explore how international and constitutional self-determination become relevant once such acts of collective deprivation challenge the existence and identity of collectivities. To investigate this effectively, I adopt a twofold methodology:

- *Interdisciplinary Analysis*: This approach focuses on deprivation as a distress factor affecting collective identity from the perspectives of sociology, social psychology, psychoanalysis, social phenomenology, and critical hermeneutics. The discussions integrate theories of social identity, intergroup relations, loss and trauma, and relative deprivation, alongside aggression and frustration from psychology. In psychoanalysis, the foundational texts of Sigmund Freud and Otto Rank are examined, particularly concerning group dynamics and the unconscious processes of removal, separation, and loss. In social phenomenology, the works of Edmund Husserl and Alfred Schütz are employed, while Paul Ricoeur's insights on memory and history inform the critical hermeneutic analysis.

- *Empirical Examination*: The subsequent expanded-induction fifth chapter investigates historically documented instances of collective deprivation and loss across various contexts, including the experiences of indigenous peoples in America, the dissolution of the Ottoman Empire (focusing on Palestine), the decolonization of Nauru, the Kosovo crisis, and the situation in Cyprus. This selection spans a wide historical, sociopolitical, and geographical spectrum, reflecting the evolution and institutionalization of self-determination. The criteria for choosing these cases aim to cover major ongoing conflicts involving collective self-determination claims relevant to both domestic and international law, utilizing a variety of historical sources.

Overall, the expanded-induction chapters attempt to describe how and under which conditions deprivation operates as a distress factor to collective identity. As it will be further elaborated, deprivation is a phenomenon that is subject to qualitative distinctions due to its being dependent on cultural variables and a natural mode of being which is enriched by the liberal connotations of the property analogy. It is of a dual nature for it normally encompasses an external and an internal element. The external element is the attribution of loss to an external source such as an act of removal, whereas the internal element corresponds to the collective psychology of loss or trauma that follows the act. Although both the external and internal elements should be normally present for deprivation to be effectuated this is not a requirement: in the sociological analysis, I will argue that deprivation may occur solely at the psychological level. In comparison to this sociopsychological framework, the expanded induction chapters are only interested in phenomena of deprivation that affect collective identities.

# From Sociology, Social Psychology, and Psychoanalysis to the Phenomenology of Deprivation

## Basic Definitions, Delimitations, Connections

Before exploring how deprivation functions as a source of distress for collective identity, it is important to begin with some key definitions and clarifications. In particular, we need to distinguish between psychology and psychoanalysis. Clarifying this distinction will help explain why both disciplines are relevant to the discussion that follows.

*Psychology and Psychoanalysis*: Although both disciplines investigate the individual and collective psyche and seek to understand the etiology of human emotions and actions, they approach their common object of study differently. Psychology is primarily a cognitive-empirical science that focuses on observable behaviors and mental processes. In contrast, psychoanalysis is a non-empirical, hermeneutical method that delves into the latent motivations, impulses, and instincts characteristic of the unconscious (Sidanius and Pratto 1999, 5). Despite traditional skepticism about its scientific validity, there is a growing consensus among academic psychologists that psychoanalysis should be integrated more closely with the discipline of psychology (Barron 1992, xv–xviii). From a psychoanalytic perspective, a behavior is considered instinctive if it "follows a recognizably similar and predictable pattern in almost all members of a species [and] it is not a simple response to a single stimulus but a sequence of behavior that usually runs a predictable course" (Bowlby 1969, 62).

*Social Psychology*: Social psychology may be broadly understood as the field concerned with the relationship between individuals and the societies to which they belong. It has been suggested that this discipline examines how individuals form and interpret their social identities, how they relate to their environments, what motivates their behaviors, under what conditions they act collectively, and what outcomes such collective actions produce. It also explores the dynamics of mutual influence among individuals and groups, as well as the social processes through which knowledge, norms, and cultural artefacts emerge (Chryssochoou 2004, xvi). From this standpoint, a shared culture is generally seen as involving a common framework through which members of a group understand their relationship with both the social and physical world. Such a framework tends to shape how individuals institutionalize relationships, express thoughts and emotions, organize collective life—including labor, communication, and resource allocation—and assign social values, honors, and authority. A common culture is therefore thought to give rise to a sense of belonging and to a shared cognitive orientation toward the world (Chryssochoou 2004, xxi).

Social psychology and sociology are distinguishable yet closely interrelated disciplines. As of May 11, 2024, the website of Encyclopaedia Britannica lists sociology as "the social science that studies human societies, their interactions, and the processes that preserve and change them." It accomplishes this by investigating the dynamics of societal components such as institutions, communities, populations, and various demographic groups, including those distinguished by gender, race, or age. Consequently, the research focus of sociology tends toward an empirical analysis of social structures, whereas social psychology adopts a more "experimental" and "laboratory-based" approach, primarily examining how individuals, group dynamics, and social structures influence individual and collective psychology (Bordens and Horowitz 2008, 8).

Despite their differing methodologies, the interplay between these disciplines is inevitable and has sparked robust debate regarding their divergences and the potential for interactionist—and even integrationist—dynamics between them (Cavaletto 2007). Both fields overlap conceptually in areas such as social deviance, reference and comparison groups, and the formation and operation of collective identities (Dovidio 2000, 3). This background sets the stage for understanding the intertwining of social psychology, sociology, and group psychoanalysis in the study of collective behavior. While the empiricism of sociology and social psychology stands in contrast to psychoanalysis—which has been criticized as overly mechanistic and unscientific—Freud's theories on group psychology have notably influenced various theories within sociology, social psychology and intergroup relations theories (Billig 1976; Sidanius and Pratto 1999, 5; Taylor and Moghaddam 1994). Several concepts of group psychoanalysis have made their way into sociology and social psychology, particularly with regard to the frustration-aggression theories that will be discussed later on (Krahé 1996, 346). For systemic reasons it is therefore both appropriate and necessary to address these three fields concurrently, while maintaining clear and explicit epistemological boundaries. This approach ensures a comprehensive understanding of the theories discussed and respects the unique contributions of each discipline.

## The Psychoanalytic Basis of Collective Loss

Given that my approach is primarily phenomenological, integrating the psychoanalysis of a key concept like collective deprivation might prompt the traditional, and indeed expected, critique that phenomenology and psychoanalysis are fundamentally incompatible. This critique generally hinges on the contention that while phenomenology focuses on the description of (naïve) conscious experiences, psychoanalysis delves into the unconscious explanations of the human psyche and behavior. Although a detailed exploration of the interplay between these two methodologies is beyond the scope of this book, it is important to clarify that psychoanalysis and phenomenology are not inherently antithetical.

Sigmund Freud himself described the unconscious as "the true psychical reality" (Karlsson 2010, 1). The process of deriving psychoanalytic conclusions about this unconscious reality relies fundamentally on consciousness. Indeed, psychoanalytic practice cannot extricate itself from consciousness, as "the psychoanalytic process both begins with the self-understanding of the analysand and is driven by means of conscious validations and verifications of interpretations of the unconscious" (Karlsson 2010, 1). In other words, this interdependence underscores that while phenomenology and psychoanalysis may focus on different aspects of human experience, they are interconnected through the continuous interaction between conscious and unconscious processes.

From the psychoanalytic point of view, human existence is fundamentally relational. Freud's claim that, in an individual's mental life, another person is always present—whether as a model, object, helper, or opponent—has been taken to indicate that individual psychology cannot be meaningfully separated from social psychology (Freud 1945, 1–2). This perspective implies that the self is not formed in isolation but emerges through engagement with the social world, an interpretation that some scholars have linked to broader phenomenological concerns with the structures of experience (Campel 2001, 137). While psychoanalysis and phenomenology remain distinct in method and focus, this shared attention to relationality suggests a certain complementarity, particularly when addressing complex psychological and sociocultural processes.

In Freud's view, group psychology addresses the individual as a member of a collective—whether defined by race, nationality, profession, institution, or a temporarily assembled crowd formed for a specific purpose (Freud 1945, 3). He maintains that conscious behavior originates from a deeper, unconscious layer of the psyche, largely shaped by inherited dispositions (Freud 1945, 8). This framework applies not only to individuals but also to collective settings, though Freud does not venture into metaphysical territory with respect to collective consciousness.

According to Freud, when individuals enter group contexts, certain repressions that ordinarily suppress instinctual drives tend to weaken. This release of the unconscious, he argues, allows traits to emerge that may appear new but in fact reflect latent predispositions—particularly those associated with aggression, destructiveness, or moral disengagement. In such conditions, the usual operations of conscience and personal responsibility are diminished (Freud 1945, 9–10).

In developing this theory, Freud draws heavily on Gustave Le Bon's work in crowd psychology. Le Bon described the transformative effect of the crowd on the individual as akin to hypnosis, wherein a person's conscious personality is temporarily eclipsed. The result, he argued, is a psychological state in which the individual loses independent will and critical judgment, becoming highly susceptible to suggestion. Under these conditions, there is a rapid and automatic spread—or "contagion"—of emotions and ideas, often followed by impulsive and uniform action (Freud 1945, 12).

Le Bon is often cited as having argued that the mere fact of belonging to a group leads individuals to regress along the "ladder of civilization." Once absorbed into a collective, people are said to exhibit traits such as spontaneity, impulsiveness, and even ferocity—characteristics that, when amplified through group dynamics, render the crowd emotionally volatile and highly reactive (Freud 1945, 14). In such a context, critical discernment tends to be suspended, and individuals become especially prone to suggestion and emotional excess, particularly when exposed to intense stimuli (Freud 1945, 16).

Freud appears to endorse Le Bon's view that membership in a group results in a substantial transformation of individual mental functioning. The group setting, in this view, facilitates a heightening of emotional responsiveness while simultaneously undermining reflective or intellectual capacities (Freud 1945, 33). Nonetheless, Freud introduces a degree of nuance by suggesting that this psychological effect is less pronounced in more structurally organized groups. In such cases, the influence of rules, roles, and hierarchies may offer some constraint on the unmediated expression of the unconscious. When considering the mechanisms behind these phenomena, Freud acknowledges a difficulty in relying exclusively on rationalist or empirical explanations. He notes that conventional reasoning cannot fully account for the compelling nature of imitation and emotional contagion as they occur within social formations (Freud 1945, 34). Such processes, while observable and recurrent, remain resistant to simple causal analysis, suggesting a need for deeper theoretical tools to grasp their function and significance. Freud reads:

> [t]here is no doubt that something exists in us which, when we become aware of signs of an emotion in someone else, tends to make us fall into the same emotion; but how often do we not successfully oppose it, resist the emotion, and react in quite an opposite way? Once more we should have to say that what compels us to obey this tendency is imitation, and what induces the emotion in us is the group's suggestive influence . . . [w]e shall therefore be prepared for the statement that suggestion (or more correctly suggestibility) is actually an irreducible, primitive phenomenon, a fundamental fact in the mental life of man. (Sigmund Freud 1945, 35)

Freud brings the idea of suggestibility into conversation with his theory of libido, grounding both in the broader framework of psychoanalysis. Libido, in this context, refers to the energy behind those instincts that fall under the wide-ranging term *love*. As Freud explains, this includes not only sexual desire with physical union as its goal but also self-love, affection for others, familial bonds, friendships, devotion to humanity, and even attachment to ideas or causes (Freud 1945, 37–8). All of these expressions, he argues, stem from the same deep-rooted drives. In sexual relationships, these drives aim directly at union, but in other forms, they are redirected or blocked from reaching that end—though they retain enough of their original nature to remain recognizable, showing up in gestures like wanting to be close or sacrificing something for the other (Freud 1945, 38). Freud connects this view of love to Plato's concept of *eros*, casting it as the basic libidinal force that binds people together in groups (Freud 1945, 38). When that force is stable, it helps maintain social ties and cohesion. But when these emotional and instinctual links are disturbed—through fear, trauma, betrayal, or breakdown of trust—those ties weaken, and people are left exposed to what Freud calls "senseless dread" (*Angst*) (Freud 1945, 46).

This idea offers a powerful way to understand what happens during moments of collective panic. For Freud, such episodes are not just reactions to external threats, but signs that the emotional glue holding the group together has come undone. The fear spreads like wildfire—not because individuals are simply imitating each other, but because the group's internal structure has collapsed. What remains is a raw, contagious fear that reflects the deeper psychic bonds now unraveling. Now, considering how psychoanalytic theory connects to the argument of collective deprivation, Freud's insights reveal that the libidinal instincts of both individuals and groups can be directed toward both concrete objects and abstract ideas. In the context of self-determination, this is particularly relevant, as peoples may direct their libidinal instincts not only toward each other but also toward places, institutions, traditions, and so forth. Disturbances to these libidinal connections between peoples and their objects of attachment produce angst. Otto Rank, a prominent psychoanalyst and one of Freud's closest colleagues, identifies anxiety as the "nucleus of every neurotic disturbance" (Rank 1973, 46). He differentiates between neurotic anxiety and traumatic anxiety, suggesting that all forms are ultimately linked to primal anxiety, which originates from the trauma of birth.

For Rank, the unconscious repercussions of the birth trauma are reflected and manifested in various ways. He notes, for example, an "increased memory capacity" in dreams concerning the recall of suppressed childhood impressions (Rank 1973, 7). This pronounced ability to recollect infancy images, Rank argues, indicates an unconscious effort to recreate the "primal scene" and the most intense of all memories—the experience of one's own birth, which paradoxically, can never truly be remembered (Rank 1973, 8). Consequently, there is a natural resistance to relinquishing the "mother-binding phase," viewed as a peaceful and undisturbed ideal state. In this psychoanalytic framework, the figure of the father (who acts as a substitute, according to Rank) is seen as the initial disruptor of this idyllic maternal tranquility, thus becoming "the first and lasting enemy" (Rank 1973, 9). Across all cultures and eras, the unconscious perceives any disturbance of the "eternal sleep" as a profound injustice and the gravest crime (Rank 1973, 198). This model of birth trauma aligns also with the psychoanalytic hypothesis of this book, that it is an act or omission that causes disturbance that gives birth to rights as the institutional substitute for the mother.

Rank extends his theory of birth trauma to encompass the phenomena of death, separation, and loss. He proposes that for children, thoughts of death evoke "a strong unconscious sense of pleasure associated with the return to the mother's womb," a yearning to retreat to a place utterly free from external disturbances (Rank 1973, 24). Friedrich Nietzsche similarly discusses a cultural and unique harmonious attribute associated with death by the Greeks, termed "Apollonian," which he contrasts with the "Dionysian" aspects of neurotic disturbances. In Nietzsche's *The Birth of Tragedy*, the philosopher narrates the myth of Silenus as thus:

> An ancient legend recounts how King Midas hunted long in the forest for the wise Silenus, companion of Dionysos, but failed to catch him. When Silenus has finally fallen into his hands, the King asks what is the best and most excellent thing for human beings. Stiff and unmoving, the daemon remains silent until, forced by the King to speak, he finally breaks out in shrill laughter and says: "Wretched, ephemeral race, children of chance and tribulation, why do you force me to tell you the very thing it would be most profitable for you not to hear? The very best thing is utterly beyond your reach not to have been born, not to be, to be nothing. However, the second best thing for you is: to die soon." (Nietzsche 1999, 22)

For Nietzsche, the ancient Greeks were acutely aware of the terrors and horrors of existence. Otto Rank interprets Nietzsche's perspective through a psychoanalytic lens, suggesting that Dionysian anxiety can be traced back to what he describes as the "nuclear symbol of primal anxiety"—the trauma of birth, epitomized by the mythical figure of the Sphinx (Rank 1973, 143). In Greek mythology, as dramatized in Sophocles' tragedy Oedipus the King, the Sphinx is depicted as a formidable creature, half-woman, half-animal, sent by the gods to devour those who fail to answer her enigmatic riddles.

According to Otto Rank, the Sphinx in the Oedipus saga symbolizes "the primal trauma itself." Its feminine form represents the desire to return to the mother, while its animal form reflects the struggle against this desire due to the peril of being consumed by it (Rank 1973, 145). By deciphering the Sphinx's riddle, Oedipus symbolically overcomes the anxiety associated with this primal trauma (Rank 1973, 144). Rank interprets the trauma of birth as providing a foundational psychoanalytical explanation for why the loss of an erotic object (in Freudian terms) triggers the mourning process: such loss evokes the "primal separation from the mother" and necessitates a painful detachment of the libido from the erotic object, reviving the primal trauma in the unconscious mind of the bereaved (Rank 1973, 25).

For Rank, the entire trajectory of civilization, human creativity, and—arguably—social institutions represent collective efforts to surmount the "enforced removal from the mother," driven by "the instinctive tendency to return to her" (Rank 1973, 103). From this psychoanalytical vantage point, one might view the legal right to self-determination and international law more broadly as psychological surrogates for the mother and concrete institutional responses to the primal trauma.

In times of distress, deprivation, and loss, the unconscious revives the birth trauma, resulting in anxiety (Rank 1973, 199). From the early Greek philosophy, notably Plato's notion of *eros*, there emerges a constant "yearning for a lost state . . . a lost union," and thus a deep-seated aversion to removal, separation, and loss (Rank 1973, 173). Rank argues that this unconscious symbolism and instinctual yearning for the lost maternal tranquility apply equally to individuals and collectivities. He illustrates this with the historical example of the Doric migration, where the Greek people were compelled to leave their native lands for Ionia and Asia Minor (Rank 1973, 161). Rank argues that for the Greeks, this forced separation from their homeland was a reenactment of the trauma of birth, profoundly influencing the evolution of Greek culture and civilization. The Homeric epics, particularly the Iliad, are seen as cultural responses to the birth trauma as re-enacted through the Doric migration, encapsulating the collective memory and psychological impact of these foundational disruptions (Rank 1973, 161).

The unconscious mind displaces primal anxiety and redirects libidinal dynamics from the mother to alternative substitute-erotic objects. In the context of group psychology, the collective libido can then be channeled toward such erotic objects as the homeland ('mother-land'), collective traditions, myths, political history, popular symbols, religion, institutions, languages, culture, and art. From a psychoanalytical perspective, international legal institutions such as the League of Nations' mandate system and the United Nations' international trusteeship system can be viewed as global, institutional imitations of the lost union with the mother, with the administering powers acting as substitutes who ostensibly protect and nurture their non-self-governing 'children.' Following this motherly psychoanalytical analogy, it might not be an exaggeration to suggest that the withdrawal of the administering 'mother-state' could induce feelings of abandonment due to the unconscious replication of maternal loss.

According to Freud's theory of emotional contagion, which we previously discussed, not every individual member of a group needs to be concretely or evenly affected by deprivation or separation; the emotions of loss and the subsequent psychological processes of mourning, bereavement, or melancholia are transmitted and amplified due to the group's suggestive influence. This dynamic illustrates how deeply embedded psychological patterns, originally formed in relation to the mother, can influence collective responses to changes in political and social structures.

## Loss and Deprivation from the Perspective of Social Psychology: The Psychological Triad of Bereavement, Anxiety, and Frustration

Although Freud's psychoanalytic attempt to connect the individual unconscious with interpersonal and social levels was met with critical responses from the mainstream sociological and psychological communities (Billig 1976, 44), his impact on sociology, anthropology, and social psychology has been substantial. Broadly, Freud's group theory is often criticized as reductionist because it interprets group psychology and social phenomena in terms of individualistic variables, which are then explained through hidden unconscious processes and pre-social instincts (Billig 1976, 45). Freud's theory of group psychology can be summarized by the claim that all collective psychological phenomena "depend on the instinctual erotic and aggressive feelings shared by all individuals" (Billig 1976, 45).

This reductionist approach is echoed in other theories within psychology and social psychology, such as attachment theory, which posits that human loss should be understood primarily in terms of the mother-infant relationship. According to this theory, separation "induces specific forms of anxiety, separation anxiety, distress, and protest," whereas "[w]ith reunion these affects settle, but when reunion does not occur, the processes of mourning do, with feelings of sadness and a sense of loss" (Raphael and Dobson n.d., 46). These theories suggest that the "love for the mother" is the libidinal, erotic force that binds groups together, leading to a continuous search for maternal substitutes in tribes, nations, and other collectivities (Billig 1976, 52). Concurrently, negative instincts are often associated with the father figure, which "gives rise to the need for enemies and the projection of aggression onto such enemies" (Billig 1976, 52).

From a psychological viewpoint, "the attribution of specialness and value follows from a recognition of potential unavailability" and "[t]hat which may be lost suddenly is perceived as valuable" (Janoff-Bulman and Berger 2000, 35). Accordingly, "we are more motivated by the thought of losing something than by the thought of gaining something of equal value" (Janoff-Bulman and Berger 2000, 35–6). Attachment theory also relates to the theories of bereavement, grief, and melancholia as direct reactions to loss. Bereavement can follow a collective loss, such as the loss of a community or a country (Raphael and Dobson n.d., 45).

Freud's influence is also significant in the psychological theories of mourning and melancholia. In his seminal essay, Freud distinguished mourning from melancholia by the direction of libidinal energy: in mourning, the libidinal bonds are withdrawn from the lost erotic object and displaced to another, whereas in melancholia, the freed libido is internalized and withdrawn into the ego, transforming the object loss into an ego loss (Freud 1989, 586).

Reductionist psychological theories of loss, which integrate Freudian concepts into the analysis of social institutions, emphasize bereavement by highlighting instinctual drives. In contrast, non-reductionist theories move away from Freud's instinctual bases to explain social phenomena using interpersonal or "genuinely social variables" (Billig 1976, 74). While diverging from Freud's innate presuppositions, some interpersonal theorists propose that human behavior is driven not by libido but by a desire to avoid anxiety (Billig 1976, 98). These theories align with another basic hypothesis of this book, namely that humans have a natural tendency of maintaining an undisturbed mode of being.

In the context of collective deprivation, some social psychologists seek to bridge Freud's ego psychology with social sciences. They challenge Freud's assertion that "[c]ultural values and normative prescriptions" operate within the individual, arguing instead that the formation of social identity should not be "reduced to the level of the instincts" (Billig 1976, 103–4). A notable non-reductionist approach within this framework is the frustration–aggression dyadic theory, which links deprivation, frustration, and aggression under a unified psychological umbrella theory. According to the frustration–aggression model, "the occurrence of aggressive behavior always presupposes the existence of frustration and, contrariwise [. . .] the existence of frustration always leads to some form of aggression" (Billig 1976, 124). A crucial aspect of the frustration-aggression model is the external stimulus that triggers frustration, such as the act of removal in instances of deprivation, subsequently leading to an aggressive response (Billig 1976, 124) (Taylor and Moghaddam 1994, 28). Frustration is defined as the psychological result "of a blocking or a prevention of a goal response" (Taylor and Moghaddam 1994, 28). The theory of frustration-aggression also introduced the concept of displaced aggression, where the frustration cannot be directly vented toward the source due to its overwhelming power. In such scenarios, "the instigation to aggress does not evaporate but ensures that some other form of aggression will take place" (Billig 1976, 125). From the perspective of social psychology, it is therefore inferred that: (a) aggression is a necessary and cathartic reaction to frustration, and (b) the impetus to aggress persists if it cannot be directed toward the source of frustration. The concept of displaced aggression stems from Freud's Mourning and Melancholia, where Freud argued that "the blocking of pleasure-seeking, or erotic impulses, causes frustration, with aggression being 'the primordial reaction' to frustration" (Billig 1976, 124).

In the context of collective and large-scale social phenomena, the frustration-aggression theorists argue that in organized societies there are various sources of frustration and therefore the imposition of social and communitarian restrictions is inevitable (Billig 1976, 150). Despite these frustrations being an integral part of communal life, social psychologists observe that revolutions and riots do not arise merely because "people coincidentally have similarly aroused emotional states" or because they channel their aggression in identical directions (Billig 1976, 151). Instead, the uniformity of aggressive mass behavior is largely influenced by its underlying motivation, namely the source of frustration and social discontent. Crucially, "the interpretation of social discontent or deprivation" is deemed more significant than "the actual feeling of suffering"; this interpretation plays a critical role in the genesis of social violence as a response to social deprivation (Billig 1976, 153). Thus, the social interpretation of deprivation becomes key to understanding frustration as a disruptor of the natural, mundane mode of being. This interpretation assumes that members of a society believe that "certain social, economic, or political ends are being denied to them, and that they should rightfully possess such ends" (Billig 1976, 153). This perspective underscores the importance of perceived justice and entitlement in the development of collective responses to deprivation. It suggests that not just the experience of deprivation itself, but how it is perceived and interpreted within the social context, catalyzes significant social movements and upheavals.

## Loss and Deprivation from the Perspective of Sociology and Phenomenology

Before exploring the phenomenology of deprivation in greater depth, it is essential to discuss another significant concept within social psychology: relative deprivation. This sociopsychological concept is applicable to both individuals and collectivities. Relative deprivation refers to a perceived, rather than actual, loss—it signifies a simulation of deprivation that departs from the notion of objective deprivation, which involves actual, attributable loss. Unlike the frustration-aggression theory, which emphasizes an external stimulus such as an act of removal or explicit denial, relative deprivation focuses on an internal element of dissatisfaction, which arises from comparative assessments between reference groups.

According to Walter G. Runciman, a sociologist and leading theorist on relative deprivation, "people's attitudes, aspirations, and grievances largely depend on the frame of reference within which they are conceived" (Runciman 1966, 9). This theory posits that the level of individual or collective satisfaction is determined by how one's situation compares to that of others within their frame of reference. This comparison can lead to self-perceptions of being either better off or worse off relative to these reference groups. Consequently, expectations adjust accordingly. Runciman explains: "if people have no reason to expect or hope for more than they can achieve, they will be less discontented with what they have, or even grateful . . . [b]ut if, on the other hand, they have been led to see as a possible goal the relative prosperity of some more fortunate community . . . they will remain discontented with their lot until they have succeeded in catching up" (Runciman 1966, 9). The concept of the reference group in this theory does not need to be literal and can range from a single person to an abstract idea.

Relative deprivation is intricately linked to Émile Durkheim's concept of *anomie*, which refers to a "vacuum of standards" that destabilizes social contexts. When societal norms or standards become unclear or absent, people struggle to establish reference groups or ideals and may become susceptible to exaggerated hopes or fears (Runciman 1966, 22). Runciman draws on Durkheim arguing that "[w]hat is needed [for] the mass of men be content with their lot . . . is not that they have more or less but that they have no right to more" (Runciman 1966, 25). While egalitarian theories and proclamations regarding the right to self-determination may elevate the ambitions of various peoples, "those at the bottom modify their ambitions in accordance with the facts of their situation" (Runciman 1966, 28). Consequently, the intensity of deprivation felt by the underprivileged may not be greater than that felt by the more prosperous, as the latter group adjusts its expectations to higher standards (Runciman 1966, 27). From the perspective of relative deprivation theory, tolerance levels are influenced by one's social status.

To examine the liberal assumptions underlying this sociological theory, a phenomenological approach is applied, contrasting the concept of relative deprivation with the structure of objective deprivation as revealed through eidetic phenomenology.

The phenomenology of deprivation focuses on the relationship between the source of disturbance (the Depriver) and the recipient of the disturbance (the Deprived). The interaction between the Depriver and the Deprived involves a deliberate or accidental act or event that, in phenomenological terms, is seen as an intentionality toward a result—such as removal, separation, forced relocation, expulsion, threat, or physical extinction—that disrupts or otherwise impedes the natural (qua undisturbed) mode of being of the Deprived. Once this intentionality is bracketed, what remains as a phenomenological residue is the effect or alteration on the natural mode of being of the Deprived, attributable to the Depriver. The divergence between the natural mode of being *ex ante* (before the disturbance) and the altered mode of being *ex post* (after the disturbance) represents the external faculty of loss (i.e., that-which-is-lost), whether temporarily or permanently. The attitude, perception, or intentionality of the Deprived toward their own altered mode of being, and particularly toward that-which-is-lost, constitutes the internal faculty of loss. Together, these aspects form the phenomenological concept of objective deprivation as actual, attributable loss.

Contrary to the phenomenology of objective deprivation, relative deprivation does not interpret loss in a literal sense, as it neither presupposes the external-material reality of an altered mode of being nor acknowledges an internal attitude and intentionality toward some presumed or concretely attributable loss. From a phenomenological standpoint, the term 'relative deprivation' might be considered a misnomer because it merely highlights the internal faculty of dissatisfaction with one's actual mode of being (I refer to the actual mode of being in order to contrast it to the natural mode of being as the ideal, undisturbed mode of being or *ataraxia*, and the desired mode of being. The triadic conception denotes that *ataraxia* necessitates the bridging of the distance between the actual and the desired.). This dissatisfaction generates frustration because it is perceived by the relatively deprived as a relative injustice and a limitation of potentiality and freedom (Hull 2007, 47–50).

In phenomenological terms, dissatisfaction itself is an intentionality directed toward one's actual mode of being in comparison with a desired mode of being. Thus, dissatisfaction entails another layer of intentionality: a desire for an addition or amendment to one's actual mode of being. This desired change is an ideal construct, which integrates ideals of relative justice (derived from interpersonal, intergroup, and other comparisons) as aspirational benchmarks against one's actual mode of being. Although relative deprivation does not *prima facie* result in an alteration of one's natural mode of being, it nonetheless constitutes a disturbance to it because it is infused with unmet expectations. In other words, even without tangible loss, feelings of deprivation can significantly affect an individual's or group's perception of their social reality and well-being.

Relative deprivation is intricately linked to the liberal objectification of legal rights, which are often viewed as quasi-properties of their holders. As discussed above, the property metaphor influences the natural mode of being by expanding individual and collective expectations and fostering a defensive predisposition among legal holders toward others perceived as potential trespassers. Consequently, the theory of relative deprivation portrays freedom as a cluster of potentialities, fostering an inherent negative and competitive predisposition among individuals and collectivities.

Although relative deprivation may be a viable concept from the perspectives of sociology and social psychology, within the phenomenology of rights, it is imperative to differentiate between disturbances understood in the above liberal or purely psychological sense and those understood in a strict material sense. Disturbances in the liberal sense overlook the material reality of loss and attribution. Previous sections have shown that loss triggers profound psychoanalytical and psychological responses, including mechanisms of bereavement, anxiety, and frustration. Thus, simulating liberal and objective deprivation is both phenomenologically and psychologically unsound.[1] Nevertheless, it is crucial not to underestimate the significance of relative deprivation, as it continues to disrupt the expectations of a liberally enriched natural mode of being, which conceptualizes legal rights as spheres of claims and acquired freedoms.

An empirical study on relative deprivation highlights that legitimacy is a crucial factor, as it "may provide a mechanism whereby group members accept their fate" (Ellemers 1999, 222). The study found that individuals who perceive their treatment as fair are "more likely to accept unfavorable decisions and outcomes" (Ellemers 1999, 222). Conversely, when a situation is seen as procedurally illegitimate, group members are more likely to recognize the injustice, regardless of their individual circumstances (Ellemers 1999, 223). This consideration is particularly relevant in the debate on self-determination, where procedural rules and normative standards remain unresolved, leading to a profound indeterminacy in the concept of legitimacy. Such indeterminacy cultivates liberal comparisons and collective feelings of relative deprivation and resentment.

Sociologists often cite the French-speaking and English-speaking Canadians of Québec as emblematic cases of relative deprivation (Taylor and Moghaddam 1994, 129). A pertinent sociological study indicated that English-speaking Canadians experienced feelings of relative deprivation due to language legislation in Québec that designated French as the official language (Taylor and Moghaddam 1994, 135). In this instance, English-speaking Canadians compared their situation to several reference groups, including Anglophones in other provinces, Anglophones in Québec from earlier times, Francophones in Québec, and other language groups within Québec.

Sociology emphasizes the importance of history, social identity, and the specific time frame in making relative deprivation comparisons. It suggests that the more positively, securely, and confidently group members view their own collective identity, the more favorably they will orient toward out-groups (Taylor and Moghaddam 1994, 190). The historical context is also crucial and must be considered in the sociological analysis of in-group and inter-group relations. For example, the history of european colonialism and english dominance in Canada is seen as having influenced the current state of inter-group relations between English-speaking and French-speaking Canadians (Taylor and Moghaddam 1994, 198). While sociology highlights the role of identity in intra- and inter-group dynamics, it lacks a concrete theoretical framework for assessing deprivation and loss from the perspective of collective identity. The following section will discuss how social phenomenology, the narrative theory of group psychology, and critical hermeneutics address this significant gap.

## The Intersection Between Loss and Collective Identity: Approaches from Social Phenomenology, Narrative Psychology, and Critical Hermeneutics

Building on the foregoing discussion, one can argue that the international right to self-determination regulates and, thus, 'preemptively' protects from disturbances and deprivations those aspects of the natural mode of being that correspond to the undisturbed expression of collective identity. Therefore, the focus of this book is not on collective deprivation and loss in general, but specifically on deprivation and loss as factors distressing collective identities. Consequently, this section explores the psychological and narrative mechanisms that collectivities utilize when deprivation, loss, and trauma are internalized and assimilated into the collective conscience. Three major approaches are pertinent to this examination: Alfred Schütz's social phenomenology, narrative psychological theory, and Paul Ricoeur's phenomenological-hermeneutical perspective on collective identity as temporality.

Collective loss and social identity are integral to theories of intersubjectivity and shared meaning within social phenomenology, which shifts the focus from the psychological and philosophical inquiry of collective consciousness to higher order intersubjective meanings. Although Edmund Husserl did not draw a direct analogy between individuals and collective unities, he posited that social objects are "the combination of some bearer of sense and a sense (meaning)" (Chelstrom 2013, 50). Husserl refrained from discussing collective consciousness, instead referring to communal sense and narrativity: "[i]n the case of a state, a people, a union, and so on, there is a plurality of bodies, standing in physical relationships something required for intercommerce, either direct or indirect. . . . Each body has its spirit, but they all are bound together by the overarching communal spirit which is not something beside them, but is an encompassing 'sense' or 'spirit'" (Chelstrom 2013, 50). For Husserl, it is not fitting to delve into the ontological dimensions of collectivities, thus eliminating the need for a bodily dimension in social categories, since these are ideal in form (Chelstrom 2013, 51). However, plural objects are distinct from individual objects and "capable of having properties distinct from their individual members" (Chelstrom 2013, 53). At the simplest level of intersubjectivity and collective intentionality, there is an immediate "we" directed toward the same object (Chelstrom 2013, 80). Yet, at larger social and collective levels, such a "we" is not directly reducible and therefore, collective intentionality and intersubjectivity should be understood in terms of "higher-order intersubjective meanings" which are constituted on the basis of shared experiences. Thus, the community should be conceptualized as a "community of monads" to which we attribute transcendental intersubjectivity (Chelstrom 2013, 80).

Alfred Schütz, a distinguished theorist of social phenomenology, developed Edmund Husserl's theory of intersubjective meaning further. According to Schütz, meaning is typically ascribed retrospectively, following the occurrence of an event, whereby a motive-oriented interpretation is basically imposed (Schütz 1967, xxiv). Schütz outlines a broad social horizon that includes varying degrees of directness, proximity, anonymity, and abstraction in social relations. Drawing on Max Weber, he argues that our understanding of contemporaries is always inferential and discursive. In situations characterized by a lack of direct interaction, we often construct "ideal types"—logical constructs of individuals that are essentially projections of our own subjective matrix of experiences (Schütz 1967, 184). The more distant these ideal types are, the more abstract their characteristics become, exhibiting repetitive and homogeneous traits. Ideal types move beyond subjective interpretation to form "a series of highly complex and systematically interrelated objective meaning-contexts" (Schütz 1967, 184). They serve various functions, such as predicting or assuming an objective course of action (Schütz 1967, 187). When it comes to groups, peoples, or entire states, the typology of ideal types reaches peak levels of abstraction and typically becomes anthropomorphic, with human characteristics and properties ascribed to these collective entities (Schütz 1967, 199).

The pressing question, then, is how experiences of deprivation and loss, inherently subjective in nature, are addressed within the framework of social phenomenology, and how these experiences are projected onto the anthropomorphic 'identities' of collectivities. This inquiry is crucial for understanding how collective identities internalize and manifest these deeply personal experiences.

For Schütz, the directness of immediate relationships (We-relationships), facilitates the direct experience of another's subjective experiences, such as personal loss (Schütz 1967, 202–3). Conversely, in the case of collective entities (They-relationships), this immediacy "is replaced by the assumption of a shared interpretative scheme" (Schütz 1967, 203). The high degree of anonymity in such relationships leads to assumed scenarios and environments which, although not identical to our own, employ similar signs and principles of comprehension (Schütz 1967, 204). This abstraction and anonymity lead to the objectification of signs and attitudes, projecting a generalized, homogeneous perception of deprivation and loss at the collective level—a sense of loss that necessarily transcends the individual variety of subjective perceptions. On the basis of this objectified understanding of deprivation and loss, we assume that an incident affecting an anthropomorphic community impacts all its individual members with the same intensity and magnitude.

Thus, in collective situations, there is a standardization of perceptions concerning other members' probable reactions and feelings toward the same source of disturbance, such as an act or event of collective deprivation. Moreover, while in everyday life our perceptions of fellow human beings are "subject to constant adjustment and revision based on the observer's experience" (Schütz 1967, 193) such immediate adjustability is not feasible for ideal types. This indicates that although the shared world "is constantly being enlarged and replenished" (Schütz 1967, 203) a possible change of attitude toward collective deprivation and loss by certain members of the community may not be—at least immediately—perceivable by the rest.

Narrative psychology suggests that individuals and collectivities strive for coherent narrativity in the experiences they live and share. From this perspective, individuals and groups actively construct a story structure in their lives "and ultimately compose themselves in the process" (Neimeyer and Levitt 2000, 402). This highlights how the act of storytelling and the formulation of identity are intricately connected, as narrativity encompasses not only stories about experiences but also narratives that define personhood and collective identity.

At the group level, "societies, peoples or nations establish a sense of their tradition and distinctiveness through the explicit creation of culture tales that capture and preserve their unique history" (Neimeyer and Levitt 2000, 402). However, this historical and narrative continuity can be disrupted and challenged by traumatic loss, which may impede the individual and collective process of "meaning-making," rendering it "chaotic or conflicted" (Neimeyer and Levitt 2000, 402). Cultural chaos is a psychological term describing the disruption of a people's or nation's narrative continuity due to "natural or human-made disasters" (Neimeyer and Levitt 2000, 406). The reestablishment of narrativity and meaning, whether individual or collective, requires "the integration of a threatening, harmful experience into one's model of the self and the world by answering questions reconstructing the causal 'why' and the teleological 'why' 'what for.'" Narrative repair often involves the creation of a new identity that incorporates the experience of loss (Neimeyer and Levitt 2000, 402).

While social psychologists note that the reconstruction of people's collective stories typically unfolds at the political rather than therapeutic level, it "nonetheless entails a process of narrative repair on a collective scale" (Neimeyer and Levitt 2000, 406). Failure to initiate such a reconstructive process may result in "a deviation-amplifying cycle of recrimination." Loss can also provoke a range of conflicting psychological responses to the source of collective disturbance or different narrative interpretations of the same traumatic events (Neimeyer and Levitt 2000, 406). Such antagonism may disrupt the coherence of collective storytelling as well as the integration of loss into the reconstruction of collective identity.

Even within the realms of culture, art, and classical literature, themes of collective deprivation, loss, and mourning are prevalent, having been narrated in many major classical works. For example, in one of the numerous analyses of Shakespeare's works, it is suggested that loss is culturally specific and that "different societies offer different narratives through which subsequent versions of deprivation are read" (Dubrow 1999, 9). Such classical works frequently weave in psychoanalytical elements of deprivation and loss, notably associating home and land with the human body, particularly the female body and the mother. This recurring motif in classical literature posits the home, like the female body, as a site of surveillance and control, as well as a vessel (Dubrow 1999, 12).

Under the framework of critical hermeneutics, Paul Ricoeur merges the phenomenological approach with psychoanalysis to construct a theory on history and collective identity. Ricoeur highlights the interdependence between memory and identity, proposing that to remember something (*se souvenir de*) inherently involves recollecting oneself (*se souvenir de soi*) (Ricoeur 2004, 3). Drawing on this analogy, Ricoeur extends the Freudian theory of mourning to the pathogeneses of collective identity, acknowledging the possibility for collective traumatisms and wounds to collective memory (Ricoeur 2004, 78). He states, "[t]he notion of the lost object finds a direct application in the 'losses' that affect the power, territory, and populations that constitute the substance of a state" (Ricoeur 2004, 78). Thus, collective loss may trigger typical mourning reactions by collective entities aimed at "reconciliation with the lost object," such as funeral celebrations that evolve into massive public events (Ricoeur 2004, 78). Ricoeur adapts Freud's theory of libidinal instincts to the scale of nationhood, suggesting that the lost object can become a matter of national or collective love (Ricoeur 2004, 79). Following this psychoanalytic framework, collective memory is compelled to confront the collective loss, relinquish its libidinal investment in the lost object (termed *cathexis* in Freudian terms), "as long as the loss has not been definitively internalized" (Ricoeur 2004, 80).

For Paul Ricoeur, there is a definitive intersection between memory and identity, as memory is mobilized "in the service of the quest, the appeal, the demand for identity" (Ricoeur 2004, 81). The issue of identity is thus inherently connected to the distribution of memory. The existential question of "who am I?" is responded in terms of "what," namely "this is what we are." This is how the problem of memory becomes a problem of identity (Ricoeur 2004, 81). Identity contains a crucial temporal component, requiring the invocation of memories for its articulation. Logically, identity results from temporal induction, incorporating the notion of "sameness" that persists over time (Ricoeur 2004, 81). Memories, therefore, ensure the "temporal continuity" of persons and peoples, consequently shaping and securing their respective identities (Ricoeur

2004, 96). Ricoeur, drawing from John Locke, discusses identity as a constant, temporal self-reference: "[f]or being at that instant what it is, and nothing else, it is the same, and so must continue as long as its existence is continued; for so long will it be the same, and no other" (Ricoeur 2004, 104). A person is a self, endowed with reason and self-reflection, capable of considering himself as "the same thinking thing, in different times and places" (Ricoeur 2004, 104). Thus, for Ricoeur, personal identity is essentially temporal identity, with consciousness acting as temporal self-reflection and memory (Ricoeur 2004, 105).

At the collective level, Ricoeur notes that "symbolic wounds calling for healing are stored in the archives of collective memory" (Ricoeur 2004, 79). The function of memory is crucial in addressing collective loss and mourning, especially in overcoming the *cathexis* with the lost object. Ricoeur emphasizes a "duty of memory" in instances of loss, which entails a "duty to do justice, through memories, to an other than the self" (Ricoeur 2004, 89). This concept of moral debt is intertwined with collective identity and especially with notions of heritage and justice, as there is an obligation to remember those who have preceded us. In this process of recollection, a particular emphasis is placed on victims and memories of loss, which are accorded moral priority over memories of victory (Ricoeur 2004, 89).

To summarize, social phenomenology, narrative psychology, and critical hermeneutics converge on the intersection between the phenomenology of objective deprivation and collective identity. Loss often imbues individual and collective memory with a sense of injustice, which, in the context of groups and peoples, disrupts communal narrativity. The process of mourning for the lost object and the subsequent narrative repair depend on the loss being 'archived' into collective memory rather than being internalized and transformed into melancholia. According to the psychoanalytic model of Sigmund Freud, melancholia represents a trauma to individual and collective identity. In cases of melancholia, peoples refuse to relinquish the libidinal attachment to the lost object, resulting in the internalization of the loss and its absorption into collective identity. However, even mourning and the typical reconciliation with the lost object do not imply that collective identity remains unaffected. A traumatic event of deprivation can still evoke a profound sense of injustice. While this feeling of injustice might not be internalized as in melancholia, it recurrently resurfaces in collective memory, driven by a community's duty to its heritage. This duty encompasses the obligation to remember both the victims and the historical losses experienced by the community.

## Note

1 There is another form of deprivation, which I do not address in this book, but I hope to address in the future: extreme deprivation of basic material resources that leads to hunger, thirst, starvation, imminent danger of survival, lack of access to decent healthcare, and generally insecure living conditions for individuals and their families. Given that these conditions produce severe anxiety, I would categorize this type of deprivation as objective rather than relative. Indeed, one could argue that this type of deprivation revives the birth trauma, for it mirrors the absence of a nurturing mother, embodying a state of abandonment and radical deprivation.

# 5

# The Empirical

## The Case Studies

This section moves into the next phase of our expanded inductive inquiry, turning to the analysis of empirical cases of collective deprivation and loss. These historical experiences are examined in light of their influence on the transformation of traditional international legal doctrines into contemporary interpretations of the international right to self-determination. It is proposed that such experiences of collective deprivation, whether political, economic, or territorial, have served as key phenomenological drivers in the evolution of international legal rights for peoples. In particular, they have shaped both the normative content of political and economic self-determination and the emergence of sovereign rights over natural resources as essential components of this right.

This part of our expanded induction begins with a historical account of selected conflicts, placing particular emphasis on ethnographic details that capture the perception of collective deprivation and loss from the perspective of the affected peoples. It further illuminates the historical dynamics of the two forms of deprivation discussed in the previous chapter: (a) objective deprivation as the phenomenological accumulation of removal and loss and (b) the liberal concept of relative deprivation as perceived inferiority resulting from intergroup comparisons. Additionally, this section touches on the doctrinal emergence of the rights of peoples as predominantly scholastic normative responses to past experiences of collective deprivation and loss, as well as the adaptation of international legal arguments to align with—or even yield to—the politics of power.

The chapter concludes by synthesizing the psychological-hermeneutic analysis of the phenomenology of collective deprivation with the historical description of the conflicts and draws general conclusions on collective deprivation as an identity distress factor.

## The Cherokee Nation

Long before the normative emergence of the international right to self-determination, numerous acts of collective deprivation and loss occurred throughout history. The section on empirical studies begins with the history of the Native Americans, specifically focusing on the expulsion of the Cherokees from their historical homeland, an event widely known as the Trail of Tears. This empirical study draws on Tim Alan Garrison's *The Legal Ideology of Removal: The Southern Judiciary and the Sovereignty of Native American Nations*, which provides a comprehensive historical and legal account of the conflict, as well as detailed ethnographic insights into the traditions and collective identity of the Cherokee Nation.

Historically, the relationship between Indian tribes and colonial governments had been structured through formal treaties. After the American Revolution and Britain's defeat, the United States initiated a process of renegotiating these treaties with various tribes, including the Cherokees, Chickasaws, and Choctaws. The resulting Hopewell Treaties, signed in South Carolina, required the tribes to accept the protection of the United States and to renounce allegiance to any other sovereign authority. These treaties also established that Congress would exercise exclusive control over trade with the tribes and the management of their affairs (Garrison 2002, 15). At the same time, the treaties acknowledged tribal land boundaries and affirmed the tribes' authority to regulate who could enter or reside in their territories.

Provisions to a similar effect appeared in the Northwest Ordinance adopted by the Continental Congress. It was stated there that tribal lands and property were not to be taken without consent and were to remain undisturbed unless in wars deemed just and lawful by Congress (Garrison 2002, 16). These legal instruments signaled a degree of recognition by the United States of tribal political autonomy and occupancy rights.

However, interpretive ambiguities emerged in light of a clause in the Articles of Confederation, which assigned Congress the sole and exclusive power to regulate Indian affairs, but did so on the condition that the legislative rights of individual states within their own boundaries would not be infringed (Garrison 2002, 16). This provision created persistent tensions, as some states interpreted it as a license to engage independently with the tribes, at times entering into their own treaties and thereby undermining federal authority. Although this conditional clause was eventually omitted during the Constitutional Convention, the constitutional text did not provide a clear demarcation of jurisdiction between federal and state powers in matters concerning Indian tribes (Garrison 2002, 16).

The constitutional crisis escalated when the state of Georgia intensified efforts to pressure federal authorities into removing the Cherokee population from its territory (Garrison 2002, 3). In response to this increasing threat, delegates representing the Cherokee Nation convened in 1827 at New Echota, where they drafted a national constitution. This act formalized and unified the tribe's existing political and legal institutions, presenting them within a distinctly constitutional framework. According to historical accounts, the Cherokee delegates articulated a clear and resolute view of themselves as an independent and sovereign nation—one that stood outside the jurisdictional reach of both federal and state governments in the United States (Garrison 2002, 34). They asserted their right to live free from harassment and unauthorized encroachments upon their territory, invoking the principle of national sovereignty as the normative basis for their claims (Garrison 2002, 34). What is particularly striking about this assertion is that it emanated from a community that did not possess a state in the conventional sense, yet nonetheless laid claim to the full normative language of sovereignty. This raises a critical question as to how the Cherokee Nation understood and deployed the concept of sovereignty within the context of their statelessness and contested legal status.

During the nineteenth century, legal scholars and political philosophers typically defined sovereignty as the ultimate and absolute political authority, a condition where the sovereign possessed legal and political supremacy over a specified geographical area and had the power to maintain this status by excluding any external nations or governments. For the Cherokees, however, the concept of sovereignty encompassed more than just political implications; it was deeply intertwined with their spiritual connection to their ancestral homelands and evoked memories of traditions and "law-ways" that predated European arrival in Cherokee territories (Garrison 2002, 35). The Cherokees' affinity and spiritual bond with their land were integral to their worldview, which envisioned the universe as consisting of three levels: the earth, or this world; the upper world above the earth, home to friendly spirits; and the underworld below the earth, inhabited by monstrous creatures (Garrison 2002, 36). The Cherokees held the responsibility of maintaining balance among these three worlds, using their traditions and rituals to exorcise any sources of disharmony.

The concept of Cherokee sovereignty was deeply rooted in their undisturbed spiritual and physical connection to their land, as also evidenced by their distinctive approach to property regulation. Unlike the Anglo-European settlers who adopted the principle of individual ownership, the Cherokee community practiced common ownership. The land utilized by an individual Cherokee was considered property of the tribe and was available for use by anyone who could build on it and cultivate it (Garrison 2002, 37). The Cherokees viewed their land not as a commodity to be measured or divided. Consequently, their expulsion meant more than just losing their birthplace; it involved relinquishing sacred ritual sites and, by extension, their ritual practices (Garrison 2002, 39).

After the Cherokees adopted their constitutional convention, the state of Georgia reacted by extending its jurisdiction over Cherokee lands. Under this extended jurisdiction, Georgia annexed Cherokee lands, disbanded the Cherokee government and courts, and invalidated the laws established by the Cherokee National Council, as indicated by historical records (Garrison 2002, 3). Alabama, Tennessee, and Mississippi followed Georgia's lead, extending their jurisdictions over Indian lands as well. This policy of removal gained substantial federal support when Andrew Jackson, a staunch advocate for the removal, became president of the United States. Two years following his election, in 1830, Congress passed the Indian Removal Act, granting Jackson the authority to negotiate removal treaties with the tribes. By 1835, while the Creeks, Chickasaws, and Choctaws had succumbed to political pressures, the Cherokees and the Seminoles resisted the removal efforts. The Seminoles opted for war, whereas the Cherokees sought legal recourse by challenging Georgia's removal laws before the Supreme Court (Garrison 2002, 3).

When the Cherokee case reached the Supreme Court, the modern principle of self-determination had not yet emerged as a recognized legal doctrine, and therefore could not guide the Court's reasoning. Instead, the justices drew upon the prevailing law of nations, shaped significantly by natural law traditions. Within this intellectual framework, rooted in Aristotelian thought, Christian theologians such as Thomas Aquinas had argued that certain basic principles of justice were universally accessible through reason. These principles, it was believed, extended to the rights of nations and peoples, including those in newly encountered territories. The prevailing view among these thinkers was that every nation was entitled to respect for its land, its capacity for self-governance, and its jurisdiction over temporal matters (Garrison 2002, 440).

In evaluating the Cherokee claims, federal judges consulted a variety of legal sources, including seminal works by Francisco de Vitoria, Hugo Grotius, Samuel von Pufendorf, and Jean Bodin. However, it was Emmerich de Vattel's *The Law of Nations* that proved most influential. Vattel's work synthesized earlier theories of international law with the pragmatic exigencies of colonial expansion. While aligned with the natural law tradition, Vattel also emphasized the necessity for international law to be practically applicable, arguing that peace and order among nations depended upon compromise (Garrison 2002, 69). As part of this pragmatic outlook, he encouraged weaker nations to enter into unequal but stabilizing alliances with more powerful states. He defined nations as political communities united for the sake of mutual safety and benefit (Garrison 2002, 67), and asserted that sovereignty required a people to be governed by their own laws and institutions (Garrison 2002, 83). This dual aspect of Vattel's theory allowed both defenders and detractors of Native American sovereignty to appeal to his work: proponents highlighting his insistence on sovereignty and natural law, opponents invoking the legitimacy of conquest and unequal power dynamics.

In *The Cherokee Nation v. Georgia* (1831), the Supreme Court declined to consider the merits of the case, reasoning that Indian tribes did not constitute "foreign states" under Article III of the US Constitution. As such, they lacked standing to bring claims before the Court. Chief Justice John Marshall clarified that tribes situated within US territory could not be treated as foreign states in the constitutional sense, thereby precluding federal jurisdiction. However, the Court's position evolved significantly the following year in *Worcester v. Georgia* (1832), where Marshall delivered a much firmer affirmation of Native American sovereignty. In that decision, he held that the laws enacted by the state of Georgia, which sought to extend its jurisdiction over Cherokee lands and authorize the removal of their residents, were unconstitutional. Marshall grounded his reasoning in the bilateral treaties previously concluded between the United States and the Cherokee Nation, observing that those treaties clearly recognized the Cherokee as a sovereign people with the right to govern themselves and to exclude non-Cherokees from their territory without their consent. Because such treaties form part of the "supreme law of the land" under the Constitution, the Court concluded that Georgia's legislation was invalid (Garrison 2002, 186).

Despite the legal clarity provided by the Worcester ruling, Georgia's response was openly defiant. State authorities reportedly characterized the Supreme Court's intervention as a violation—or "usurpation"—of Georgia's sovereignty (Garrison 2002, 191). The federal executive offered no assistance; President Andrew Jackson is widely attributed with having responded to the decision with the now-infamous phrase: "John Marshall has made his decision, now let him enforce it" (Garrison 2002, 193). Meanwhile, Southern state courts continued to rely on the doctrine of discovery to justify their legal positions. In *Tennessee v. Forman* (1835), for example, Judge John Catron significantly downplayed the precedential weight of *Worcester*. Upholding the constitutionality of state extension laws, Catron affirmed the continued applicability of the discovery doctrine, asserting that it was for the United States to determine whether the continent should be settled by Europeans or remain, in his words, "the haunt of savage beasts" (Garrison 2002, 222). Between 1830 and 1835, the highest courts in three Southern states ruled in favor of Indian land expropriation (Garrison 2002, 5). In stark contrast to Marshall's recognition of tribal sovereignty, these state-level judgments refused to acknowledge a distinct collective legal identity for Native American nations. Instead, they treated Indians as individual persons subject to the jurisdiction of the states in which they resided (Garrison 2002, 5).

Before departing for the Trail of Tears, the Cherokee Council issued the following statement:

> The title of the Cherokee people to their lands is the most ancient, pure, and absolute known to man, [. . .] its validity confirmed and illustrated by possession and enjoyment antecedent to all pretense of claims by any other portion of the human race. [T]he natural, political and moral relations existing among the citizens of the Cherokee nation toward each other and toward the body politic; cannot in reason and justice be dissolved by the expulsion of the nation from its territory by the power of the U.S. Government. [The] inherent sovereignty of the Cherokee nation, together with the Constitution, laws and usages of the same [remain] in full force . . . in perpetuity. (Garrison 2002, 2)

There is a widely held agreement among scholars that approximately four thousand Cherokees—nearly a quarter of the population—perished on the Trail of Tears due to exposure, starvation, and disease (Garrison 2002, 234). The forced relocation inflicted an immeasurable psychological and sociological impact on the tribe. The Cherokees were compelled to relinquish their homeland, resulting in a profound disconnection from their ancestors and sites of significant spiritual importance. According to Garrison, "[r]emoval required the Cherokees to leave behind places that fostered feelings of cultural and personal identity," and "Cherokee families and clans left behind the graves of their ancestors and rode and marched to a land holding absolutely no spiritual or personal familiarity" (Garrison 2002, 235). Having lost what they considered the center of their universe, the surviving Cherokees developed intense feelings of sadness, anger, and disorientation.

## Nauru

Nauru, a small island nation situated in Micronesia, came under German control in 1888 and remained within the German Empire until the onset of the First World War. Although no formal treaties were concluded with the island's traditional leaders, the German administration effectively established a governing presence. This included the creation of land registers, the issuance of ordinances, and the assumption of control over Nauru's phosphate resources, an asset of considerable economic value due to its widespread use in fertilizer production (Weeramantry 1992, 8). Phosphate mining began under German rule and continued beyond the war under an international mandate, eventually concluding only upon Nauru's independence in 1968 (Weeramantry 1992, 2).

During German administration, mining rights were transferred to Jaluit Gesellschaft and subsequently to the Pacific Phosphate Company. By the end of the First World War, approximately 630,000 tons of phosphate, valued at nearly one million pounds, had been extracted, with Nauruan landowners receiving a meager £1,320 in total—merely a halfpenny per ton (Weeramantry 1992, 8). Throughout the period of exploitation, both before and after the war, the Nauruans were neither consulted nor consented to the legal, political, and commercial arrangements on their territory (Weeramantry 1992, 22–3).

Following the war, Nauru was designated as a mandated territory under the League of Nations, governed collectively by Australia, New Zealand, and the United Kingdom, who were accountable to the League. Article 22 of the League's covenant stipulated that "[to] peoples not yet able to stand by themselves under the strenuous conditions of the modern world, there should be applied the principle that the well-being and development of such peoples form a sacred trust of civilisation." This mandate system was essentially an institutional remedy to the exploitation and suffering inflicted by the German Empire (Weeramantry 1992, 84). It reflected a broader, historically entrenched European notion of trust and guardianship over dependent peoples, a concept that can be traced back to the fifteenth and sixteenth centuries following the discovery of the West Indies and America. This discovery sparked extensive debates about the rights of indigenous peoples, similar to the scholarly responses seen in our empirical study of the Cherokee Nation. European jurists and medieval theologians deliberated whether non-Christian native peoples retained rights to their lands amidst the harsh realities of colonial conquests and acquisitions, thereby gradually shaping the discourse on the rights of peoples in response to the potential or actual acts of collective deprivation by colonial powers.

From the early stages of international legal development, there was a growing recognition that the property rights of indigenous peoples ought to be respected—an idea that emerged as a foundational principle, albeit often indirectly. This respect for indigenous title was also embedded in the doctrine of *terra nullius*, which assumed that only lands unoccupied by organized political communities could be subject to lawful claim. Where such communities were present, their pre-existing rights were, at least in principle, to be acknowledged.

Parallel to this international norm, the concept of trust evolved from domestic legal traditions. Francisco de Vitoria, drawing from scholastic and Roman legal thought, discussed the fiduciary dimension of power exercised over others. In his writings on guardianship (*tutela*), he stressed that the guardian does not own the ward's property; rather, ownership remains with the ward, and the guardian merely administers it on their behalf (Weeramantry 1992, 79). This concept of fiduciary stewardship found resonances across various legal traditions. In the civil law system, the Roman law principle of *mandatum* operated similarly, establishing that the person entrusted with another's goods must act solely to fulfill the terms of the mandate and may not derive any benefit from this arrangement unless expressly permitted (Weeramantry 1992, 151).

In the realm of international law, these concepts of *mandatum* and *tutela* were embodied in the international mandate and trusteeship systems, linking to the later development of the right to self-determination. It was deemed a duty of the trustees to guide colonial peoples and non-self-governing territories toward independence. The abuse of this international *tutela* or *mandatum* subsequently spurred the decolonization process and affirmed the international right of peoples to self-determination.

Even prior to receiving the official mandate, Australia, New Zealand, and the United Kingdom engaged in confidential negotiations culminating in the Nauru Island Agreement. This agreement, which effectively transferred control over Nauru's valuable phosphate deposits to the three powers, was never submitted to the League of Nations for ratification (Weeramantry 1992, 55). According to Article 6 of the Agreement, ownership of the phosphate deposits and all associated infrastructure was to be vested in the British Phosphate Commissioners (Weeramantry 1992, 56). These Commissioners obtained the phosphate rights from the Pacific Phosphate Company at cost, a transaction that raised concerns about a conflict of interest. The mandatory powers, entrusted under international law with fiduciary obligations to act in the best interests of the Nauruan people, simultaneously stood to benefit economically by securing phosphate at minimal cost. This conflict was made explicit during parliamentary debates on the Nauru Island Agreement Bill in Australia. Prime Minister Billy Hughes openly acknowledged the financial advantage the agreement offered to the signatories, stating that its primary objective was to ensure phosphate access at cost price for the United Kingdom, Australia, and New Zealand. He emphasized the economic benefits, noting that the phosphate supply would meet Australia's agricultural needs for the foreseeable future and asserting that the arrangement guaranteed "an assured supply at the cheapest possible rates that can be obtained in the world" (Weeramantry 1992, 58). Although concerns were raised within the United Kingdom's Parliament, the momentum behind the Nauru Island Agreement proved overwhelming. Ultimately, all three participating parliaments,the United Kingdom, Australia, and New Zealand, passed legislation to confer legal validity on the Agreement.

Not only were the Nauruans excluded from any participation in the phosphate industry, but their rights as landowners were also significantly curtailed. Under the terms of the Agreement, landowners were required to obtain prior consent from the colonial Administrator before undertaking any transactions involving their land, thus stripping them of the freedom to lease or sell their property (Weeramantry 1992, 101). The structure of the Agreement thus ensured that Nauruan lands could be accessed exclusively by the British Phosphate Commissioners, effectively foreclosing the possibility of independent economic engagement by the local population. Similar to the Cherokees, Nauruans possess a profound connection to their land—a bond transcending mere financial or utilitarian value, linking families, tribes, or broader community groups (Weeramantry 1992, 164). Land in Nauru was not only named but also culturally bound to the group to which it belonged, rarely passing outside of it except under extraordinary circumstances (Weeramantry 1992, 164). The Nauru Island Agreement represented not only an inequitable arrangement for the Nauruans but was also "incomprehensible and diametrically opposed to their cultural traditions" (Weeramantry 1992, 165). Phosphate mining significantly altered the Nauruan lifestyle, and the collective sense of loss toward their damaged land has been expressed in various popular songs, underscoring the deep cultural and emotional impacts of such exploitation (Weeramantry 1992, 22).

The profound attachment of the Nauruan people to their land was unmistakably evident in a 1924 episode, when a group of Nauruans resisted further leasing of their territory to the British Phosphate Commissioners. As Weeramantry recounts, the emotional intensity of the moment was palpable: the people "wept bitterly" upon learning their land would be taken and, as reported by Chief Dabe, declared they would "rather die" than surrender it (Weeramantry 1992, 166). This reaction, far from being an isolated display, reflected a deeper cultural worldview rooted in land-based identity.

Upon gaining independence in 1968, the Nauruan state raised the issue of environmental devastation as a principal dispute with the former administering powers, Australia, New Zealand, and the United Kingdom. The Nauruan Constitution makes a clear distinction between mining carried out before and after independence, placing accountability for the environmental damage during the earlier period squarely on these three states (Weeramantry 1992, 12). Decades of intensive phosphate extraction had left large sections of the island ecologically barren and uninhabitable. In response, Nauru established an Independent Commission of Inquiry in 1986, which concluded that the principles governing international mandates and fiduciary obligations had been fundamentally breached. The report found that the administering powers had exploited their fiduciary position to derive economic benefit from phosphate resources while neglecting the long-term welfare and environmental interests of the Nauruan people (Weeramantry 1992, 14–15).

Given the scale of ecological degradation, the idea of relocating the population was considered. Australia proposed resettlement on Curtis Island, but this was conditioned upon the Nauruans relinquishing their sovereignty and adopting Australian citizenship (Weeramantry 1992, 292–3). The proposal was ultimately rejected.

## Filastin/ Eretz Yisrael

> We and they want the same thing. We both want Palestine.
> David Ben-Gurion, first Prime Minister of Israel. (Dowty 2012, 82)

The Israeli-Palestinian conflict is one of the most profound conflicts in modern history, representing a significant international legal challenge. It embodies a failure to justify, demarcate, or accommodate the claims of two distinct groups over the same territory, referred to as Eretz Yisrael by the Zionist movement and as Filastin within the bounds set by the British Mandate for Palestine (Dowty 2012, 82). The core of the conflict can be simplified into two contrasting narratives: Israel asserts that the Arabs do not recognize the legitimacy of a Jewish state in its historic homeland, while Palestinians argue that the creation of Israel has led to serious violations of their human and humanitarian rights, particularly the denial of their right to self-determination and sovereignty over their ancestral lands (Dowty 2012, 4). Before delving deeper, it is crucial to understand the distinct narratives of both Arabs and Israelis, as these form an essential part of the collective memory and identity of both peoples.

The Jewish connection to the land is steeped in a millennia-long history marked by the persistence of collective identity through religion, culture, and language, despite widespread dispersion (Dowty 2012, 23). This identity is anchored in powerful narratives of common history and ancestry, and an emotional attachment to Eretz Yisrael (Dowty 2012, 25). According to Jewish tradition, this connection began with the exodus from Egypt and the divine commandments received by Moses in the Sinai. This narrative includes the conquest of Canaan, termed a "geotheological" concept, signifying a Holy or Promised Land assigned to the Chosen People through the Abrahamic Covenant (Krämer 2008, 19).

Jerusalem holds a special place in Jewish mythology, significantly shaped by King David's conquest and the historical events that followed, including the destruction and subsequent rebuilding of Solomon's Temple, the exile following its second destruction, and the enduring theme of exile and return. Zion, often synonymous with Jerusalem, evolved into a powerful symbol of hope for return and redemption throughout Jewish history, a sentiment deeply embedded in religious practices, art, and literature (Krämer 2008, 25). This historical narrative denotes the profound connection Jews have maintained with the land, framing their collective identity around themes of displacement, return, and divine providence, culminating in the messianic hope of ultimate redemption for Jews and all mankind (Dowty 2012, 26).

From the third to the tenth centuries, the majority of the Jewish population resided in Babylonia. During the subsequent Muslim era, Jews generally enjoyed a degree of autonomy as a protected minority. However, this relative tolerance deteriorated in the twelfth century with the rise of the Muslim Almohad dynasty. The Almohads invaded Spain and imposed harsh conditions that forced Jews to migrate massively to Christian-dominated regions of the country. Within these Christian areas, Jews faced extreme pressures to convert to Christianity (Dowty 2012, 27). By 1483, they were confronted with a dire ultimatum: convert or face expulsion. This led to a significant exodus of Jews, known as Sephardim, many of whom sought refuge in the Ottoman Empire (Dowty 2012, 27).

Eastern Europe also emerged as a sanctuary for Jews during and after the First Crusade, especially as they faced bans from Western Europe. The Jewish communities in Eastern Europe underwent a "demographic miracle" during the eighteenth and nineteenth centuries, with the population expanding from approximately one million to an estimated ten million over two centuries (Dowty 2012, 28). Almost 90 percent of this Jewish population was concentrated in Poland. Following the partition and annexation of Poland into Tsarist Russia, nearly half of the world's Jewish population found themselves under Russian sovereignty (Dowty 2012, 28).

In the Muslim narrative, on the other hand, Jerusalem is revered as one of the holiest sites in Islam. According to the Qur'an, Abraham is the spiritual ancestor of Muslims, Jews, and Christians. It was in Jerusalem that Prophet Muhammad embarked on his nocturnal journey, as narrated in Islamic tradition. Riding Mount Buraq to the Temple Mount, he is said to have ascended to Heaven from this spot, praying alongside the Prophets Abraham, Moses, and Jesus (Krämer 2008, 35). After "the correct form of obligatory prayer was revealed to him," Muhammad returned to invite his followers to embrace Islam (Krämer 2008, 35). Initially, the *qibla*, or direction of prayer, was toward Jerusalem; this changed to Mecca in 622, likely due to a "violent conflict between Muhammad and the Jewish tribes in Medina" (Krämer 2008, 31). Subsequent Caliphs constructed the Dome of the Rock (qubbat al-sakhra) and the Al-Aqsa Mosque on the site of the then-destroyed Second Jewish Temple, forming the noble district of Jerusalem's Old City (Krämer 2008, 33).

After Muhammad's death, Palestine's population was a mix of Jews, Semitic and non-Semitic peoples like the Philistines, who transitioned from Christianity to Islam, with Aramaic eventually replaced by Arabic (Dowty 2012, 49). During the eighth to the twelfth centuries, known as the Golden Age of Islam, the region experienced significant cultural and scientific advancements while Europe was mired in the Dark Ages. From 1516 to 1918, under Ottoman rule, Palestine was predominantly Arabic (Krämer 2008, 40). The Ottomans defined Palestine's boundaries mainly for administrative and tax purposes (Krämer 2008, 41). The Crusades' traumatic legacy engendered a deep-seated caution toward non-Muslim foreigners, leading to restrictions like prohibiting Europeans from residing or maintaining a diplomatic presence in Jerusalem, although these were relaxed under Muhammad Ali's rule (Dowty 2012, 62). Nevertheless, Muslim aversion to foreigners persisted. The Ottoman Empire's rapid decline branded it the "sick man of Europe," intensifying Palestinian fears of political instability and threats to their land. This era, as noted by a scholar, marked the onset of Palestinism—the emergence of a distinct Palestinian identity alongside a broader Arab national identity (Dowty 2012, 63).

In the meantime, the Jewish religious theme of exile and return to Zion was augmented by the political reality of anti-Semitism and perpetual persecution. Under Tsar Alexander II, a resurgence of conservatism and political violence against Russian Jewish communities manifested in pogroms. These pogroms triggered a massive exodus of approximately 2.6 million Jews between 1882 and 1914 from Russia to America and Western Europe, with less than 5 percent settling in Ottoman Palestine, joining the pre-existing Jewish community known as the Old Yishuv (Dowty 2012, 32–3; Krämer 2008, 104). This migration marked the first *aliyah*, the initial wave of Jewish immigration to Palestine.

The concept of returning to Zion, though not initially widespread, became increasingly politicized. The repeated failures of assimilation in foreign societies, juxtaposed with other national groups achieving political independence, rekindled the desire for Zion, now as a political solution (Dowty 2012, 33). Theodor Herzl, founder of the Zionist movement, outlined his vision in his 1896 publication, *The Jew's State: An Attempt at a Modern Solution to the Issue of the Jews*. Herzl did not initially insist on Palestine as the location for a Jewish State. He argued, "[w]e naturally move to places where we are not persecuted, and there our presence produces persecution. . . . I think the Jewish question [. . .] is a national question, and in order to solve it we must above all make it a political world-question to be settled by the civilized nations of the world. . . . Palestine is our ever-memorable historic home. The very name of Palestine would attract our people with a force of marvelous potency" (Dowty 2012, 108).

The subsequent *aliyahs* drew attention within the Ottoman Empire. The rise of the Young Turks led to measures to control Jewish immigration, driven by concerns that a Jewish question could provoke Arab resistance or European intervention (Dowty 2012, 122). Zionists, meanwhile, underestimated the implications of the indigenous Arab population for the establishment of Eretz Yisrael. They held an uncontested historical claim over Palestine and adopted the notion of "a land without a people for a people without a land," treating the land as if it were terra nullius (Dowty 2012, 42). Initially, Arab opposition to Jewish immigration, viewed merely as isolated property disputes, was not recognized as indicative of broader resistance to a Jewish homeland in Palestine (Dowty 2012, 64).

After the collapse of the Ottoman Empire, British interests in the region led to the issuance of the 1917 Balfour Declaration by the British Foreign Secretary. This statement supported the establishment of a Jewish national home in Palestine and was later incorporated into the British Mandate for Palestine. Lord Balfour stated:

> His Majesty's Government view with favor the establishment in Palestine of a national home for the Jewish people and will use their best endeavors to facilitate the achievement of this object, it being clearly understood that nothing shall be done which may prejudice the civil and religious rights of existing non-Jewish communities in Palestine or the rights and political status enjoyed by Jews in any other country. (Dowty 2012, 74)

While the Jewish community saw this as a significant diplomatic victory and the first international acknowledgment of their historical claim over Eretz Yisrael, it also introduced a dual obligation for Britain: to facilitate a Jewish national home while preparing the indigenous Arab population for self-government (Dowty 2012, 74). In 1918, the Muslim-Christian Association of Jaffa articulated the sentiments of the Arab population with a statement emphasizing their identity and opposition to Zionist plans:

> Palestine is Arab, its language is Arabic, we want to see this formally recognized. It was Great Britain that rescued us from Turkish Tyranny and we do not believe that it will deliver us into the claws of the Jews. We ask for fairness and justice. We ask that it protects our rights and not decide the future of Palestine without asking our opinion. (Krämer 2008, 158)

Despite Arabs in the former Ottoman Empire and particularly in Syria and Iraq qualifying for an A-type Mandate, indicating readiness for independence with international support, Palestine was not granted this status. This was ostensibly because the inhabitants of Palestine were not recognized as a distinct people with a common culture, history, and collective identity (Krämer 2008, 166). Yet, Arabs comprised 89 percent of the population according to a 1931 census (Krämer 2008, 182).

The British Mandate was viewed by Arabs in Palestine as a betrayal and a denial of their right to self-determination, interpreting it as a demand to "pay for the sins of others" referencing Jewish suffering in Europe and Russia (Dowty 2012, 80). This perception fueled unrest and riots in the early 1920s, driven by opposition to Zionist land acquisition policies and the leadership's aggressive land purchases (Pappe 2006, 94). The British and Zionist policies under Ben-Gurion had severe repercussions for rural Palestine, notably the practice of buying land from big landlords and evicting tenants without compensation (Pappe 2006, 97–8). British agricultural experts expressed shock at their government's neglect of rural areas, leading to calls for intervention against such expansionist policies (Pappe 2006, 99).

The degradation of rural standards of living and the loss of land fueled Arab resentment. Unlike the Zionist national movement, the Arabs lacked effective political leadership. The Arab Higher Committee, the sole representative body for the Arab population at that time, failed to provide guidance or counter Zionist expansion effectively, leading to sporadic and disorganized riots (Pappe 2006, 103). However, in May 1936, the Committee called for a general strike, igniting an uprising in the Palestinian countryside. While some Zionists sought to frame the resistance as religious and anti-Semitic, the uprising clearly had a political character (Krämer 2008, 268). This led to the formation of a commission of inquiry under Lord Peel, which concluded that the Mandate's conflicting promises necessitated a partition of Palestine into two states: an Arab state covering 80 percent of the territory and a Jewish state in the remaining 20 percent (Dowty 2012, 84). The proposal, however, met with strong Arab opposition, leading the British to propose a white paper in 1939 asserting that "the framers of the Mandate . . . could not have intended that Palestine should be converted into a Jewish State against the will of the Arab population of the country" (Krämer 2008, 293).

The Second World War and the Holocaust profoundly impacted the situation, generating widespread sympathy and a robust moral case for establishing a

Jewish homeland in Palestine. In 1947, the matter was referred to the United Nations, which, after a special committee's recommendations, adopted Resolution 181. This resolution proposed a partition plan granting the Jewish people 56 percent of Palestine, even more favorable than the Peel Commission's proposal. However, without concrete implementation plans and lacking Arab consent, the British government withdrew, leaving a vacuum that escalated into violence (Dowty 2012, 89).

Resolution 181 marked a significant diplomatic victory for the Jewish people but was seen as a political catastrophe by the Arabs, who viewed it as the West compensating the Jews with land that did not belong to them (Krämer 2008, 307). The ensuing violence worsened after the British withdrawal, leading to widespread reprisals and reconsiderations by the UN (Pappe 2006, 127), but it was too late to prevent atrocities like those at Deir Yassin, which became a potent symbol of Zionist aggression in Palestinian collective memory (Krämer 2008, 313). As the Arab uprising gained momentum, Arab cities, towns, and villages formed national committees to organize resistance, highlighting the deepening division and escalating conflict in the region (Krämer 2008, 310).

The 1948 Arab-Israeli conflict had profound impacts on the indigenous Arab population of Palestine. Under the auspices of the infamous Plan D, approximately 300 villages were erased, and around 750,000 Arab Palestinians were expelled, becoming refugees in neighboring countries like Syria, Jordan, Lebanon, and Egypt (Pappe 2006, 138). This figure represented about 90 percent of the Arab population residing in the areas allocated for the Jewish state under the UN partition plan. The expulsion followed a pattern of terrorizing local Arab residents, executing a few to incite flight among the majority, and forming committees to assess the abandoned properties (Pappe 2006, 137).

Within just a year and a half, the Jewish population in the region surged from 600,000 to one million (Krämer 2008, 320). By the war's end, Israel occupied 78 percent of what was formerly Palestine, with the 1949 armistice lines becoming its de facto borders following its declaration of independence on May 14, 1948 (Dowty 2012, 95; Pappe 2006, 131). Shortly after, Israel introduced its currency, the Israeli lira, replacing the existing currencies and eventually assuming control over public and private bank accounts, a process completed when the British transferred Palestine's remaining public accounts to Israel in the early 1950s (Pappe 2006, 134).

For the Arab population, the 1948–9 conflict is remembered as *al-nakba* (the catastrophe), a period of profound loss and displacement. In contrast, Israelis commemorate it as a moment of national liberation and the realization of the Zionist aspiration for a sovereign homeland (Krämer 2008, 323). Post-war, Palestine emerged as a geopolitical entity comprising the West Bank and Gaza Strip, managed by Jordan and Egypt, respectively (Pappe 2006, 140).

The trauma of *al-nakba* galvanized the formation of a robust Palestinian national movement, with collective identity increasingly centered around the lost homeland (Pappe 2006, 141). This identity was further solidified through a "literature of exile" produced in refugee camps, echoing a sentiment of enduring presence despite displacement (Dowty 2012, 101). One poignant poem from this period expresses the deep-rooted connection to their homeland:

Tent #50, on the left, that is my present,
But it is too cramped to contain a future.
And "Forget!": they say, but how can I?
Teach the night to forget to bring
Dreams showing me my village
And teach the wind to forget to carry to me
The aroma of apricots in my fields!
And teach the sky, too, to forget to rain.
Only then may I forget my country. (Dowty 2012, 101)

As refugee camps became hotbeds of political activity, a new, revolutionary Palestinian identity emerged, aimed at rectifying the injustices of *al-nakba*. This identity prioritized the right to return as a fundamental political goal, alongside the establishment of a Palestinian state (Dowty 2012, 102). The rejection of Israel's existence became a corollary of this radicalization, epitomized by the "mythical figure of the Palestinian fighter" or *fida'i*, willing to sacrifice for the cause of repatriation (Dowty 2012, 102). This ethos spurred the rise of guerrilla warfare, exemplified by groups like Fatah under Yasir Arafat's leadership, which conducted systematic raids on Jewish settlements (Dowty 2012, 109). This resistance crystallized a distinct Palestinian identity, merging the aspirations for statehood with the imperative of refugee repatriation (Pappe 2006, 151). The enduring sense of collective loss fundamentally transformed the Arabs of Palestine into Palestinians.

Over the years, various discriminatory measures have been implemented against the Arab minority in Israel. Since the 1950s, the Knesset has passed several laws focused on immigration and fiscal matters, including loans, mortgages, and university fees, which disproportionately affect this group (Pappe 2006,

159). Most notably, Palestinian land was nationalized, designated as public land available exclusively "to be sold or leased only to Jews" (Pappe 2006, 160).

The 1967 Six-Day War brought further devastation to Palestinian refugees and the Arab minority in Israel, resulting in a significant defeat for the Arab states involved. Israel captured the Gaza Strip and Sinai from Egypt, the West Bank from Jordan, and the Golan Heights from Syria (Dowty 2012, 114). The conflict concluded with the United Nations Security Council Resolution 242, which introduced the "land for peace" formula. This resolution called for Israel's withdrawal from occupied territories and the repatriation of refugees in exchange for recognition of Israel and peace agreements with Arab countries (Dowty 2012, 122–3).

Palestinians were notably absent from international discussions and resolutions for over two decades post-British Mandate (Pappe 2006, 204). They were excluded from the 1967 Khartoum summit of the Arab League and were not invited to the first conference between Israel and Arab countries after the Six Day War in 1973 (Dowty 2012, 130). It was not until the 1974 Rabat Arab summit that the Palestine Liberation Organization (PLO) was recognized as "the sole legitimate representative of the Palestinian people" (Dowty 2012, 134). Following this, Yasser Arafat addressed the UN General Assembly, which later granted the PLO observer status and passed in 1975 resolution 3379 denouncing Zionism as "a form of racism and racial discrimination."

The Israeli government, particularly under the Likud party, did not recognize the PLO as a legitimate negotiating partner (Dowty 2012, 138). When Ariel Sharon became defense minister, he initiated the 1982 Lebanon invasion, termed "Peace for the Galilee," aimed at dismantling the PLO (Pappe 2006, 215). This military action led to the massacre of hundreds of civilians in the Sabra and Shatila refugee camps and significant bombardments in Beirut. It also contributed to the rise of Hezbollah, a Shiite militant group backed by Iran, on the Lebanese political scene (Pappe 2006, 219–20). This invasion indirectly set the stage for the first *intifada*.

The *intifadas*, large-scale Palestinian uprisings, are seen as spontaneous mass responses to various forms of collective deprivation, fitting into the aggression and frustration psychological theory. Groups such as Hamas and Jihad, classified unequivocally as terrorist organizations by many countries, emerged as significant players during these periods (Dowty 2012, 144). Following the first *intifada*, the Israeli government, led by Likud, recognized the PLO as a negotiating partner for the first time (Dowty 2012, 147). This recognition was formalized with an exchange of letters between Yitzhak Rabin and Yasir Arafat in the 1993 Oslo Accords, which established a framework for conflict resolution and the creation of a "Palestinian Interim Self-Governing Authority" in the West Bank and Gaza (Dowty 2012, 154). Under the accords, Israel agreed to withdraw from occupied territories, and the PLO recognized Israel's right to exist, renouncing articles in the Palestinian Covenant that called for Israel's destruction and accepting the pre-1967 armistice lines (Dowty 2012, 155).

The peace process initiated by the Oslo Accords ultimately faltered. Following the assassination of Yitzhak Rabin in 1995 by Israeli extremists, Benjamin Netanyahu's administration was perceived as less conciliatory. Critics argue that Netanyahu aimed to "stall the process" such that the interim solution would become permanent (Dowty 2012, 165). Palestinians felt that Oslo broke down due to Israel's failure to withdraw from the West Bank and Gaza and because of the expansion of Israeli settlements, which they viewed as illegal. Conversely, Israel accused the Palestinian Authority and Yasir Arafat of tacitly supporting terrorist attacks against Israeli targets (Dowty 2012, 168–9). Despite attempts at reconciliation, like the 2000 Camp David Summit and the 2001 Taba negotiations, no lasting agreement was reached, leading to the declaration of the second *intifada* at the end of 2000. This *intifada* was widely seen as a manifestation of frustration over the stalled peace process and a rejection of Israel's policies (Dowty 2012, 172). The failure of negotiations also boosted support for Hamas and other Islamic extremist organizations.

During the second *intifada*, Israel's Defense Cabinet approved the construction of a separation wall between Israel and the Palestinian territories, citing security reasons. Intended to stretch 440 miles, the wall was not officially designated as a political barrier by Israel but resulted in the de facto annexation of about 15 percent of the West Bank to protect large blocs of Israeli settlements (Dowty 2012, 185). In 2004, in its Advisory opinion about the *Legal Consequences of the Construction of a Wall in the Occupied Palestinian Territory*, the ICJ declared the wall's construction illegal, stating that it violated Palestinians' rights by restricting movement and creating enclaves.

The political landscape shifted significantly when Hamas won a political victory in the Palestinian National Council after the failure of law and politics (Dowty 2012, 199). For both Israelis and Palestinians, international law has appeared inadequate. Israel contends that international law fails to adequately address its right to self-defense against unconventional and asymmetric warfare (Dowty 2012, 206). Palestinians, meanwhile, demand Israeli withdrawal from occupied territories and the safe return of refugees, whose numbers grew from about 750,000 in 1949 to almost 5 million by 2010 (Dowty 2012, 243). The right of return remains a core principle for Palestinians, deeply embedded in their identity.

In negotiations, a proposal by former Israeli Prime Minister Ehud Olmert for a "symbolic return" of 15,000 refugees was seen by Palestinians as insufficient (Dowty 2012, 248). From the Israeli perspective, however, there is no statute of limitations on restoring historical rights or rectifying past injustices.

## Cyprus

> "We have done it your way for 10 years.
> Now we are going to try it our way."
> Bülent Ecevit, former Prime Minister of Turkey (Stern 1975, 62)

Since Greece's declaration of independence in 1821, Greek Cypriots have harbored a strong desire for *enosis*, or union, with Greece, a sentiment intensified by their participation alongside Britain in the First World War (Mallinson 2009, 737–8). This aspiration was rooted deeply in Greek Cypriot identity, fostered by centuries of Hellenistic influence and the Greek Orthodox Church's role in nurturing a Hellenistic consciousness (Holland 1998, 6).

Despite the historical coexistence of Greek and Turkish Cypriots during Ottoman and British colonial rule, the prospect of Greek political supremacy evoked suspicion and hostility among Turkish Cypriots (Holland 1998, 12). The British administration's efforts to maintain peace often involved balancing the interests of both ethnic groups, sometimes resulting in tension and conflict. For example, in 1931, a riot led to the burning of the Government House in Nicosia, prompting the British to suspend constitutional governance and implement repressive measures against Greek Cypriots (Holland 1998, 5).

After the Second World War, the British initially promised self-government for Cyprus, but substantial local representation failed to materialize (Holland 1998, 13). By the late 1940s, amid escalating regional tensions in the Middle East, the British rejected more substantive proposals for Cypriot self-governance (Holland 1998, 16). In 1949, Archbishop Makarios emerged as a prominent leader for Greek Cypriots, advocating strongly for *enosis*. The Orthodox Church conducted a plebiscite in January 1950, resulting in overwhelming support for union with Greece among Greek Cypriots, though Turkish Cypriots remained largely disengaged (Holland 1998, 18).

As Cyprus' strategic importance to Britain increased post-war, any movement toward *enosis* was staunchly opposed. Yet, by 1952, the campaign for union with Greece gained momentum, fueled by comparisons with other British colonies like Malta, which had advanced toward self-determination. Archbishop Makarios then sought to internationalize the issue by bringing the Cypriot cause to the United Nations, coinciding with rumors of his collaboration with Colonel George Grivas (widely known by the code name Dighenis), leader of EOKA,[1] a group engaged in anti-British activities. The exact nature of the relationship between Makarios and Grivas remained ambiguous, though it was clear that Grivas' actions intensified the push for *enosis* (Holland 1998, 118, 187).

In 1952, Archbishop Makarios lobbied in New York for Cyprus' self-determination, arguing that the international right should apply to Cyprus as well (Holland 1998, 30). However, British geopolitical interests significantly countered these efforts. Sir Charles Peake, the British Ambassador to Athens, explicitly warned Greece against supporting Cyprus' UN appeal, stating it would disastrously affect Greek-British relations (Holland 1998, 32). During a meeting on June 29, 1954, the British Foreign Office clarified that while self-government was possible for Cyprus, self-determination was not (Holland 1998, 35). This stance was starkly articulated in the House of Commons, where it was stated that "certain territories in the Commonwealth . . . owing to their particular circumstances, can *never* expect to be fully independent," effectively dismissing any possibility of Cypriot independence (Holland 1998, 38).

This rigidity prompted Greece to take the matter to the United Nations, arguing for the Cypriots' right to self-determination. Despite British efforts to frame this as a domestic issue, their lack of constitutional progress in Cyprus weakened their position (Holland 1998, 41). The British then tried to involve Turkey to counter the self-determination drive, emphasizing Turkish-Cypriot opposition to *enosis*. A UN vote on Cypriot self-determination was deferred due to the Anglo-Turkish collaboration and, in the end, the required majority for a decisive recommendation was not met (Holland 1998, 44). In the wake of this UN failure, severe riots erupted in Greece and Cyprus, reflecting deep frustration and feelings of discrimination by the British and the broader international community. The Greek Cypriots, in particular, felt aggrieved, seeing other colonial populations granted self-determination that was denied to them (Holland 1998, 53).

In 1955, a tripartite conference among Britain, Greece, and Turkey discussed strategic Mediterranean issues, including Cyprus, without any Cypriot representation (Holland 1998, 59). Although Turkey had not governed Cyprus since 1878, its involvement as well as Greece's presence at the conference were secured through American pressure and British support (Holland 1998, 66). It is noteworthy that Ankara was at first reluctant to engage in a diplomatic battle for the Turkish Cypriots. With persistent British patronage for Turkish Cypriot differentiation in Cypriot politics, a small group of political figures emerged, with Rauf Denktaş as the most promising among them (Holland 1998, 66, 68).

During the conference, the diplomatic escalation came quickly when Prime Minister Menderes publicly declared that *enosis* would be a "day of massacre" for the Turkish Cypriots and then referred to the Turkish triumph against Greece in 1922 (Holland 1998, 70). Turkish foreign minister Fatin Rüştü Zorlu went even further and suggested that Cyprus was closer to Anatolia and therefore should be considered part of Anatolia (Holland 1998, 73). He rejected the Greek demographic argument by noting that "when we take into account the state of the population in Cyprus, it is not sufficient to say . . . that 100,000 Turks live there. One should rather say that 24,000,000 Turks live there" (Holland 1998, 73). He concluded that if self-determination were ever to be applied for Cyprus, the guiding principle should not be the demographic distribution between the two ethnicities, but rather the principle of full equality that would bring the 18 percent of the Turkish Cypriot population on equal footing with the 80 percent of the Greek Cypriot majority (Holland 1998, 73).

The tripartite conference's breakdown was followed by severe anti-Greek riots in Istanbul, fueled by inflammatory statements from Turkish officials like Zorlu. These riots involved widespread violence against Greek properties and individuals, underscoring a brutal display of animosity toward Greeks (Holland 1998, 75). British officials viewed these events as a demonstration of Turkey's serious claims over Cyprus, although Turkish state records suggest British involvement as well (Holland 1998, 76).

Amidst ongoing tensions, the British faced persistent demands from Archbishop Makarios and continued insurgent activities by EOKA under the leadership of Colonel Grivas and Gregoris Afxentiou, who was Grivas' chief lieutenant. The British were compelled to offer some prospect of self-determination or risk escalating violence (Holland 1998, 91). Governor John Harding attempted to negotiate with Makarios, proposing a self-government plan that ostensibly maintained British and Turkish interests. Makarios was skeptical, viewing the proposal as a potential perpetuation of British control and a doorway to a Turkish veto over Cypriot constitutional progress (Holland 1998, 94). Though he presented the plan to the Ethnarchy Council, it was ultimately rejected.

In response, on November 26, 1955, Governor Harding declared a state of emergency in Cyprus, imposing curfews and other severe measures aimed at quelling resistance but criticized even within Britain for their harshness (Holland 1998, 153, 159). These actions mirrored oppressive tactics used previously in Palestine, including the forced displacement of Greek suspects (Holland 1998, 255). Under significant American pressure to resume diplomatic talks and facing growing support for EOKA, Harding sought to negotiate with Makarios again, this time for a denouncement of violence in exchange for concessions toward self-determination. Makarios showed openness to a new British proposal, contingent on assurances that any restored Legislative Assembly would feature a Greek elected majority (Holland 1998, 110). However, British Colonial Secretary Lennox-Boyd and Prime Minister Anthony Eden were reluctant to agree to such terms, with Eden ultimately dismissing the idea of majority rule. Makarios criticized the British counterproposal as insufficient, highlighting ongoing disputes over the appropriate level of self-determination and representation for Greek Cypriots relative to the Turkish minority (Holland 1998, 113–14).

Following this meeting, Governor Harding communicated with the Colonial Office, recommending the immediate deportation of Archbishop Makarios to quell unrest, using the pretext of restoring civil order (Holland 1998, 123). During a trip planned by Makarios to Athens, his flight was covertly redirected. Simultaneously, British troops searched his office and private quarters for incriminating material but found none (Holland 1998, 118). Despite these actions, diplomatic tensions escalated, particularly with Turkish leaders Menderes and Zorlu threatening invasion should *enosis* proceed. To alleviate Turkish concerns, the British secretly promised that Turkey could station troops in Cyprus if Cypriot self-determination were realized (Holland 1998, 137).

In Makarios' absence, the British sought to implement an interim constitutional structure to ease Greek Cypriot demands with a mild self-government proposal while conceding constitutional advantages to the Turkish side. In November 1956, Lord Radcliffe presented a proposal that rejected Turkish demands for co-equality and partition but acknowledged the legislative majority of Greek Cypriots in a proposed single-chamber legislature with a significant representation advantage, namely twenty-four Greek Cypriots to six Turkish

Cypriots (Hoffmeister 2006, 3). The plan also proposed significant safeguards for Turkish Cypriots, including a dedicated Ministry of Turkish Affairs.

On December 19, 1956, Colonial Secretary Lennox-Boyd stated that the United Kingdom would consider self-determination when conditions were favorable, ensuring that both communities could independently determine their futures, hinting at partition as a potential outcome:

> When the international and strategic situation permits, and provided self-government is working satisfactorily, Her Majesty's Government will be ready to review the question of application of self-determination. When the time comes for this review, (. . .) it will be the purpose of Her Majesty's Government to ensure that any exercise of self-determination should be effected in such a manner that the Turkish Cypriot community, no less than the Greek Cypriot community, shall, in the special circumstances of Cyprus, be given freedom to decide for themselves their future status. In other words, Her Majesty's Government recognise that the exercise of self-determination in such a mixed population must include partition among the eventual options. (Hoffmeister 2006, 3)

This promise fueled Turkish expectations for partition (*taksim*), complicating future diplomatic efforts between the Cypriot communities.

The British hoped that Makarios' exile would sever his emotional ties with the Greek Cypriots, simplifying British governance. However, this plan backfired, and they eventually released him, although they remained unwilling to engage in dialogue with him (Holland 1998, 180, 183). The diplomatic isolation of Makarios continued as the United Kingdom viewed his advocacy for *enosis* and self-determination as a threat to their military interests in Cyprus (Holland 1998, 185). His release was unfavorably received by Turkey and Turkish Cypriots. Fazıl Küçük, a leading Turkish Cypriot politician, even requested the Governor for Makarios' removal (Holland 1998, 198). Furthermore, Turkish Cypriots demonstrated their discontent by resigning en masse from Cypriot municipalities shortly after Makarios' return, reflecting their deep-seated aversion to what they perceived as Greek expansionist threats (Holland 1998, 198, 221).

As Greek Cypriots were unwilling to settle for anything less than *enosis* or full independence, it became apparent that any agreement would need to be externally imposed on the Cypriot majority (Holland 1998, 221). Turkish Cypriot representatives, enjoying regular access to the British Governor, were assured that their interests would be protected; yet, they pressed for outright partition. A wave of orchestrated violence and riots advocating for partition swept through areas with significant Turkish populations, aiming to enforce a *de facto* partition by driving Greek Cypriots from Muslim quarters (Holland 1998, 229, 251).

Following the failure of Radcliffe's plan, the British government, led by Prime Minister MacMillan, proposed a new plan that suggested a joint administration of Cyprus by Britain, Greece, and Turkey, with each community managing its affairs through separate parliaments and citizenships (Hoffmeister 2006, 4). The plan maintained the implicit possibility of partition but excluded any role for Archbishop Makarios and lacked consultation with Cypriot populations (Holland 1998, 260). MacMillan believed the decision-makers on Cyprus' future were external to the island. This led to the plan's rejection by both Greek and Turkish parties, the latter upset by the absence of a clear pathway to partition (Hoffmeister 2006, 4). Turkish expectations, set by the earlier British promise of partition, meant any retraction or ambiguity from this promise was met with resistance (Holland 1998, 256). Despite opposition, the British moved forward with the unilateral implementation of the MacMillan Plan. This action triggered a surge of violence in Cyprus, with Turkish Cypriot leaders engaging in ethnic cleansing tactics, including intimidation and displacement of Greek Cypriot families, while simultaneously ceasing to pay rents to Greek landlords (Holland 1998, 263). These actions, orchestrated by Ankara, aimed to achieve a *de facto* partition (Holland 1998, 290). Greek Cypriots sought intervention from the British Governor against these aggressions, but their appeals were dismissed by Prime Minister MacMillan (Holland 1998, 263). In response, EOKA, primarily an anti-colonial and anti-British movement, adapted its mission to address the ethnic cleansing of Greek Cypriots, marking a significant shift in its operational focus (Holland 1998, 286).

In a surprising diplomatic shift, a political rapprochement occurred between Turkish Foreign Minister Zorlu and Greek Foreign Minister Evangelos Averoff during a conference in Paris. This unexpected warming in relations, reminiscent of the historical "great rapprochement" between Ataturk and Venizelos, led to a collaborative effort by Zorlu and Averoff to halt the execution of two Greek Cypriots by the British (Holland 1998, 296). Zorlu then saw the issue of Cypriot independence as secondary, envisioning the island as a shared Turkish-Greek entity. This approach set the stage for the "miracle of Zurich," a pivotal agreement between Greece and Turkey concerning Cyprus' future (Holland 1998, 299, 304).

The agreement included a provision allowing for intervention by all parties if specific legitimate interests in an independent Cyprus were threatened, particularly from a Turkish perspective, by an internal Greek coup (Holland 1998, 304). Crucially, Cypriots were once more not involved in the Paris and Zurich discussions. Nonetheless, Greek consent, symbolically represented by Archbishop Makarios, was deemed diplomatically necessary. Greek Prime Minister Karamanlis ensured Makarios would endorse the Zurich conclusions as an "agreed foundation," marking the first significant involvement of Greek Cypriots in diplomatic negotiations, albeit still marginal (Holland 1998, 310). To balance the reintegration of Makarios into the tripartite talks, the British ensured the presence of Turkish Cypriot representatives during the follow-up negotiations in London, although they were given no substantial role in the discussions (Holland 1998, 311). After considerable pressure from Karamanlis and Averoff, Makarios formally accepted the Zurich terms in a communication to the Colonial Office (Holland 1998, 316).

On August 16, 1960, Cyprus declared its independence, with Makarios as President and Küçük as Vice-President. The 1960 Constitution of Cyprus, incorporating the Treaty of Establishment, the Treaty of Guarantee, and the Treaty of Military Alliance, has been noted by many scholars as one of the most rigid and complex constitutions of the post-decolonization era (Chrysostomides 2000, 30–2). Shortly after Cyprus declared its independence, significant constitutional and legislative challenges emerged, particularly around tax law and municipal delimitation (Hoffmeister 2006, 13). The requirement for consensus between Greek and Turkish Cypriots led to a deadlock when no agreement could be reached on new taxation policies, forcing each community to adopt separate tax rules. In response, President Makarios proposed 13 amendments to the Cypriot Constitution aimed at eliminating the veto powers of the president and the vice-president and unifying municipalities and security forces, among other changes (Chrysostomides 2000, 33). These proposals were seen by Turkey as an attempt to abolish the 1960 Treaties, leading to their swift rejection (Chrysostomides 2000, 34).

Tensions escalated dramatically between the two communities. In 1963, a violent incident involving the refusal of Turkish Cypriots to show identification to Greek Cypriot police resulted in deaths on both sides and sparked further violence, including attacks by paramilitary groups from both communities (Hoffmeister 2006, 14). This conflict led to significant destruction and displacement, with estimates of 109 villages being damaged or destroyed and around 25,000–30,000 Turkish Cypriots becoming internally displaced, culminating in the establishment of the Green Line in Nicosia (Hoffmeister

2006, 15; Chrysostomides 2000, 35). Amidst this violence, Küçük and all Turkish Cypriot members of the House of Representatives withdrew from the Cypriot government, declaring it illegitimate. They formed a General Committee to manage Turkish Cypriot affairs and directed Turkish Cypriot civil servants to resign from the Cypriot Government (Hoffmeister 2006, 17). Turkish Cypriots were also reorganized into enclaves, a process that was largely accepted by city dwellers but resisted by rural populations, who were coerced by the paramilitary group TMT.[2] By 1964 the enclaves covered only two percent of the island, but the Turkish Cypriot population residing there counted for 59,000, including the 25,000–30,000 refugees (Hoffmeister 2006, 19).

Efforts at international reconciliation faltered as Greek Cypriots sought revisions to the Zurich/London agreements, while Turkish Cypriots continued to push for geographical separation (Hoffmeister 2006, 15). Amid these failed talks, the UN Security Council, with its Resolution 186, urged all states to respect Cyprus' territorial integrity and independence. Despite this, intercommunal violence persisted, and Turkey made several threats to invade, which were deterred by American intervention. In response, Greece deployed some thousands of troops to Cyprus along with Grivas, who took command of Cypriot forces. This period of tension included a notable incident where Grivas' forces attacked Turkish Cypriots in Kokkina, prompting Turkish retaliation against Greek Cypriot towns (Hoffmeister 2006, 16–17).

In 1967, a military junta in Greece significantly altered Cyprus' political landscape. Under this new regime, Grivas established the right-wing organization EOKA-B, aiming to overthrow Archbishop Makarios. Makarios and the majority of Greek Cypriots had, in the meantime moved away from supporting *enosis* (O'Malley and Craig 1999, 134). By 1974, Makarios had declared EOKA-B illegal and requested the withdrawal of Greek officers from Cyprus (Hoffmeister 2006, 34). In response, the junta orchestrated a coup, installing Nicos Sampson as the head of a short-lived puppet government. Makarios managed to escape to London. On July 20, 1974, Turkey invaded Cyprus, citing the Treaty of Guarantee as its justification (Chrysostomides 2000, 36). Despite a United Nations Security Council demand for an immediate cessation of military actions and a brief ceasefire, Turkish forces occupied an initial 5 percent of Cyprus, in what is known as Operation Attila I.

Meanwhile, constitutional order was restored in both Greece and Cyprus. Karamanlis returned to Greece from his exile in Paris, while in Cyprus, Sampson resigned and Glafkos Clerides assumed the role of acting President under the

1960 Constitution. Following the Security Council Resolution, representatives from Turkey, Greece, and Britain met in Geneva from July 25 to July 30, 1974. It was agreed during these meetings that there would be a gradual reduction of armed forces in Cyprus and further negotiations to establish a unified constitutional government that included the return and participation of Turkish Cypriots (Hoffmeister 2006, 36). The requested negotiations began on August 8, 1974. Denktaş demanded a "bicommunal and bizonal State," where Turkish Cypriot territory would comprise 34 percent of Cyprus (Hoffmeister 2006, 36). Clerides requested a 36- to 48-hour break to consult with both Greece and Makarios, still in London. Bülent Ecevit refused the request, fearing, according to one commentator, that the break was intended to "to buy time to mobilise an international coalition against Turkey" (Hoffmeister 2006, 36).

After the collapse of the tripartite talks, despite the restoration of constitutional order in Cyprus, Turkey launched Operation Attila II. From August 14 to 16, 1974, reinforced Turkish troops expanded their control from 5 percent to 36.4 percent of Cypriot territory. This area included 60 percent of the island's industry, 65 percent of its agriculture, and 80 percent of its tourism. The invasion resulted in approximately 6,000 Greek Cypriot deaths (according to Greek sources), 1,619 missing persons (both Greek and Turkish Cypriots, according to official records), and the displacement of between 105,000 (according to Turkish sources) and 200,000 (according to Greek sources) Greek Cypriots—equating to about 95 percent of the Greek Cypriots previously living in Northern Cyprus (Hoffmeister 2006, 37; Chrysostomides 2000, 37). Additionally, the European Commission of Human Rights cited severe violations of human rights committed by the Turkish army against the Greek Cypriot civilian population (Hoffmeister 2006, 37).

Under the Vienna III Agreement, the Republic of Cyprus allowed Turkish Cypriots, at their discretion, "to proceed to North with their belongings under an organized programme and with the assistance of UNFICYP." The vast majority of the Turkish Cypriots living in the south (40,000–45,000) willingly relocated to the northern part of the island (Hoffmeister 2006, 37–8).

Subsequently, Turkey actively encouraged the migration of about 160,000 illegal settlers from Anatolia (Mallinson 2009, 741). On February 13, 1975, Turkish Cypriots declared the foundation of the Turkish Federated State of Cyprus, which was envisioned as part of a future federation with the Greek Cypriots (Hoffmeister 2006, 38). On November 15, 1983, the Turkish Cypriot Legislative Assembly declared the establishment of the Turkish Republic of

Northern Cyprus (TRNC), recognized only by Turkey. Following this, the Security Council issued Resolution 541 condemning the declaration as null and void. Due to its international isolation, the TRNC relies almost entirely on Turkey for financial support (Hoffmeister 2006, 38–9).

The tragedy of Atilla has profoundly shaped Greek Cypriot life and collective identity since 1974. "I do not forget" or "*δεν ξεχνώ*" (*den xechno*) has become a popular motto among Greek Cypriots, symbolizing their refusal to erase the memory of the catastrophic invasion and their lost or forcibly divided homeland (Philippou and Varnava 2009, 209).

Bi-communal talks resumed in 1974 under UN auspices but have yet to yield a successful outcome. Resolving the territorial disputes and securing the return of refugees remain top priorities for the Greek Cypriots. In 1980, they made a significant concession by accepting the concept of bi-zonality for the first time, but Denktaş' counteroffer to hand over just 2.6 percent of the occupied territories was deemed unacceptable (Hoffmeister 2006, 64). Under diplomatic pressure from President Ronald Reagan, Denktaş showed greater flexibility, and in 1984, he accepted the Pérez de Cuéllar draft plan for Cyprus, which proposed returning 7 percent of the occupied territories (Hoffmeister 2006, 65). However, Greek Cypriot Prime Minister Kyprianou did not consider de Cuéllar's draft to be final and proposed additions, including a detailed timetable for the withdrawal of the Turkish army, explicit guarantees for free movement within the unified state, and a new form of international guarantee that would presumably restrict Turkey's right to intervene in the domestic affairs of the new state (Hoffmeister 2006, 65).

In 1990, Denktaş requested that the term "communities" be used synonymously with "peoples," asserting that both groups had a right to self-determination (Hoffmeister 2006, 67). However, UN terminology remained unchanged despite Denktaş' request. Denktaş also opposed Cyprus joining the EU, a union of which Turkey is not a member (Hoffmeister 2006, 69). The advanced EU accession status of the Republic of Cyprus, contrasted with the stagnation of Turkey's EU candidacy, led to Turkish resentment and a refusal to engage further with the Greek Cypriots. Moreover, Denktaş argued that Cyprus's application to the EU violated the Treaty of Guarantee (Hoffmeister 2006, 98). Against this political backdrop, Turkish Cypriots have hardened their stance, demanding a confederation for Cyprus since 1998 (Hoffmeister 2006, 100).

In 2003, as Turkey's EU accession negotiations approached and aware that Cyprus could exercise its veto power, Turkey became more proactive in seeking a resolution to the Cyprus issue. On April 21, 2003, the TRNC opened three crossing points along the Green Line (Hoffmeister 2006, 162). Negotiations between the two communities resumed at the end of the year. New UN Secretary General Kofi Annan declared that if the two parties failed to agree on a mutual text, he would finalize the plan himself and call for both leaders to submit it to simultaneous referendums. As no agreement was reached, the Secretary General introduced his own version of the plan. The final iteration of the Annan Plan (Annan IV) was embraced by Turkey and the Turkish Cypriots but met with concern and skepticism from the Greeks and Greek Cypriots (Hoffmeister 2006, 176).

According to the Annan Plan, Turkish military forces would remain on the island, and virtually all Turkish Cypriot refugees and about 120,000 Greek Cypriot refugees would have the right to return (Loizides and Antoniades 2009, 612). This arrangement denied the right of return to another 100,000 Greek Cypriot refugees. For these dispossessed owners, Article 10 of the Foundation Agreement under the Annan Plan excluded any judicial resolution of property claims and established a claims committee to determine appropriate compensations. The plan stipulated that these compensations be handled by the unified Cypriot federation, effectively absolving Turkey of liability and contradicting established case law from the ECtHR and, more recently, the European Court of Justice (Bryant 2009, 3). Additionally, the property settlement terms created a paradox for Greek Cypriot refugees who, as taxpayers, would contribute to their own compensations.

The referendums took place on April 24, 2004, with 64.9 percent of Turkish Cypriots supporting the plan and 75.8 percent of Greek Cypriots opposing it. Consequently, the Republic of Cyprus joined the EU on May 1, 2004, as a *de facto* divided island. The Annan Plan remains the most recent international effort to resolve a conflict that has persisted for more than half a century. The opening of the three crossing points by the TRNC in 2003, just months before the referendums, is thought to have backfired. The initial euphoria over the newfound freedom of movement quickly turned to shock and resentment among Greek Cypriots when they saw the profound changes to their homes, hometowns, and villages—places they had been forced to abandon thirty years earlier (Bryant 2009, 3). This realization that a return to their villages would not mean a return to their lost past directed substantial anger and opposition toward the Annan Plan.

## Kosovo

> No one should dare to beat you.
> Slobodan Milošević, addressing Serbian crowds in Kosovo (Judah 2008, 65)

Very much like Cyprus, the Kosovo conflict captivates both international and constitutional legal scholars. It has ignited intense academic debates on international self-determination, constitutional self-determination, and remedial secession. Kosovo represents a notable case of constitutional self-determination, as it becomes evident from its history that Kosovar claims to this right largely arose from collective feelings of constitutional deprivation. Initially, Kosovars experienced what can be described as liberal characteristics of relative deprivation, feeling deprived compared to other Yugoslav nations which, unlike Kosovo, were granted explicit rights to self-determination and secession under the 1946 Yugoslav Constitution. This sense of deprivation deepened into objective deprivation following the unilateral revocation of Kosovo's autonomous status by Slobodan Milošević.

According to the 1981 Yugoslav census—the last to include the participation of Kosovar Albanians—out of a total population of almost one and a half million in Kosovo, 77.4 percent were Albanians, while only 14.9 percent were Serbs and Montenegrins (Judah 2008, 2). The political history of Kosovo is highly complex and is intertwined with two divergent nationalist narratives. Kosovo has never experienced long-lasting ethnic homogeneity due to the continual movement of ethnic populations since the Ottoman era. Although Albanians claim historical precedence in Kosovo, asserting that the Slavs arrived later and occupied their land, Serbs counter with evidence that during the Middle Ages, the Kosovar population was predominantly Serb (Judah 2008, 18). They also point out that many place names in Kosovo are Slavic, such as the Patriarchate of Peč/Peja, and even the name Kosovo itself, which derives from the Slavic word "Kos," meaning blackbird (Judah 2008, 19, 31).

Except for certain Albanian scholars, there is a broad historical consensus that when the Ottomans arrived in Kosovo in the fourteenth century, the majority of its inhabitants were Serbs (Judah 2008, 14). Prior to this, the Nemanjić Dynasty played a pivotal role in shaping the collective identity of the Serbian nation. In the thirteenth century, the Nemanjićs significantly expanded the Serbian Kingdom and fortified Serbian national identity by constructing churches and monasteries, embedding Orthodoxy as a key component of their culture (Judah 2008, 19). Stephen Dušan ascended to power in 1346 and expanded the Serbian

Empire to include regions from Greece to Albania and Bulgaria. Under Dušan, the Serbian army even posed a threat to invade Constantinople (Judah 2008, 20). However, following his death, the empire began to wane. The Ottoman invasion in 1389, led by Sultan Murad, culminated in the famed Battle of Kosovo at Kosovo Polje/Fushë Kosova (the "Field of Blackbirds"). Despite their defeat by the numerically superior and wealthier Ottomans, this battle entrenched Kosovo as a vital element of the Serbian nationalist narrative (Judah 2008, 21). For Serbs, Kosovo holds the revered status of their Jerusalem. On the 500th anniversary of the Battle of Kosovo, Serbia's Foreign Minister declared:

> an inexhaustible source of national pride was discovered on [sic] Kosovo. More important than language and stronger than the Church, this pride unites all Serbs in a single nation. . . . The new story of Serbia begins with Kosovo—a history of valiant efforts, long suffering, endless wars, and unquenchable glory. . . . We bless Kosovo because the memory of the Kosovo heroes upheld us, encouraged us, taught us and guided us. (Judah 2008, 23)

Albanians hold a different perspective on the Battle of Kosovo. A prominent Albanian writer stated, "[t]he Battle of Kosovo was not a confrontation solely between Serbs and Turks. It was a Battle fought by all the people of the Balkans united against an invader" (Judah 2008, 21, 24). Unlike the Serbian narrative, where religion plays a central role, the Albanian nationalistic narrative largely eschews religious themes and instead celebrates a medieval hero, Skanderbeg. In 1443, Skanderbeg rebelled against the Ottomans, liberating much of what is today Albania (Judah 2008, 25). Initially converted to Islam by the Ottomans, Skanderbeg later reverted to Christianity. However, since most Albanians were Muslims at the time, the Christian aspects of their hero's story were downplayed (Judah 2008, 26). Skanderbeg is revered as a national hero by all Albanians, and the Albanian flag, believed to be derived from Skanderbeg's seal, probably symbolizes this Byzantine connection (Judah 2008, 27). Adem Jashari, a hero of the KLA, has often been likened to Skanderbeg. It has been suggested that through his martyrdom, Jashari rekindled the "continuous resistance" emblematic of both the medieval Albanian hero and the storied Battle of Kosovo (Judah 2008, 27).

During the Ottoman period, Serbs gradually migrated to Serbia, Hungary, Bosnia, and Croatia (Judah 2008, 14). The populations in these areas were predominantly Muslim, but demographics began to shift following the Serbian revolution. Newly liberated Serbia drew many Serbs from the countryside, as

Kosovo, still under Ottoman control, was less attractive to Christians. Conversely, Albanians, having converted to Islam, received preferential treatment in Kosovo and were more likely to attain high positions within the Ottoman Empire (Judah 2008, 14). This favored status also delayed the emergence of a revolutionary consciousness among Albanians compared to other Balkan nations. Initially, as nationalistic movements stirred in the Balkans, Albanians sought autonomy within the weakening Empire. However, as their relationship with the Ottomans soured, this quest for autonomy evolved into a demand for independence, culminating in its proclamation on November 28, 1912 (Judah 2008, 36).

By the end of the First Balkan War, Serbia and Montenegro had occupied much of Kosovo (Judah 2008, 38). In 1912, during a conference in London, the frontiers of the newly formed Albanian state were determined, leaving Kosovo out of the new delineation (Judah 2008, 38). Dissatisfied with their shares and the new geographic arrangement in the Balkans, both Albanians from Kosovo and Bulgarians revolted. In 1913, Bulgaria initiated the Second Balkan War but failed to annex additional territories. Two years later, during the First World War, Austro-Hungary, Germany, and Bulgaria invaded Serbia, triggering a massive exodus of Serbian refugees who had to traverse Kosovo to be rescued by the Entente. Many died in the mountains during this exodus, others were captured by the Central Powers, and some suffered from Albanian reprisals (Judah 2008, 40).

For the Kosovar Albanians, who had missed the opportunity to unite with Albania during the Balkan Wars and still remembered Serbian atrocities, the Austro-Hungarian invasion was initially welcomed (Judah 2008, 41). However, after the war's end and the Allies' victory, Serbian forces returned to Kosovo. The Balkan Wars and the First World War had brought widespread devastation to the region, causing significant population shifts and forced dislocations. Following the Serbian uprising against the Ottoman Empire, about 50,000 people, mostly Albanians, had moved to Kosovo (Judah 2008, 35). By the end of the First World War, Serbs comprised only 30–40 percent of Kosovo's population (Judah 2008, 39). Nevertheless, Kosovo's return to Serbian control was emotionally charged, symbolizing the realization of a long-held Serbian aspiration.

After the end of the First World War, representatives from the Serbs, Croats, and Slovenes convened in Corfu where they issued a declaration to form "a constitutional, democratic and parliamentary monarchy headed by the [Serbian] Karađorđević dynasty" (Pavković 1997, 21). The declaration affirmed the equality of the three nations and their major religions—Orthodoxy, Roman

Catholicism, and Islam. The new federation, governed by the principle of self-determination, was declared territorially indivisible (Pavković 1997, 21). The National Council of Yugoslavia officially proclaimed the independence of the federation on October 29, 1918, in Zagreb. Following the establishment of Yugoslavia, Serbs, and Montenegrins were encouraged to settle in Kosovo. An estimated 70,000 "colonists" arrived during this period, receiving land confiscated from Albanians who had been on the losing side of the war (Judah 2008, 45). Despite these incentives, the challenging economic conditions of the early communist era drove many Serbs to migrate north to Serbia, where there was a higher demand for labor in both agricultural and industrial sectors (Judah 2008, 15).

During the Second World War, Kosovo was partitioned among Germany, Bulgaria, and Albania (Judah 2008, 16). Kosovar Albanians favored the Axis powers and supported the creation of a "Greater Albania" that would include Kosovo (Judah 2008, 47). The collapse of Yugoslavia wrought significant devastation upon the Serbs in Kosovo, with many Serb villages destroyed and between 30,000 and 100,000 people either becoming refugees or being sent to concentration camps (Judah 2008, 47). When Italy withdrew from the region, Albania sought to annex Kosovo, but the Axis powers denied this request (Judah 2008, 48).

In 1943, a pivotal meeting presided over by Josip Broz Tito took place in Bosnia to decide the future of the new Yugoslavia, without any representation from Kosovar Albanians (Judah 2008, 48). Conversely, during a political meeting in Albania, it was declared that "Kosovo-Metohija is an area with a majority Albanian population, which, now as always in the past, wishes to be united with Albania" (Judah 2008, 48). Despite strong resistance from Kosovar Albanians, Kosovo was annexed to Serbia in 1945 as an "autonomous region" at the request of the Serbian-dominated regional council (Judah 2008, 49).

By the 1950s, Yugoslavia was more centralized than truly federal. Efforts were made to foster a common Yugoslav identity promoting "brotherhood and unity" intended to transcend yet not invalidate national identities (Pavković 1997, 61). However, this cultural experiment by the Socialist Party largely failed, partly because many Croat and Slovene intellectuals perceived Yugoslavism as a veiled form of Serbian hegemony threatening their national identities (Pavković 1997, 62). Another reason cited for this failure was Tito's inability to reconcile the "conflicting memories" of the Second World War among the Yugoslav nations (Ramet 2005, 163).

Although still formally attached to Serbia, Kosovo was "promoted" in 1963 from an autonomous region to an autonomous province of Yugoslavia (Judah 2008, 53). By the late 1960s, communist elites in the Republics began demanding more power (Pavković 1997, 65–6). In 1968, the Muslims of Bosnia-Herzegovina were allowed to identify themselves as "Muslims in the ethnic sense," subsequently declaring themselves a separate nation within Yugoslavia (Pavković 1997, 66). Inspired by Bosnia-Herzegovina, Kosovar Albanians formally requested their constitutional upgrade to a separate republic within Yugoslavia. However, according to the Yugoslav Constitution, Kosovar Albanians were classified as a nationality, not a nation (Independent International Commission on Kosovo 2000, 36). Large demonstrations occurred in Kosovo during Albania's National Day in 1968, leading the Communist Party to concede more financial, educational, and industrial benefits to the province (Pavković 1997, 67). Despite these concessions, nationalistic sentiments persisted.

In 1974, a new Yugoslav Constitution was drafted, transforming Yugoslavia into a less centralized and more "confederal" state (Pavković 1997, 69). Each republic gained substantial self-governing powers, and a system was introduced allowing them to veto most federal decisions. This veto could only be overridden by Tito himself (Pavković 1997, 57). The Constitution also reaffirmed the right to self-determination for all nations and granted significant autonomy to Vojvodina and Kosovo within both Serbia and Yugoslavia (Pavković 1997, 71). This enhanced autonomy placed the two provinces in a position similar to the republics, as they both gained "full legislative autonomy," effectively allowing them to veto Yugoslav and Serbian legislative acts (Pavković 1997, 71).

While Tito's political presence seemed to alleviate most nationalistic grievances, his death in 1980 disrupted the cohesion among the republics and their commitment to the federal structure. This became particularly evident during the 1981 student protests in Kosovo. Initially triggered by trivial issues like a canteen mismanagement and resulting long queues, the situation escalated as Kosovar Albanian demands for Kosovo to become a Yugoslav republic resurfaced (Judah 2008, 58). Protesters, including students and other community members, chanted slogans such as "We are Albanians, not Yugoslavs!" and "We want a unified Albania!" (Judah 2008, 58). The protests led to severe clashes with the police and were ultimately suppressed by the communist regime. The harsh suppression of the protests and the imprisonment of future KLA members catalyzed a radical shift in Kosovar Albanian sentiment against Yugoslavia and Serbia, exacerbating hostilities toward the Serbs (Judah 2008, 58). Additionally, the demographic explosion of Albanians in Kosovo intensified harassment against Serbs, who were increasingly viewed as a "ruling minority" (Judah 2008, 58–9).

In 1987, Serbian President Ivan Stambolić sent Slobodan Milošević, then head of the Serbian Communist Party, to Kosovo to address the grievances of Kosovar Serbs (Judah 2008, 64). Stambolić was particularly concerned about Kosovo's veto power over Serbian legislative matters. During Milošević's visit, Kosovar Albanian police attacked a group of 15,000 Serbian and Montenegrin protesters near Pristina, calling for Milošević and Serbian authorities to protect them from ongoing harassment (Pavković 1997, 83–4). The incident led Milošević to publicly declare, "No one is allowed to beat you" (Pavković 1997, 84). Upon returning to Belgrade, he called for immediate action to ensure the effective protection of Kosovar Serbs and Montenegrins. This response marked a significant breach of the 1974 Yugoslav Constitution's division of powers, as it removed what was essentially an internal Kosovar issue from local jurisdiction to be addressed by Serbian authorities (Pavković 1997, 84).

Slobodan Milošević intensified his campaign to affirm the Serbian identity of Kosovo. In 1989, he famously addressed Serbian crowds, declaring, "Every nation has a love which eternally warms its heart. For Serbia it is Kosovo. That is why Kosovo will remain in Serbia" (Judah 2008, 66). That same year, the Serbian Assembly began stripping away various legislative powers from Kosovo until it completely revoked the province's autonomous status in 1990 (Independent International Commission on Kosovo 2000, 41). Prior to this revocation, the Serbian government passed several laws aimed at altering Kosovo's demographic composition. These included shutting down Kosovar Albanian media outlets, renaming streets, implementing Serbian curricula in schools and universities, dismissing thousands of Kosovar Albanians from public sector jobs, providing financial incentives for Serbs to move to Kosovo, and imposing property restrictions on Kosovar Albanians (Independent International Commission on Kosovo 2000, 41–2).

Violent protests erupted following the revocation of Kosovo's autonomy. In response, Albanian members of the Kosovo assembly voted to establish Kosovo as a republic within Yugoslavia—a move that Serbia swiftly annulled (Judah 2008, 69). The Albanian deputies then convened secretly to draft a new constitution for the "republic," though they did not seek full independence at that time. However, the disintegration of Yugoslavia soon accelerated. In 1991, Slovenia and Croatia declared independence, and the conflict spread to Bosnia-

Herzegovina, where the Srebrenica massacre, the most atrocious event of the Yugoslav wars, took place (Judah 2008, 68). In light of these developments, Kosovo declared its independence in September 1991 based on a referendum, which Serbia declared illegal (Judah 2008, 69). The KLA was founded in 1993, with notable figures such as Hashim Thaçi and Ramush Haradinaj, some of whose members received military training in Albania (Judah 2008, 78). The Bosnian War concluded with the signing of the Dayton Accords in 1995, and the European Union recognized the new states, as well as Serbia and Montenegro, as the legal successors of the former Yugoslavia (Judah 2008, 79). By 1995, all of Kosovo's reference groups were internationally recognized states.

In 1997, massive student demonstrations occurred in Pristina. That year, the KLA began making public appearances at funerals and launching attacks against the Serbian police (Independent International Commission on Kosovo 2000, 67). Serbia responded with increased repression, deploying Yugoslav troops and heavy military assets to Likoshan/Likosane (Independent International Commission on Kosovo 2000, 68). The conflict persisted in the Drenica region, a stronghold of the KLA. The Yugoslav government's claims that the situation was a manageable internal conflict were challenged in 1997 when the UNHCR reported that 200,000 Kosovars had been displaced (Judah 2008, 81–2).

Peace negotiations were held in Rambouillet, France, under the auspices of NATO to normalize the situation in Kosovo. The proposed agreement stipulated a complete disarmament of the KLA and a full withdrawal of Yugoslav forces, supervised by approximately 30,000 NATO troops (Independent International Commission on Kosovo 2000, 82). Additionally, the agreement sought to restore Kosovo's autonomy and ensure the effective operation of its independent institutions, while deferring a decision on Kosovo's final status "for reconsideration after three years." The Kosovar Albanians signed the agreement, but the Serbian delegates refused. From March 24, 1999, to June 10, 1999, Serbia, Kosovo, and some targets in Montenegro were subjected to severe NATO air strikes (Independent International Commission on Kosovo 2000, 92). Even after four weeks of bombardment, Slobodan Milošević refused to negotiate the status of Kosovo. In a controversial military decision, NATO intensified and expanded its operations to include industrial infrastructure, media, bridges, airports, and telecommunications (Independent International Commission on Kosovo 2000, 93). When the bombing ceased, it was estimated that approximately 10,000 people had died in Kosovo during the conflict (Judah 2008, 91). The UNHCR reported that 848,100 Kosovar Albanians had fled Kosovo, and a total of 1.45 million people had been displaced (Judah 2008, 88). Security Council Resolution 1244 called for the withdrawal of all Yugoslav forces from Kosovo, the deployment of NATO forces (KFOR), and the establishment of a UN interim administration mission (UNMIK). Although it was initially envisioned that some Serbian forces might later be allowed to return, this never materialized (Judah 2008, 91). Moreover, KFOR struggled to prevent violent reprisals against Serbs and some Romas suspected of collaborating with Yugoslav forces during the war, prompting many to flee (Independent International Commission on Kosovo 2000, 104). The remaining Serbian population withdrew into enclaves.

Overall, Resolution 1244 aimed to restore normalcy for Kosovars. Specifically, it tasked UNMIK with establishing and overseeing "provisional democratic self-governing institutions [in order] to ensure conditions for a peaceful and normal life for all inhabitants in Kosovo." A primary goal of UNMIK was to facilitate the safe return of all refugees, a goal largely achieved as nearly all of the 848,000 Kosovar Albanian refugees returned safely. However, about 100,000 Serbs were forced to leave Kosovo after the arrival of KFOR (Independent International Commission on Kosovo 2000, 119).

Resolution 1244 reaffirmed the sovereignty and territorial integrity of Yugoslavia but also called for a final solution that would consider the will of the Kosovar people (Judah 2008, 94). In 2005, Secretary-General Kofi Annan appointed Martti Ahtisaari to oversee negotiations between Kosovo and Serbia. Ahtisaari advocated for a "supervised independence" for Kosovo and a special status for Serbian enclaves in the north, suggesting autonomy for northern Kosovo that would maintain special cultural, religious, and financial links with Serbia (Judah 2008, 113). The Ahtisaari plan was submitted to the Security Council on March 27, 2007, but was vetoed by Russia, although it received support from all EU member-states (Judah 2008, 114).

On February 16, 2008, under its European Security and Defense Policy, the EU approved the deployment of a civil mission to Kosovo known as EULEX, tasked with monitoring, mentoring, and advising on all aspects related to the rule of law in Kosovo (Judah 2008, 114). One day after EULEX was endorsed, Kosovo declared its independence. The unanimous declaration was immediately condemned by Serbia as null and void, leading to massive demonstrations in Belgrade (Judah 2008, 146).

Despite its independence, Kosovo has not sought union with Albania. A 2005 poll showed that only 9.1 percent of the population favored such a union, likely because Kosovar Albanians have developed a distinct Kosovar identity, separate from their ethnic Albanian identity (Judah 2008, 119). Similar to the Palestinians and Greek Cypriots, the war in Kosovo and acts of objective deprivation against Kosovar Albanians have contributed to a profound transformation of their identity.

## Deprivation and the Traumatisms of Collective Identity

The five empirical studies examined above have disclosed two distinct forms of collective deprivation that have significantly shaped the historical and normative evolution of the right to self-determination: (a) objective deprivation, characterized as a phenomenological amalgamation of removal, separation, and loss; and (b) the conceptualization of collective deprivation as perceived inferiority stemming from inter-group comparisons and other relative assessments. This perspective includes the experiences of Jews, Greek Cypriots, Turkish Cypriots, and Albanian Kosovars.

The collective consciousness of the Jewish people has been influenced by both forms of collective deprivation. Historically, they have endured objective deprivation through recurrent persecutions across Europe and Russia, from forced relocations and expulsions in Spain and the Ottoman Empire to the extensive pogroms in Tsarist Russia. Although the aspiration for Zion has been a longstanding cultural and religious motif, it only crystallized into a definitive political demand with Theodor Herzl and the Zionist movement in the nationalistic milieu of the nineteenth century. In the context of the post-Westphalian world order, Jews drew new parallels with national groups that had achieved full independence and sovereign statehood, particularly following the disintegration of the Ottoman Empire. These comparisons fostered a fundamentally liberal Jewish assertion that, in light of their persistent maltreatment, they deserved the equal right to establish a state within the historical boundaries of Eretz Yisrael. While this claim holds strong moral justification, especially post-Holocaust, it is improbable that such a claim would have been articulated outside the nineteenth-century nationalist framework and without other nationalist examples as reference points.

In Cyprus, both Greek Cypriots and Turkish Cypriots have made liberal comparisons, albeit with starkly different benchmarks. For Greek Cypriots, a fair application of the international right to self-determination, as shaped within the nationalist context of the nineteenth and twentieth centuries and particularly during the decolonization era, would imply a recognition of their right to self-identify as Greeks. This would allow them to either unite with Greece or establish their independent statehood. As highlighted in the empirical analysis, Greek Cypriots consistently compared their situation to other British colonies that had progressed to advanced levels of self-government. Their resentment intensified as these reference groups eventually achieved full self-determination and independent statehood. The Greek Cypriots perceived this as a form of discrimination, believing that the principles of self-determination were being applied selectively, favoring other groups over them.

Turkish Cypriots, in contrast, have consistently employed the Greek Cypriot community as a standard for political juxtaposition. This inclination is notably evident in the Turkish Cypriot response to the *enosis* campaign, which was the latter's diametrical opposite: *taksim*. Despite their numerical disadvantage, Turkish Cypriots insisted on nothing short of equal treatment alongside the Greek Cypriots. This demand for parity, as perceived by Turkish Cypriots, necessitated, at minimum, absolute legislative parity between the two communities. Under the sway of British political pressure and diplomatic maneuvering, the Turkish Cypriot aspiration concretely materialized in the form of extensive veto powers enshrined within the 1960 Constitution. Consequently, given that both the foundations of the Zurich agreement and subsequently the 1960 Constitution of Cyprus epitomized this political equilibrium, Makarios' ill-fated proposition to revisit the issue of legislative equality in 1963 through his 13 constitutional amendments was perceived by Turkish Cypriots as an affronting and demeaning proposal. Denktaş' retort to Makarios during the London negotiations epitomized the sentiments of relative deprivation among Turkish Cypriots, as he openly declared his refusal to acquiesce to a scenario where Turkish Cypriots would be perceived by Greeks as a mere "minority" (Holland 1998, 315).

Even following the *de facto* partition of the island in 1974, Turkish Cypriots continued to employ Greek Cypriots as a reference point for their political comparisons. As outlined in the historical narrative of the conflict, immediately after the initial stage of the Turkish invasion, Denktaş demanded the creation of a bicommunal-bizonal state, envisioning distinct territory for the Turkish Cypriots. From that moment on, there was a discernible surge in Turkish Cypriot aspirations and political demands. Particularly noteworthy is the evolution of the initial Turkish Cypriot demand for a bicommunal state into a call for a federal state in 1975, followed by an insistence on an independent state in 1983. Subsequently, after the political setback and ensuing international isolation of the TRNC, there emerged a demand to be recognized as a distinct people with full self-determination rights during the UN approximation talks in 1990. Finally, after the UN's rejection of the Turkish Cypriot self-determination claim, there was an adjustment toward advocating for a very loose confederation with the Greek Cypriots in 1998—a stance that still underscores the Turkish Cypriot diplomatic redline. The escalating demands of Turkish Cypriots during prolonged and complex diplomatic negotiations are deeply intertwined with growing feelings of relative deprivation from their perspective. Unlike the TRNC, which is widely regarded as a pseudo-state, the Republic of Cyprus stands as the sole legitimate and operational government on the island. It is a fully independent and internationally recognized state with diplomatic representation in most international organizations. This political asymmetry inevitably leads to constant and profoundly disheartening comparisons between the TRNC and the Republic of Cyprus.

What is particularly notable in the case of Turkish Cypriots is that the *de facto* partition did not ameliorate or fortify their relative status vis-à-vis Greek Cypriots. Quite the contrary, the *de facto* partition not only globally isolated Turkish Cypriots but also significantly exacerbated their relative political standing, as their pre-invasion point of comparison—the Greek Cypriots as a politically equal community under the 1963 Constitution—became a hardly comparable post-invasion benchmark: an independent and fully functional state. Hence, it is hardly surprising that any political or diplomatic gesture perceived to perpetuate or endorse this political inequality is met with vehement opposition by Turkish Cypriots. One might cite, for instance, the strong reaction of both Turkey and the TRNC following Cyprus' acceptance as a candidate country by the EU in 1993, which provoked Turkish resentment and, notably, Denktaş' diplomatic outburst, essentially announcing that henceforth, Turkish Cypriots would not entertain negotiations for a federation but, at best, a very loose confederation with Greek Cypriots.

Kosovo, conversely, presents a striking contrast to the case of Jewish self-determination. Unlike the Jewish people, Kosovo's collective sense of deprivation initially bore relative characteristics, primarily manifesting as collective feelings of deprivation stemming from ongoing political comparisons with other Yugoslav nations. Unlike the Kosovar Albanians, these nations enjoyed an explicit right to self-determination as stipulated in the 1946 Yugoslav Constitution. Despite Kosovo's elevation from an autonomous region to an autonomous province of

Yugoslavia in 1963, political comparisons persisted. The political achievements of the Muslims of Bosnia-Herzegovina, who secured recognition as a separate nation within the Yugoslav federation in 1968, served as an additional point of reference and a source of resentment for the Kosovar Albanians.

Only after the constitutional amendments of 1974, which effectively placed Kosovo and Vojvodina in a politically analogous position to the other Republics, did the situation in Kosovo begin to stabilize. From 1974 onwards, Kosovo, although not formally a Republic, possessed full legislative autonomy, enabling it to effectively veto the adoption of virtually any Yugoslav and Serbian legislative measures. However, the circumvention of Kosovo's constitutional rights following the 1981 student protests, along with discriminatory measures imposed on Kosovar Albanians by the Milošević regime, and ultimately, Serbia's unilateral revocation of Kosovo's autonomous status, transformed the perceived inferiority of Kosovar Albanians into objective deprivation through the actual removal and loss of autonomy. Nevertheless, alongside these objective changes, sentiments of relative deprivation persisted and indeed fueled the unwavering Kosovar demand for political independence. This demand was reinforced by the fact that, following the conflicts in Yugoslavia, all of Kosovo's reference groups had achieved international recognition as sovereign states.

Additionally, the case studies reveal the significance of norms and political promises as reference points that engender collective sentiments of relative deprivation. Liberal comparisons are accentuated or introduced anew due to two primary factors: (a) the ambiguous content of legal norms (e.g., the precise scope of international and constitutional rights to self-determination) and (b) the psychological impact of political, diplomatic, and/or legal affirmations and commitments that validate or reward the collective actor making the comparison. In such instances, political pledges can either establish a new reference point for the comparing group or confer credibility and legitimacy upon an existing comparison. These political commitments elevate collective expectations to a perceived level of entitlement.

For example, the catalytic effects of the Balfour Declaration, the Peel Report, and the 1947 UN partition plan were pivotal for both Israel and Palestine. The Balfour Declaration formally and explicitly endorsed the British government's support for the Zionist endeavor of Jewish resettlement in Eretz Yisrael. Despite Arab opposition, the Balfour Declaration was subsequently enshrined within the British Mandate for Palestine, thereby reiterating and institutionalizing the initial political commitment. This declaration effectively bolstered the plausibility of Jewish nationalist comparisons and reference points, ultimately affirming the right of the Jewish people to establish a sovereign state within the historical boundaries of Eretz Yisrael. Consequently, Jewish liberal expectations were validated and intensified by the ensuing psychology of acquisition: within a mere three years of the Balfour Declaration, Ben-Gurion initiated a quasi-colonial policy in Palestine through extensive acquisition of Palestinian land, resulting in the disruption of rural Palestinian life (Pappe 2006, 94).

Furthermore, following the Arab uprising, the Peel Report recommended the partition of Palestine into two distinct states—one Arab, encompassing 80 percent of the territory, and one Jewish, comprising the remaining 20 percent (Dowty 2012, 84). Although ultimately retracted due to Arab objections, the report nonetheless introduced a new reference point. This reference point was substantially broadened and formalized through the 1947 UN partition proposal, which envisioned the establishment of a Jewish state covering 56 percent of Palestine's territory (Dowty 2012, 89). The subsequent 1948 Arab-Israeli conflict led to the expulsion of approximately 90 percent of the Arab population residing in the area designated to become the Jewish state under the UN plan (Pappe 2006, 138).

In the context of Cyprus, Colonial Secretary Lennox-Boyle asserted in 1956 that the exercise of self-determination within the mixed population of Cyprus "must include partition among the eventual options" (Hoffmeister 2006, 3). Lennox-Boyle's political commitment to *taksim* significantly shaped subsequent political dynamics in Cyprus, as it heightened the collective expectations of Turkey and the Turkish Cypriots, who found formal political backing for their secessionist aspirations. The British pledge of *taksim* essentially validated for Turkish Cypriots the plausibility of their comparisons with the Greek Cypriot majority and their ensuing contention that *taksim* would constitute a just response to *enosis*. However, what the British did not anticipate was that the desire for *taksim* would become entirely disconnected from, and independent of, the Greek Cypriot *enosis* campaign. Even though Greek Cypriots ultimately abandoned their aspirations for union with Greece, the Turkish Cypriot demand for *taksim* persisted as a distinct political claim.

Psychological and hermeneutic analyses have revealed that, unlike its relative counterpart, the phenomenon of objective deprivation represents a considerably more profound form of emotional turmoil, penetrating deeper layers of collective psychology. Collective separation and loss, particularly when imposed forcibly, imbue collective memory with a profound sense of injustice and, under certain circumstances, can disrupt communal narratives and traumatize collective identity. According to Paul Ricoeur, "symbolic wounds calling for healing are stored in the archives of collective memory" (Ricoeur 2004, 79). We have also seen that collectivities tend to construct a coherent narrative of their historical continuity to reconcile both triumphs and traumatic losses. Moreover, the hermeneutic examination of deprivation suggests that the process of collective recollection prioritizes victims and memories of loss over memories of triumph and victory. Benedict Anderson contends that this form of narrative construction or collective imagination is not a mere social fabrication or invention, but rather the political analog of religious reflections on immortality, as collectives tend to transmute "fatality into continuity" (Anderson 1991, 11). Narrative repair plays a crucial role in this process.

However, the process of narrative repair does not always yield a coherent account of collective history or a healed collective identity. Instances of collective deprivation and loss can disrupt the process of narrative restoration or ultimately traumatize collective identity, particularly when *cathexis*, namely, the libidinal investment in the lost or forcibly removed object, persists within the collectivity. We have observed that an almost reflexive psychological response to the phenomenological dyad of removal and loss is political and/or military aggression. Both forms of collective deprivation fit into this pattern: the actions of EOKA in Cyprus, for instance, largely constituted a guerrilla response to Greek Cypriot relative deprivation, while the *intifadas* in Palestine were spontaneous, massive expressions of anger against the phenomena of removal and loss perpetrated by the Zionists. What lends the phenomenology of objective deprivation its distinctive psychological and emotional weight is its profound psychoanalytic foundation: collective loss instinctually evokes the primal trauma and engenders emotions of forced separation. Forced separation and loss are therefore inherently traumatic, contingent upon the libidinal ties one maintains toward their lost object. When separation and loss entail the psychoanalytic surrogate of the mother (such as a people's homeland), traumas to collective identity appear to become inevitable.

The five case studies have demonstrated that the forcible separation from the motherland normally produces collective denial to let go of the *cathexis*, namely, the libidinal investment in the lost land. If the collective denial to redirect *cathexis* to another erotic object persists, then the loss of the motherland is internalized and produces melancholia. In such a case, the communal narrative repair processes cannot heal the loss, for the latter ultimately transforms into an identity loss. Almost all peoples and communities who have been forcibly separated from their motherland have expressed denial to let go of the *cathexis*. Before departing for the Trail of Tears, the Cherokee Nation declared that they would not relinquish their libidinal ties to their ancestral homeland.

Although Nauru did not present a typical example of forced expulsion, Nauruans nevertheless endured collective loss and developed customary mourning responses to the expropriation and devastation of their land. Nauruan expressions of grief over their ravaged land are evident in various folk songs, which serve as instruments of narrative repair. The loss has thus been ingrained into Nauruan collective memory and culture, alongside recollections of the injustices inflicted upon them by Germany and the three mandatory powers. Australia's proposition to the Nauruans to abandon their homeland and relinquish their cultural identity by resettling on Curtis Island as Australian citizens not only interfered with the emotional ties between the Nauruan people and their land but also attempted to disrupt the emotional bonds among them.

As explored in the historical section, following the destruction of the Second Temple of Jerusalem, Jews coped with the realities of their exile by transforming Zion into a religious symbol of return. Throughout the process of narrative repair, Jews retained their emotional attachment to their lost motherland while managing to address the trauma of loss by endowing Zion with religious rather than political significance. For the Jewish people, exile symbolized divine punishment, while the return to Zion was associated with the advent of the Messiah and the opportunity for redemption (Dowty 2012, 25). Consequently, all synagogues were oriented toward Zion, and the yearning for Jerusalem found expression in liturgy, ritual, visual art, and poetry (Krämer 2008, 25). The psychoanalytical and hermeneutic analysis of history supports the Jewish contention that there are no "limitations on the restoration of historical rights or the rectification of past injustice for an entire people" (Dowty 2012, 257). Jews were indeed deprived of their homeland, and the ensuing trauma was mitigated through the redemptive, religious promise of return.

Likewise, Palestinians and Greek Cypriots refuse to relinquish their emotional connections to their lost or forcibly divided motherland. Unlike the Jewish people, who successfully repaired their narrative continuity and coped with the trauma of separation by transforming Zion into a religious symbol, the collective trauma of loss remains an open wound for Greek Cypriots and Palestinians. Similar to the case of Nauru, Palestinian deprivation began with the widespread appropriation of land, resulting in the degradation of rural areas in Palestine. The 1936 revolt marked the initial significant Arab reaction to Zionist expansionist policies and exemplifies the psychological dynamics of the aggression-frustration dyad. Following the British withdrawal, the Jewish leadership responded to Arab rejection of partition by implementing Plan D, which culminated in the ethnic cleansing of approximately 90 percent of the Arab population residing in the area designated for the Jewish state under the UN partition plan. This act of objective deprivation, which resulted in the displacement of some 750,000 Palestinian refugees, was compounded by the appropriation of Palestinian public and private assets (Pappe 2006, 134).

In Palestinian collective memory, the 1948 war is remembered as *al-nakba*, translating to the catastrophe, arguably catalyzing the solidification of a more robust Palestinian identity centered around the theme of the lost motherland. For Palestinians, the loss has been internalized, with objective deprivation culminating in an identity crisis. The Palestinian collective identity now resonates profoundly with revolution, embellished with the mythical persona of the *fida'i*, the Palestinian fighter committed to reclaiming the motherland and rectifying historical injustices (Pappe 2006, 147). Notably, in the cases of Palestinian, Kosovar Albanian, and Greek Cypriot deprivation, the internalized loss has fundamentally reshaped their respective identities: the Arabs of Palestine evolved into Palestinians, the Albanians of Kosovo into Kosovars, and for the Greek Cypriots, the motherland now encompasses Cyprus instead of Greece. Psychoanalytically, this internalization of collective loss and profound identity transformation stems from the unconscious transference of the archetypal mother substitute from Greece to Cyprus for Greek Cypriots, from Albania to Kosovo for Kosovar Albanians, and from the abstract notion of the Arab world to Palestine for Palestinians. In all three instances, and according to this psychoanalytical approach, objective deprivation and loss have resuscitated, in the collective unconscious, the trauma of birth. This unconscious revival acted as a psychoanalytical mechanism that displaced the archetype of the mother from the initial surrogate (nation) to the lost or divided land.

Similar to the Zionist Plan D, Operation Attila in Cyprus resulted in the ethnic cleansing of 95 percent of the Greek Cypriot population residing in Northern Cyprus, along with the forcible appropriation by Turkish Cypriots of the lion's share of Cyprus' industry, tourism, and agriculture. For Greek Cypriots, the denial of *cathexis* has been internalized and epitomized in the motto *I do not forget* or *δεν ξεχνώ* (*den xechno*), particularly evident in their diplomatic tenacity and political insistence to reunify their forcibly divided country decades after the *de facto* partition. The Greek Cypriot anguish stemming from Operation Attila has engendered profound collective disorientation, fear, and a disrupted communal narrative. This narrative disruption is especially conspicuous in various Greek Cypriot textbooks where, unlike the Jewish optimistic eschatology of redemptive return to Zion, there is no vision for a conclusive solution or a settled, peaceful future for Cyprus. In the sparse references to such a solution, it is often construed as a gift from God, a historical inevitability, or as dictated by fate (Philippou and Varnava 2009, 209).

Among Palestinians and Greek Cypriots, the deeply internalized sense of loss means that any attempt to obstruct the peace process or establish a *de facto* situation in either Palestine or Cyprus, as systematically pursued by Netanyahu and Denktaş, will not mitigate the profound psychological impact of loss embedded in their collective identities. While time may eventually help heal and reshape traumatic narratives, as seen with the Jewish narrative and the transformation of Zion into a religious symbol of return, the loss of the motherland is deeply enshrined in the collective memories, narratives, and self-identification processes of Palestinians and Greek Cypriots. This loss will not simply fade away; it continues to hold a central place in their collective consciousness.

In light of this psychological and hermeneutic framework, one can discern how the construction of the wall separating Israel from Gaza and the West Bank, the expansion of illegal settlements in the occupied territories of Palestine, and the influx of illegal settlers from Anatolia to the TRNC rekindle the trauma of initial deprivation. These measures essentially seek to cement the initial separation, loss, and detachment from the motherland. Loss has become an inherent aspect of Palestinian and Greek Cypriot collective identities. Therefore, any political or diplomatic approaches that either ignore or diminish the significance of loss in the Palestinian or Greek Cypriot collective consciousness may provoke collective sentiments of humiliation and disrespect. For example, when Ehud Olmert proposed in negotiations with Abbas the "symbolic return" to Israel of a maximum of 15,000 refugees, the offer was not taken seriously (Dowty 2012, 248). Similarly, when in 1980 Denktaş countered the Greek Cypriot concession of bi-zonality with the proposal that Turkish Cypriots would relinquish 2.6 percent of the occupied territories, the offer was deemed unacceptable and summarily rejected (Hoffmeister 2006, 64).

The Turkish Cypriot situation presents a nuanced complexity. Alongside feelings of relative deprivation, Turkish Cypriots faced tangible removal and loss.

In 1963, responding to Makarios' proposal for reviewing the 1960 Constitution of Cyprus, Nicos Sampson, later known as the "Turk Killer" (Hoffmeister 2006, 15) instigated brutal paramilitary actions against the TMT and Turkish Cypriots. The ensuing inter-communal conflict resulted in significant Turkish Cypriot casualties, damage to 109 mixed and Turkish Cypriot villages, and the displacement of 25,000–30,000 Turkish Cypriot refugees within Cyprus (Hoffmeister 2006, 15). Following these political and paramilitary incidents, Küçük and all the Turkish Cypriot members of the House of Representatives withdrew from the Cypriot government and organized the resettlement of Turkish Cypriot populations in enclaves. Turkish Cypriots living in cities were generally "willing" to resettle to such enclaves, contrary to farmers who "were more or less forced by the TMT" (Hoffmeister 2006, 19). By 1964 the enclaves covered only two percent of the island, but the Turkish Cypriot population residing there counted 59,000 people, including the 25,000–30,000 refugees (Hoffmeister 2006). Moreover, after Operation Attila, the vast majority of Turkish Cypriots that had remained in the southern parts of Cyprus (40,000–45,000) willingly left for the northern part of the island in accordance with the Vienna III agreement (Hoffmeister 2006, 37–8).

Distinguishing between forced expulsion and voluntary relocation, particularly pursuant to the Vienna III agreement, sheds light on the Turkish Cypriot response. While one might anticipate some initial resistance or a melancholic longing or desire to return in the years following expulsion, Turkish Cypriot emotional reactions have been paradoxical. Unlike Palestinians, Kosovar Albanians, and Greek Cypriots, objective deprivation did not seem to prompt a collective identity shift among Turkish Cypriots, transposing the archetypal mother symbol from Anatolia or the Turkish nation to Cyprus. Despite emotional bonds to their land, most Turkish Cypriots seemingly accepted the partition, facilitated by the Turkish Cypriot leadership post-MacMillan plan, leading to significant population movements. The eruption of riots favoring *taksim* before the 1963 Greek Cypriot paramilitary attacks further challenges psychological interpretations.

While Greek Cypriots' emotional attachment to Cyprus ultimately outweighed desires for *enosis* with Greece, Turkish Cypriot sentiment consistently favored *taksim* as the desired outcome, except for a brief period preceding the Annan plan referendum and Cyprus' EU accession. This emotional contrast invites an analogy with the biblical judgment of King Solomon (Kings 3:16), where each woman claimed a living child as her own: what Greek Cypriots perceive as a traumatic division of their motherland, Turkish Cypriots view as a just solution to the Cyprus question. Turkish Cypriot acceptance and support for Cyprus' dichotomization suggest that, in their collective unconscious, Cyprus is not the archetypal mother, but rather, the Turkish nation or Anatolia.

The Turkish Cypriot departure from the expected psychoanalytical pattern regarding birth trauma requires examination through the lens of different identity dynamics distinguishing Turkish Cypriots from the broader Turkish populace. This deviation necessitates acknowledgment of potential scenarios: either Turkishness supersedes Turkish Cypriot emotional ties to their land, or land plays a secondary role in Turkish or Turkish Cypriot collective consciousness, or perhaps land holds no defining significance at all in these contexts.

In contrast to the Greeks and Greek Cypriots, who ground their identities in Benedict Anderson's paradigm of historical genealogical continuity encompassing national, cultural, religious, and linguistic dimensions, Turkish Cypriots define their collective identity through a more dynamic, Kemalist lens. Their identity is viewed as constructed within a historical process characterized by choice and change, suggesting openness to reformulation (Papadakis 2008, 142). This revisionist stance, rooted in anti-essentialist arguments, challenges the deterministic notion of identity tied inexorably to historical continuity and its connection to land, culture, or nationhood. This departure from essentialism has intriguing implications, particularly concerning notions of blame and trauma (Papadakis 2008, 143). Turkish Cypriot historical revisionism diverges from Paul Ricoeur's hermeneutic argument equating identity with memory and historical sameness. Instead, it isolates blame and trauma within specific historical contexts, breaking the chain of collective memories. This anti-essentialist perspective negates the moral charge historically associated with collective memory, thus liberating history from binary perceptions of good or bad, just or unjust. Consequently, the future is not predetermined but left open as a political choice (Papadakis 2008, 143).

Prior to the referendum, Turkish Cypriot curricula in Northern Cyprus exhibited a more nationalistic and ethnocentric tone, yet still presented the island's history from an emotionally detached, utilitarian perspective. Notably, a secondary school book emphasized Cyprus' connection to Anatolia from historical, geographical, strategic, and economic viewpoints, contrasting with Greece's perceived lack of historical or strategic significance for Cyprus (Papadakis 2008, 135). The geopolitical argument echoes Zorlu's 1955 speech during a tripartite conference, wherein he asserted Cyprus' Anatolian proximity, implying its rightful inclusion within Anatolia (Holland 1998, 73).

The anti-essentialist stance in historical interpretation aligns with the formal position of Turkish Cypriots. During the Annan Plan negotiations, Greek Cypriots advocated for the political continuity of Cyprus, while Turkish Cypriots emphasized the principle of "virgin birth," proposing the establishment of an entirely new federal state (Kaymak 2009, 146). Exploring the liberal conceptualizations of history and communal narrativity, which may seem enigmatic to Greek Cypriots due to their genealogical and essentialist perspective, requires examination through the prism of Kemalism and the Turkish ambivalence toward collective identity.

Kemalism, also known as Atatürkism, embodies a set of ideas that have shaped Turkish identity and nationhood since the conclusion of the Turkish War of Independence (1919–1923). Central to Turkish collective identity is Mustafa Kemal, revered as Kemal Atatürk or the Father of Turks, often likened to Max Weber's concept of a charismatic leader (Demirtaş-Bağdonas 2008, 99). Atatürk is venerated as the historical figure who liberated and safeguarded Turkey from Western imperialism. His legitimacy stems not from traditional sources but from faith in his exemplary character, as articulated by various commentators (Demirtaş-Bağdonas 2008, 101).

Following the collapse of the Ottoman Empire and the Treaty of Lausanne, Kemalist elites undertook a deliberate effort to distance Turkey from its Ottoman past. Despite inheriting a state tradition and bureaucratic structure from the Ottoman era, the concept of a "Turkish nation" was nascent (Taşpınar 2006, 815). Atatürk articulated a modernist vision in 1919, emphasizing the imperative for a nation to assert its sovereignty and independence (Kili 1980, 385). He envisioned a modern, secular nation-state aligned with Western European standards, aimed at elevating Turkey "above" contemporary civilization levels (Demirtaş-Bağdonas 2008, 100). Kemalist reforms, including the adoption of the Latin alphabet, linguistic purification, secularization of the legal system, and Westernization of societal norms such as the calendar and dress code, sought to break away from Ottoman legacies perceived as hindrances to progress (Mellon 2006, 67).

Paradoxically, the reconstruction of Turkish history, through the adoption of Western values and the rejection of Islamism and Ottoman traditions, required a form of historical validation. This need for a new narrative to legitimize the emerging national identity led to numerous Turkish congresses on history and language. At these congresses, history was revisited and reinterpreted to emphasize a Turkish ethnicity that predated the advent of Islamism (Mellon 2006, 70). According to the Turkish History thesis propagated in these congresses, Turks were portrayed as a venerable and ancient race, tracing their roots to Central Asia (Cagaptay 2004, 88). Despite their nomadic history and interactions with diverse peoples, Turks purportedly preserved their collective memories, cultural distinctiveness, and national identity, chiefly through their common language, which has been celebrated as a cornerstone of Turkishness (Cagaptay 2004, 88).

Within the framework of Kemalism, the Turkish language holds paramount importance in defining Turkish identity. Atatürk asserted that true Turks are those who speak Turkish, prioritizing linguistic criteria over racial lineage. This emphasis on language highlights its significant role in contributing to civilization, yet Turkish national identity is portrayed as non-essentialist—dependent not on ethnic origins but on adherence to the ideals of the Turkish Republic and commitment to its independence and modernization (Kili 1980, 388). Despite the secular principles of Kemalism, Turkishness has become closely associated with the Turkish-speaking Muslim population, with a tacit integration of Sunni Muslim heritage into Turkish identity (Neyzi 2002, 138).

Atatürk's modernist reforms aimed to strengthen the connection between the Turkish people and Anatolia (Mellon 2006, 71), focusing on unity in political existence and historical and ethical affinity as foundational elements of Turkishness (Cagaptay 2004, 89). This rhetorical emphasis on geographical ties was intended to support the Turkish history thesis and legitimize Turkey's territorial claims. Consequently, the Turkish national narrative seems to marginalize or downplay the importance of historical attachment to an ancestral homeland. This could reflect either the influence of Turkey's nomadic past or the anti-essentialist ethos of Kemalism, where the psychological attachment to a shared historical homeland is either absent or deemed secondary in the Turkish collective consciousness.

My aim is neither to endorse nor challenge the Turkish history thesis but rather to elucidate the distinct identity dynamics shaping the collective psyche of Greek Cypriots and Turkish Cypriots. While the forceful detachment from their homeland has profoundly impacted the collective identity of Greek Cypriots, the abandonment of southern Cypriot cities and villages appears to have evoked less pronounced emotional reactions among Turkish Cypriots. A closer psychoanalytical examination of Turkishness reveals that, unlike the maternal symbol prevalent in other narratives, the paternal figure of Mustafa Kemal occupies a central role in the Turkish communal narrative.

Drawing from Otto Rank's psychoanalytical theory on unconscious birth trauma analogies, the absence of a maternal symbol or the dominance of a powerful paternal figure inhibits the unconscious evocation of birth trauma analogies, potentially explaining the Turkish Cypriot response to the historical separation from southern Cyprus. According to this hypothesis, the Turkish people seem to still seek a collective maternal substitute—a source of belonging. Atatürk's assertion that Turkey belongs to the West suggests that Western culture, civilization, and alliances may serve as such a substitute, as previously proposed by Turkey's Prime Minister Recep Tayyip Erdoğan. According to the latter, Turkey's goal to enter the EU is the "most important project in order to realize Atatürk's goal of reaching the level of contemporary civilization" (Demirtaş-Bağdonas 2008, 102). Extending Rank's psychoanalytical hypotheses to Turkish collective psychology suggests that any Western challenge to Turkey's position on the global stage, such as a potential failure to join the European Union (which is now very likely), could trigger feelings of traumatic rejection by the desired archetypal motherly substitute. In contrast, while Kosovar Albanians revere Skanderbeg as a national figure and Jews regard Abraham as a patriarch, these paternal figures have not overshadowed the motherly archetype symbolized by Kosovo and Israel in their respective collective psyches. In both cases, the historical and religious significance of the land transcends political considerations, with the libidinal connections to Kosovo and Israel remaining distinct from the influence of Skanderbeg or Abraham. Indeed, in the Kosovar Albanian and Jewish collective unconscious, the libidinal connections to Kosovo and Israel have not been subsumed under the fatherly figure of either Skanderbeg or Abraham because the historical and psychoanalytical role of the latter is subordinate and in fact one to either secure (Skanderbeg), or safely lead to (Abraham), the archetypal motherly substitute, namely Albania or Canaan.

There exists a secondary form of collective disturbance, which, while not as traumatic as the loss of a people's homeland, can engender collective angst and disorientation under certain circumstances. This form of disturbance manifests as the degradation, defamation, assault, political or diplomatic exclusion, and psychological or physical attack against a people's leader.[3] Beyond the libidinal ties among group members and the primitive suggestive influence that synchronizes a group's emotional reactions to sociopolitical stimuli, leaders hold a central position in the collective psyche and communal narrative.

As noted by Le Bon, there is "a thirst for obedience that it submits instinctively to anyone who appoints himself its master" (Freud 1945, 21). A leader is idealized by the group, imbued with certain qualities and irresistible powers corresponding to their prestige. This prestige paralyzes the critical faculty of the group, eliciting astonishment, fascination, and respect akin to a state of hypnosis (Freud 1945, 21). The connection between a leader and a group is firmly established through a "noetic synchronism" based on the ideas conveyed by the leader, which the group strongly supports. Examples such as Atatürk's modernist ideals and Makarios' call for *enosis* illustrate this phenomenon.

Empirical analysis reveals instances of collective disturbance, particularly against the leadership of Palestinians, Greek Cypriots, and Kosovar Albanians. These instances follow a phenomenological typology distinguishing between relative disturbance arising from comparisons of a leader's status and actual attacks or forceful separations.

Following the Six Day War, Palestinians were notably absent from the 242 UN Security Council Resolution, which concluded peace treaties among the belligerents. For over two decades, the Palestinian leadership found itself excluded from international talks. It was not until 1974 that Arab countries recognized the PLO, led by Yasir Arafat, as "the sole legitimate representative of the Palestinian people" (Dowty 2012, 134). During this period, Likud "declared that there was no Palestinian negotiating partner" (Dowty 2012, 138). These historical occurrences are best understood as instances of relative deprivation. The resentment felt by the Palestinian leadership did not stem from objective deprivation or loss but rather from feelings of perceived inferiority arising from comparisons with other entities or states whose leadership enjoyed international recognition. This sentiment becomes particularly apparent when considering events such as the peace conference in Madrid, where the Israeli Prime Minister and a Palestinian delegation sat at the same negotiating table. At this conference, Head of the Palestinian delegation Hayder Abd al-Shafi claimed, "We have been denied the right to publicly acknowledge our loyalty to our leadership and system of government" (Dowty 2012, 152). Similarly, an act of relative deprivation occurred in 1943 when Josip Broz Tito convened a conference in Bosnia for the future of Yugoslavia and Kosovo without inviting any Kosovar Albanian delegation.

Objective deprivation was inflicted upon the Palestinian leadership and people in 1982 with Ariel Sharon's euphemistic "Peace for Galilee," which constituted a direct attack against the PLO in Lebanon (Pappe 2006, 215). Similarly, objective deprivation was imposed upon the Greek Cypriot leadership by various actors, including the British government, the Greek junta, and EOKA-B. These entities either attempted or successfully executed the forceful removal of Archbishop Makarios. One notable instance occurred in 1956 when the British decision to divert Makarios' flight led to his actual deportation. However, the deprivers failed to anticipate that this separation would not magically resolve the situation. The absence of Makarios did not diminish the demands for *enosis* nor did it quell the activities of EOKA against the British. This was due not only to the overwhelming desire for *enosis* at the time but also to the fact that there was no redirection of Greek Cypriot emotional ties from Makarios and his enosist vision to another leader or focal point. Similarly, Greek Cypriots carry a traumatic memory of the Greek junta's decision to overthrow and even assassinate Makarios with the help of EOKA-B due to his cessation of support for *enosis*. Makarios' subsequent escape to London in 1974 further solidified this collective memory, which continues to cast a shadow over the relationship between Greece and Greek Cypriots.

In summary, the application of psychological, psychoanalytical, and hermeneutic theories to the empirical analysis of the five major case studies illustrates that collective narrativity is disrupted and collective identity reshaped by acts of objective deprivation and loss, which often subconsciously evoke the primal trauma. Relative deprivation does not significantly impact collective identity because its phenomenology lacks actual loss. In contrast, instances of forceful removal, such as land confiscation, or separation from a leader, activate deep psychological and psychoanalytical mechanisms of bereavement and the aggression-frustration dyad. This is particularly evident in cases like the Palestinian *intifadas* and the historical violence between Kosovar Albanians and Serbs, where denial to abandon attachment to the lost object leads to internalized collective loss, eventually resulting in melancholia and identity loss, common across all five case studies.

Collective deprivation often fails to lead to narrative repair and instead generates angst and disorientation, as seen in the initial reactions of the Cherokees and the textbooks of the Greek Cypriots. Even when there is no disruption of communal narrativity, mourning and reconciliation with the lost object do not prevent the preservation of a strong sense of injustice in collective memory, as seen in Nauru. Relative deprivation, according to Paul Ricoeur's theory, cannot fit into this category because the feeling of injustice is recurrent in collective memory due to people's duty to their heritage, including the remembrance of victims and historical losses. To assess objective deprivation and loss as identity distress factors, one must also consider the particular ethnographic characteristics and identity dynamics of a people, especially the place of the lost object in their collective consciousness or unconsciousness, as exemplified by Kemalism.

## Deprivation as Middle Term

This chapter endeavored to evaluate a collection of empirical data through the analysis of five case studies, aiming to discern patterns of deprivation in the context of the emergence and implementation of the international right to self-determination of peoples, with the overarching goal of shedding light on our international legal framework. This endeavor involved a logical inquiry entailing a psychological and historical examination of prominent self-determination cases, departing from established legal typologies and thematic frameworks. It entailed a shift in perspective from the traditional legal subject-centric approach to a focus on the legal object, moving from abstract legal definitions and frameworks to tangible instances of deprivation that have deeply affected collective identities.

The initial historical selection scrutinized two forms of collective deprivation, objective and relative, through the lens of the Cherokee Nation's history, the decolonization process in Nauru, the dissolution of the Ottoman Empire with a focus on Palestine, the Kosovo crisis, and the situation in Cyprus. This selection aimed to encompass self-determination studies of both international and constitutional legal significance, illustrating how international law, particularly the early scholastic discourse on the rights of peoples, has evolved in response to acts or threats of objective deprivation against indigenous peoples. Special attention was given to ethnographic details regarding the reception of collective loss by the affected peoples and communities.

The subsequent section synthesized the findings of the first two parts, applying the previously discussed psychological, psychoanalytical, and hermeneutic theories to the empirical and ethnographic data. Employing an expanded induction, this section identified a common underlying theme of objective deprivation across all five case studies, exploring the conditions under which objective deprivation disrupted communal narrativity or inflicted trauma on collective identity through the internalization of loss. The empirical analysis revealed that the phenomenology of objective deprivation varies depending on identity dynamics. Therefore, determining whether an act of objective deprivation has been definitively internalized necessitates an examination of the concrete libidinal connections, namely, the relative significance of the deprived object in the collective consciousness of the affected people, group, or community.

The empirical chapter concluded the expanded induction process aimed at identifying the middle term crucial for the logical reconstruction of the relationship between the international right to self-determination and constitutional law. The objective was to pinpoint the necessary condition for self-determination to be claimable. The lack of a robust middle term within the legal positivist sphere prompted a series of logical fallacies. The empirical case studies yielded a new, concrete definition for the middle term, suggesting that objective collective deprivation serves as the catalyst that moves both legal concepts from potentiality to actuality. The inductive syllogism can now be formalized as follows:

P1: All the relevant empirical events (S) are cases of objective collective deprivation (M).
P2: All the relevant empirical events (S) are serious disruptions of self-determination (P).
C: Therefore [typically], cases of objective collective deprivation (M) are serious disruptions of self-determination (P).

This inductive conclusion, though not deductively certain, establishes an essential relation between the predicates M and P at the level of phainomena. Within the Aristotelian framework, such an induction provides the major premise for a subsequent demonstrative syllogism (apodeixis). Once the definitional equivalence between "objective collective deprivation" and "serious disruption of self-determination" is established, we can formalize the deductive syllogism in the valid Barbara form:

P1: All cases of objective collective deprivation (M) are serious breaches of self-determination (P);
P2: [Suppose that] the treatment of the province of Québec (S) represents a case of objective collective deprivation (M);
C: The treatment of the province of Québec (S) represents a serious breach of self-determination.

The final chapter advances the logical synthesis, replacing the social contract metaphor with acts of objective deprivation and completing the logical reconstruction of the international legal syllogism concerning the relationship between self-determination and constitutional law. However, before moving to this stage, it is essential to first explore how the deprivation-rectification dyad is integral to the fundamental structure of the phenomenology of rights. The examination of this topic will reveal that a foundational understanding of corrective justice is crucial for rationalizing legal reasoning.

## Notes

1 The initials of EOKA (Εθνική Οργάνωσις Κυπριακού Άγώνος) stand for National Organization of Cypriot Struggle.

2 Abbreviation for Türk Mukavemet Teşkilatı (Turkish Resistance Organization).

3 From the perspective of psychoanalysis, the effect on collective identity will depend on the vigor of the libidinal ties between a group and its leader. For the Turkish people, for instance, one would naturally expect that an assault directed against Atatürk, even post-mortem would be collectively perceived as an attack against the Turkish nation. Indeed, according to Turkish Law 5816, insulting or cursing the memory or legacy of Kemal Atatürk is a criminal offense. The same applies to any denigration against the Turkish nation according to Article 301 of the Turkish Penal Code.

# 6

# The Ethical

## Loss and Rectification as Central Concepts of Law

The duty to repair a harmful loss stands as a cornerstone in the philosophy of tort law and is integrally linked to the broader concept of restorative or corrective justice (Coleman, The Practice of Corrective Justice 1995, 53).

In his *Nicomachean Ethics*, Aristotle delineates two types of justice: distributive and corrective. Distributive justice, according to Aristotle, is founded on the principle of political equality and possesses a public dimension. It involves the state's role in determining the criteria for the just distribution of wealth and social resources among the community members, which can be allocated in both equal and unequal measures. Corrective justice, conversely, serves a rectifying function within the realm of private transactions, which can be either voluntary or involuntary, and is aimed at addressing disruptions to the natural mode of being of at least one of the parties involved. Aristotle describes it thus:

> Particular Justice . . . is divided into two kinds. One kind is exercised in the distribution of honour, wealth, and the other divisible assets of the community, which may be allotted among its members in equal and unequal shares. The other kind is that which supplies a corrective principle in private transactions. This corrective justice again has two sub-divisions, corresponding to the two classes of private transactions, those which are voluntary and those which are involuntary. Examples of voluntary transactions are selling, buying, lending an interest, pledging, lending without interest, depositing, letting for hire; these transactions being termed voluntary because they are voluntarily entered upon. Of involuntary transactions some are furtive, for instance, theft, adultery, poisoning, procuring, enticement of slaves, assassination, false witness; others are violent, for instance, assault, imprisonment, murder, robbery with violence, maiming, abusive language, contumelious treatment. (Aristotle, The Nicomachean Ethics 1926, 12)

Modern legal scholars such as Richard Posner and Ernest Weinrib argue that these two modes of Aristotelian justice are interconnected. Posner suggests that within the *polis* (or any legal system), a set pattern of entitlements exists. When this pattern is disturbed, corrective justice is employed to restore the disrupted equilibrium (Posner 1995, 108). Posner's interpretation of Aristotle adopts an anti-essentialist, liberal perspective, implying that both types of justice are posited—socially constructed and/or agreed upon. Similarly, Weinrib maintains that both distributive and corrective justice operate under the same fundamental principle of equality among parties (Weinrib 2003, 446). He contends that corrective justice presupposes the existence of politically endowed entitlements that are distributed and potentially violated (Weinrib 2003, 463). However, Aristotle's conception of justice, which encompasses both distributive and corrective justice, offers a more profound and morally nuanced understanding than these modern interpretations suggest.

The liberal interpretation of Aristotelian corrective justice suggests that the duty to repair a harmful loss in involuntary transactions, such as rape or murder and their subsequent punishment, is legally addressed and regulated not necessarily because these acts are inherently unjust or morally wrong, but because the *polis* has conferred upon its citizens rights and freedoms, such as the right to life, which should not be violated. However, it is important to recognize that in Aristotelian and ancient Greek philosophy, the concept of rights as understood in the Enlightenment does not exist (Wright 1995, 166).[1] The ancient Greek term *δίκαιον*, akin to the Latin *jus*, translates as "right" but not as "a right."[2] For Aristotle, law or *νόμος* (nomos) is posited—either enacted or accepted as customary law—while justice is considered natural (*φύσει κοινόν δίκαιον καί ἄδικον*) (Schroeder 2003, 44).

Aristotle's justice is often interpreted as not being pre-political. According to this perspective, justice is only realizable within a political association. Aristotle himself notes that a person who is isolated from the *polis*, not by accident but due to their nature, must be self-sufficient and is therefore "either a poor sort of being, or a being higher than man" (Aristotle, The Politics 1995, 11). This has led to the assertion that justice can only be realized within the *polis*, as apolitical beings are considered "brutal and savage" (Heyman 2003, 472). However, Aristotle's philosophy significantly deviates from the notion that justice is merely a social construct. On the contrary, he asserts that the *polis* itself is natural and precedes the individual, as "the whole is necessarily prior to the part" (Aristotle, The Politics 1995, 11). According to Aristotle, all humans have a natural impulse to form political associations, and it is within these associations that they can achieve their fullest potential (Aristotle, The Politics 1995, 10–11). Justice, therefore, is essentially political in that it belongs to the *polis* and is actualized within it (Aristotle, The Politics 1995, 12). This view is underscored by Aristotle's characterization of justice as the perfect or complete virtue (*τελεία ἀρετή*), which is perfect "because its possessor can practice it toward others and not merely by himself . . . [and] that is a difficult task" (Aristotle, The Nicomachean Ethics 1926, 259, 261). Thus, while justice belongs to the *polis*, it does not originate from it; rather, it derives from nature and exists naturally (Schroeder 2003, 44). Natural justice may not have the formal standing of law unless explicitly enacted or agreed upon, but it should serve as both a standard for and be embodied in the written and/or customary law of the *polis* (Schroeder 2003, 44). Thomas Aquinas later developed the Aristotelian theory of justice, suggesting that its concrete content can be discerned through Reason—a concept resonant with Scheler's aprioristic phenomenology of human values.

The purpose of written laws, or *nomoi*, is to embody the justice that exists in nature, aiming to uphold peace, order, and political harmony within the *polis* (Schroeder 2003, 39). This reflection of natural justice should also be evident in the unwritten laws, such as customs, traditions, and rituals, collectively known as customary law or *ἄγραφοι νόμοι* (Schroeder 2003, 40). Aristotle introduces a concept akin to *jus gentium*, recognizing that both written and unwritten laws exist which are universally applicable across communities, known as general law or *δίκαιον κοινόν*. These general laws hold a superior status due to their foundation in our common political nature and adherence to the principles of natural justice (*τό κατά φύσιν*). However, it is crucial to note that Aristotle does not equate these with natural law; indeed, his philosophy does not explicitly endorse a concept of natural law (Schroeder 2003, 44–5).

Natural justice is considered prior to both law and custom. While laws and customs are human constructs and can aspire to reflect (political) natural justice, they do not inherently possess it. Aristotle articulates this distinction:

> Now there are two kinds of laws, particular and general. By particular laws I mean those established by each people in reference to themselves, which again are divided into written and unwritten; by general laws I mean those based

> upon nature. In fact, there is a general idea of just and unjust in accordance with nature, as all men in a manner divine, even if there is neither communication nor agreement between them. This is what Antigone in Sophocles evidently means, when she declares that it is just, though forbidden, to bury Polynices, as being naturally just: "For neither to-day nor yesterday, but from all eternity, these statutes live and no man knoweth whence they came." And as Empedocles says in regard to not killing that which has life, for this is not right for some and wrong for others, "But a universal precept, which extends without a break throughout the wide-ruling sky and the boundless earth." (Aristotle, Art of Rhetoric 1926, xxii)

In distributive justice, political rulers determine the allocation of wealth and resources based on criteria such as origin, merit, or need. Corrective justice, on the other hand, addresses immediate interactions that cause loss or injury. Jules Coleman argues that corrective justice is "pre-political," in that the moral duty to repair exists independently of political institutions and legal enforcement mechanisms. This implies that while the mechanisms of reparation require political and legal decisions, the occurrence of loss and the duty to rectify are objective: the former is a fact, and the latter a duty by nature. Coleman's interpretation aligns with Aristotle's views in the *Nicomachean Ethics*, where Aristotle differentiates corrective justice from distributive justice, emphasizing its objectivity and detachment from political considerations. Corrective justice, according to Aristotle, is concerned solely with the nature of the damage and the equality of the parties involved, irrespective of their moral character:

> Corrective Justice . . . operates in private transactions, both voluntary and involuntary. This justice is of a different sort from the preceding . . . the just in private transactions . . . is not the equal according to geometrical but according to arithmetical proportion. For it makes no difference whether a good man has defrauded a bad man or a bad one a good one, nor whether it is a good or a bad man that has committed adultery; the law looks only at the nature of the damage, treating the parties as equal, and merely asking whether one has done and the other suffered injustice, whether one inflicted and the other has sustained damage. Hence the unjust being here the unequal, the judge endeavours to equalize it: inasmuch as when one man has received and the other has inflicted a blow, or one has killed and the other been killed, the line representing the suffering and doing of the deed is divided into unequal parts,

> but the judge endeavours to make them equal by the penalty or loss he imposes, taking away the gain. (Aristotle, The Nicomachean Ethics 1926, 272–5)

The passage has sparked significant scholarly discussion, largely because Aristotle appears to depart from his more familiar focus on virtue and ethics. Thomas Aquinas remarked on this departure, observing, somewhat paradoxically, that in the context of corrective justice, the law treats individuals as equals "however much they may be unequal" (as cited in Weinrib 2003, 463). Ernest Weinrib has offered a detailed interpretation of Aristotle's position, identifying three central elements in his account: an emphasis on the formal equality of the parties involved, a deliberate disregard for factors such as social status or moral character, and a conception of agency that is defined strictly by the immediate interaction between parties (Weinrib 2003, 463–4). Weinrib contends that within this framework, human agency is understood in amoral terms, and the notions of gain and loss are reduced to abstract, algebraic quantities that must be balanced. He draws a distinction between the proportional equality characteristic of distributive justice and the arithmetic equality that underpins corrective justice. In cases of injury or unjust enrichment, he suggests that the gain of one party is understood as being precisely equal to the loss suffered by the other. The objective of corrective justice, then, is to restore equilibrium by nullifying the discrepancy, effectively returning both parties to the position they occupied prior to the injurious event or transaction (Weinrib 2003, 450). Weinrib contends that Aristotle aimed to strip away all particulars to establish an abstract norm of corrective justice, essentially creating an amoral, abstract individual as the foundation of a principle of algebraic human equality. This interpretation stems from Aristotle's assertion that "it makes no difference whether a good man has defrauded a bad man or a bad man a good one, nor whether it is a good or a bad man that has committed adultery; the law looks only to the difference made by the injury, and treats the parties as equal" (Heyman 2003, 477).

However, Weinrib's interpretation has faced criticism, particularly for not adequately considering the distinction between the person and the action. While distributive justice evaluates the moral qualities of individuals, corrective justice focuses on the moral quality of actions. This view is supported by another perspective that argues Aristotle's corrective justice is not "indifferent to virtue altogether, but rather it focuses on the virtue of the act [*sic*] rather than on that of the agent" (Heyman 2003, 478). Aristotle himself states that actions are inherently morally charged and should be evaluated on their own merits, independent of the character of the individual involved. He elucidates, "a man may commit injustice without actually being unjust" (Aristotle, The Nicomachean Ethics 1926, 291).

Aristotle also elaborates on how virtuous actions lead to the formation of virtuous character, contrasting the acquisition of virtues with that of sensory faculties, which are inherent and not developed by use:

> The virtues therefore are engendered in us neither by nature nor yet in violation of nature; nature gives us the capacity to receive them, and this capacity is brought to maturity by habit. Moreover, the faculties given us by nature are bestowed on us first in a potential form; we exhibit their actual exercise afterwards. This is clearly so with our senses: we did not acquire the faculty of sight or hearing by repeatedly seeing or repeatedly listening, but the other way about—because we had the senses we began to use them, we did not get them by using them. The virtues on the other hand we acquire by first having actually practiced them, just as we do the arts. We learn an art or craft by doing the things that we shall have to do when we have learnt it: for instance, men become builders by building houses, harpers by playing on the harp. Similarly, we become just by doing just acts, temperate by doing temperate acts, brave by doing brave acts. This truth is attested by the experience of states: lawgivers make the citizens good by training them in habits of right action—this is the aim of all legislation, and if it fails to do this it is a failure; this is what distinguishes a good form of constitution from a bad one. (Aristotle, The Nicomachean Ethics 1926, 70–3)

In Greek, the connection between *ἦθος* (ēthos), meaning virtue, and *ἔθος* (ethos), meaning habit, highlights the profound linguistic and philosophical relationship between character and the repeated actions that form it. This link underscores the Aristotelian principle that a single bad act does not define a person as inherently bad. Rather, it is the habitual practice of such acts that molds a person's character. A person becomes virtuous or vicious over time, through a pattern of behavior that cultivates a specific state of mind—this is where moral demerit or merit becomes attached.

Aristotle's philosophy of corrective justice avoids any predetermined notions about human nature and ethical predispositions, positing instead that individuals are born with the potential for ethical development. He famously stated, "it is clear that none of the moral virtues is engendered in us by nature . . . nature gives us the capacity to receive them, and this capacity is brought to maturity by habit" (Aristotle, The Nicomachean Ethics 1926, 71). In the context of legal systems, legislators play a critical role in nurturing this ethical potentiality.

The legal framework they establish, which focuses on identifying, sanctioning, and rectifying acts of injustice, serves not only to maintain order but also to cultivate a culture of justice. This, in turn, creates an environment conducive to virtuous living and interaction. Corrective justice, therefore, becomes a vehicle through which legal authorities promote moral development. By delineating what constitutes unjust behavior and enforcing appropriate remedies, laws act as educational tools that guide citizens toward virtuous behavior. A commentator insightfully notes, "[b]y requiring citizens to act justly in their private dealings with others, corrective justice inculcates the disposition to act in this way" (Heyman 2003, 478).

Laws, in this Aristotelian framework, are more than mere regulatory instruments; they are the means through which legal authorities foster a virtuous society. Effective laws are those that not only prevent unjust acts but also promote ethical behavior and understanding among legal subjects. Conversely, laws that fail to accurately identify and condemn injustices or that provide ineffective remedies can undermine the process of ethical maturation, leading to a legal culture that either tolerates injustice or fails to guide individuals toward moral improvement. Hence, the alignment of laws and legal institutions with the principles of natural and corrective justice is essential. Such alignment ensures that the laws not only prevent and rectify injustice but also actively contribute to the moral education of society. In doing so, laws help to cultivate the perfect virtue of justice, encouraging legal subjects to consistently act justly toward one another, thereby reinforcing the ethical foundations of the community (Heyman 2003, 477).

Aristotle's perspective sharply contradicts Richard Posner's liberal interpretation that views corrective justice merely as a reaffirmation and preservation of distributive equality. Aristotle posits that, unlike distributive justice which is deeply embedded in social conventions and susceptible to governmental influence, corrective justice is inherently objective and independent of such influences. It exists by nature, asserting that the (moral) obligation to repair a loss does not hinge on governmental decisions. However, the formal legal recognition of wrongdoing is crucial for cultivating justice as an ethical norm within society.

Jules Coleman introduces the notion that in the realm of corrective justice, damage or loss should be considered as "diminished welfare" (Coleman 1995, 66). Yet, he distinguishes between being harmed and not being benefited, highlighting that not all disadvantages constitute harm (Coleman 1995, 57).

Aristotle's own discussion in the *Nicomachean Ethics* about loss and rectification is particularly instructive:

> inasmuch as when one man has received and the other has inflicted a blow, or one has killed and the other been killed, the line representing the suffering and doing of the deed is divided into unequal parts, but the judge endeavours to make them equal by the penalty or loss he imposes, taking away the gain. (Aristotle, The Nicomachean Ethics 1926, 275).

Aristotle emphasizes that corrective justice seeks to address actual losses, i.e.tangible alterations to one's situation and natural mode of being, by equating the actions of the doer and the sufferings of the victim. This approach starkly contrasts with instances of relative deprivation, which, although they may invoke feelings of injustice under the umbrella of distributive justice, do not typically fall within the purview of corrective justice unless there is direct interaction and tangible harm or loss. Distributive justice, which often involves subjective criteria for allocating state resources such as wealth and social benefits, cannot be inherently 'objective.' Governments or political bodies determine the criteria for what is considered a just distribution. Therefore, feelings of relative deprivation arising from liberal comparisons do not inherently possess a natural moral basis for correction, unlike cases of objective deprivation where actual loss or harm has occurred. In such instances, corrective justice does not apply unless the government itself violates its established criteria for distribution, thus necessitating reparation or adjustment to restore equality according to its own standards.

Corrective justice does not ensure absolute legal protection against all acts of deprivation and their consequential losses. It primarily mandates that individuals who have unjustifiably harmed others by their actions rectify the situation, regardless of fault (Honore 1995, 94). The foundational aspect of corrective justice is the recognition of deprivation and loss as wrongful and deserving of repair, rather than penalizing the perpetrator. As such, the focus in assessing corrective justice claims lies on the nature of the loss suffered by the victim rather than the character or morality of the injurer (Coleman 1994, 58). While loss or actual harm are pivotal to corrective justice, legal doctrines, especially within tort law, incorporate additional elements like responsibility, causation, fault, intentionality, and liability for negligence to determine compensatory measures. The integration of fault highlights that not all acts of deprivation are legally actionable or compensable and that there is no automatic legal assumption of wrongfulness.

Tort law defines a tort as a "civil wrong which arises from a transaction and/or relation . . . [whereby] one party acquires something she does not deserve, and the other is deprived of something she is due" (Calnan 1997, 119). In this framework, tort litigation serves as the civil implementation of corrective justice, where wrongfulness is defined as the violation of specific legal rights. This definition depends on the legal recognition and scope of these rights (Coleman 1994, 57). The rationale behind this association is that loss can be incidental, or, in the words of a commentator, "just an unfortunate consequence of social intercourse" (Calnan 1997, 30).

The connection between wrongfulness and legal rights, particularly viewed through the lens of the property metaphor, suggests that wrongfulness involves an infringement of one's power to exclude or alienate their possessions: "[i]f I take something of yours over which you have the power to exclude and alienate, then I wrong you" (Coleman 1994, 57). Thus, for a victim to claim tort damages, more than just experiencing loss or injury is required; there must be an established wrongfulness—a violation of a recognized legal right, which then creates a secondary claim-right to compensation (Calnan 1997, 120). Tort law synthesizes two core liberal principles: that legal rights encapsulate clusters of legally protected personal interests (Coleman 1994, 57), and that loss or injury constitutes an infringement of these interests (Calnan 1997, 31). This synthesis leads to a shift where wrongfulness is disentangled from its moral underpinnings and becomes strictly a legal concept. In tort law, conduct is deemed wrongful if it violates a legal right, not merely because it causes harm or loss. Consequently, a victim is entitled to reparations only if such a legal right is breached.

Although legal wrongdoing is no longer inherently tied to moral wrongdoing, the obligation to amend a harmful loss retains its foundation as a natural moral duty. Corrective justice inherently demands that if we harm someone, we are morally obliged to make amends. Aristotle himself acknowledged the role of the legislator in giving corrective justice its legal form by specifying which acts of deprivation should be sanctioned and which losses warrant repair, along with the conditions for such reparations.

The overarching goal of tort law aligns with the ethical objective of corrective justice, which aims to diminish undesirable behavior (Honore 1995, 95). Consequently, legislators are not entirely free in their determinations of wrongfulness for acts of deprivation, or in their assessment of harm for the ensuing losses. These determinations are intrinsically linked to the broader ethical mission of the law, which must recognize that certain acts of deprivation and their resultant losses, mirrored in moral responses like Antigone's defiance of Creon to fulfill her moral duty, are fundamentally connected to the principles of natural justice. The preference for *restitutio in integrum* (restoration to the original state) in awarding tort damages underlines this ethical imperative. This principle aligns with the broader aim of restoring *ataraxia,* i.e. the victim's undisturbed natural mode of being, by seeking to place the plaintiff in the position they would have occupied had the wrongful act not taken place (Chapman 1995, 409). Framing acts of deprivation as wrongful thus invites lawmakers to consider not only legal causation but also the experiential and existential dimensions of harm. It calls for a careful engagement with the phenomenology of deprivation and the logic of corrective justice, particularly in evaluating whether an individual's conduct creates a foreseeable and substantial risk of producing a specific kind of suffering (Chapman 1995, 413). However, legislators may not always adhere strictly to the principles of deprivation and corrective justice. There are instances where wrongfulness is attributed excessively, in situations devoid of actual disturbance, or conversely, where wrongfulness is insufficiently assigned to acts that cause significant disturbance.[3]

To summarize, the obligation to rectify a harmful loss is fundamentally a moral duty rather than a purely legal one. While it may be encapsulated within the laws of the *polis,* its origins are not derived from these laws. The moral wrongness associated with objective deprivation originates from the harmful act itself, irrespective of the character of the perpetrator(s). This foundational principle of Aristotle's corrective justice permeates the general theory of tort law, although it often carries significant liberal implications.

Corrective justice, in itself, does not have legal binding force. It requires the legislator to enact laws that specifically delineate the conditions under which acts of deprivation are considered wrongful and losses harmful. However, in drafting these laws, the legislator is not entirely free to act according to discretion. Rather, there is a moral imperative to consider both the ethical mission of the law, which aims to cultivate justice as a virtuous habit among citizens, and the distinct moral wrongs associated with specific acts of deprivation and the resultant losses that demand rectification in accordance with natural justice.

## From Corrective Justice to the Pragmatics of International Law

Unlike national systems, there is no global legislator to define wrongfulness for international acts of deprivation, nor an effective international judiciary or executive body to enforce international legal rights and ensure compliance. This gap renders both distributive and corrective justice in international law susceptible to arbitrariness, as they rely on the elusive requirement of international consensus.

Distributive justice in international law faces particular challenges due to the lack of predefined criteria for the allocation of global resources and wealth. States must voluntarily consent to create legal frameworks that ensure fair trade, economic cooperation, and equitable distribution of natural resources. Corrective justice encounters even greater obstacles, as it demands legislation that defines the conditions of wrongfulness. The absence of an international legislator complicates the process of legal specification, highlighting the inherent dissonance between the consensual nature of international law and the objective, unconventional demands of corrective justice. While distributive justice might accommodate a degree of volitional consensus among states on distributive criteria (which become binding once agreed upon), the consensus required for corrective justice is considerably more constrained.

From a critical legal standpoint, international law often overlooks ethical and moral considerations, instead serving as a tool to advance the political, geostrategic, military, and financial interests of powerful states, particularly those in the West. This practice highlights a key critique of legal positivism, which is that it is not truly morally neutral. Critics contend that international legal rhetoric, including the principles of self-determination, *jus cogens*, and human rights law, often serves as a form of disempowerment (Carty 2007, 195). Legal rights are deployed as instruments or Trojan horses to advance the agendas of powerful Western states and their alliances, rather than to genuinely promote corrective justice (Carty 2007, 225).

In international law, the principle of *pacta sunt servanda*—that treaties must be honored—is frequently invoked to validate agreements, even those negotiated under conditions of significant power imbalances. This practice has drawn criticism for concealing the lack of genuine consent often present in treaties concluded between dominant and subordinate states. Anthony Carty has argued that this legitimization of coerced agreements reveals a broader hypocrisy at the heart of international law, where diplomacy and legal order serve to veil the disorder and aggression that frequently characterize interstate relations (Carty 2007, 195; Carty 2011, 146). Carty introduces the notion of "imposed legal acquiescence" to describe how the mere passive acceptance of legal structures by a majority is often sufficient to constitute a legal system. Under this framework, there is no requirement for active endorsement or full legitimacy—just acquiescence (Carty 2007, 196). This perspective casts a critical light on the treatment of individual and collective rights, such as the right to self-determination, arguing that such rights cannot be meaningfully examined apart from the larger coercive dynamics of the international legal and political order—an order largely shaped by the hegemonic influence of Western powers (Carty 2007, 197).

The philosophical foundations of this concept of lawful coercion are traceable to thinkers such as Hobbes and Kant. Hobbes described the state of nature as fundamentally violent, necessitating the imposition of legal structures to prevent disorder. Similarly, Kant held that states, like individuals, exist in an antagonistic state of nature. Even if humans or states were presumed to be well-intentioned and law-abiding, Kant maintained that the rational idea of law still requires coercion, since in the absence of a public legal order, none can be assured of protection from others who act according to their own judgment (Kant 1991, 124). In both thinkers' views, rights have no inherent moral substance; law is not grounded in objective moral principles but in the need to contain disorder.

This line of thought stands in sharp contrast to the aims of corrective justice, which presupposes that some acts of deprivation and loss are not merely disruptive but are wrong and demand redress. In this sense, the philosophical underpinnings of international legal coercion undermine the moral component of justice-based theories that seek to affirm the intrinsic wrongfulness of harm and the ethical necessity of repair. Additionally, the adjudication of international wrongfulness is not overseen by an objective legislator interested in the welfare of legal subjects, but rather is subject to the interests of powerful states. These states, acting as quasi-legislators, are often in a position to determine the harmfulness of their own actions, leading to a biased application of international wrongfulness that favors their interests. This clash of interests is exemplified in treaties like the Vienna Convention on the Law of Treaties, which failed to categorize economically and politically coercive actions (likely undertaken by powerful Western states) as wrongful. Thus, the system allows powerful states to penalize weaker ones for harmful conduct while exempting their own, exploiting political and economic disparities to enforce an international order that reflects their interests through coerced consensus.

The absence of a global legislator in international relations is a profound source of *anomie*, leaving a vacuum where ethical guidance should be. This gap allows Western states to avoid the moral responsibilities typically associated with the role of a global ethical leader. Consequently, international law often fails to fulfill its foundational mission of corrective justice and, by default, transmits negative moral signals. States learn from this framework that imposing their views or harming others to protect national interests is a routine part of diplomacy. This tolerance of amoral behavior by international law suggests that a habit of domination and injustice has been established within international relations. This habit involves both powerful states, which assume the role of the Master, and weaker states, which find themselves in the role of the Slave. However, unlike the Hegelian dialectic where the Slave eventually reverses the power imbalance through mutual recognition and self-consciousness (Hegel 2005, 520), international relations do not support such a simplistic transposition of this analogy. The dependency of Western states on third-world resources, for example, is insufficient to fundamentally alter the dynamics of power.

Even if we were to assume that mutual recognition, collective freedom, and the formulation of a mature collective consciousness are a priori feasible, such maturity should ultimately characterize both the Master and the Slave. Powerful states, however, have shown a persistent unwillingness to recognize weaker states as sovereign equals,[4] treating them instead as politically weak corporeal entities within a broader geopolitical game. These weaker states, often politically unstable and lacking robust infrastructure, face not only coordination challenges but also existential threats from Western interests and practices. Unlike the Hegelian ideal, these states confront real and immediate dangers.

States operate in a state of nature, lacking genuine mutual recognition based on respect rather than fear (Carty 2007, 221). This dichotomy of coercion and fear has profoundly influenced the development of international law. Powerful states often resort to both unlawful and lawful coercion to establish *de facto* situations or to formalize their own values, which they then promote globally through norms such as the right to humanitarian intervention, preemptive strikes, and the war on terror. As a result, international law becomes a tool for enforcing a world order that aligns with their subjective definitions of good and evil, making it essentially an imperial law (Carty 2007, 527).

The morality of international law, therefore, is not grounded in values but rather in its usefulness to powerful states.[5] What is considered 'good' is often what is useful for these states, not what is universally valuable. This hegemonic usefulness is ideologically transformed from a subjective, national-centric basis into global norms, facilitated by the mainstream legal community's approach, which dismisses anything outside the strict legal framework as merely moral or political, and therefore irrelevant. This silence and lack of engagement by international jurists contribute to the ideological transformation of these norms, masking their origin in power dynamics as universal principles.

Despite claims of amoral and apolitical objectivity, the reality is that legal positivism has been instrumental in rationalizing and purifying legal discourse from metaphysical or essentialist considerations. This supposed legal purity often serves to legitimize a hegemonically defined global order under the guise of international norms and principles. In particular, the implementation of Kelsen's neo-Kantian pure theory in international law suggests that normative coercion is necessary due to states acting primarily out of self-interest, similar to Freud's view of individuals being driven by dangerous instincts and desires. In domestic contexts, coercion serves to subdue individual impulses for the sake of survival under a superior coercive power (Carty 1994, 1239). However, this mechanism is absent in international law, leading states to comply with international norms only when these align with their interests.

Kelsen's theory underwent a hegemonic transformation, detaching from its German cultural origins to become a universal paradigm within international legal thought. This evolution preserved the Hobbesian notions of fear and insecurity, shaping a global legal mentality that emphasizes rigidity and control. This autocratic approach has permeated legal education and practice, fostering a generation of legal professionals trained to prioritize technical proficiency over moral or political considerations. Law schools often dissuade students from engaging with the moral or political implications of the law, promoting a strictly apolitical, amoral approach to legal reasoning (Carty and Baka 2017). This educational emphasis produces lawyers who excel in a robotic, detached mode of legal operation, where those who best adopt this detached professionalism gain recognition and success.

The belief among law students, practitioners, and academics that law belongs to the social sciences provides a comforting illusion of objectivity. This notion, shaped by academic propaganda, positions law as a pseudo-science, reinforcing an uncritical acceptance of rigid intellectual habits within classrooms, courts, and political forums. Lawyers are often seen, and see themselves, as scientists by virtue of their profession, trained to equate legal reasoning with rational thinking. However, this perspective is fundamentally flawed. The prevailing mindset of rigidity and control among international jurists and scholars hinders the proper application of syllogistic logic and inductive reasoning methods. Legal education typically warns against the creative and perceived dangerous aspects of induction, such as drawing legal analogies, under the pretense that lawyers should not create law but merely attest to it. Conversely, the standard legal reasoning model of deductively describing the facts, finding the law, and applying it is promoted as the safest approach—being automatic, predictable, and easily controlled.

In the context of international law, all methods of logical reasoning are ultimately subservient to formal law-creating processes that hinge on the principle of state consent (Schwarzenberger 1965, 19, 50). This approach limits the dynamic application of legal thought and reinforces a conservative, status quo-preserving framework that prioritizes control over innovation and ethical engagement.

The intellectual atrophy and moral apathy prevalent among international jurists stem largely from an over-reliance on deductive reasoning and a lack of engagement with the more challenging inductive reasoning. This dynamic has led to a stagnation in the development of new knowledge within international law, as such knowledge is typically contingent upon state consent. Judges and legal practitioners find themselves confined to a limited set of international legal arguments, heavily reliant on established deductions and a narrow range of accepted inductions like customary law and general legal principles.

A telling example of this intellectual stagnation is the international legal community's failure, or perhaps indifference, to effectively connect the dots between self-determination and constitutional law, despite their clear relevance to each other. This was exemplified by the International Court of Justice in the Kosovo Advisory Opinion, which skillfully avoided providing clear legal guidance on issues such as the right to self-determination or remedial secession and their potential ties to Serbia's constitutional framework. This intellectual passivity supports a broader habit of injustice that characterizes international relations. By failing to challenge the politics of coercion, international lawyers inadvertently legitimize them. If new knowledge and insightful understanding are to be achieved, they must come through inductive reasoning—a method that encourages deeper insight and self-awareness.

The failure of international lawyers to interrogate their own role within the legal order reflects a deeper existential disconnection. Without a renewed awareness of their ethical and intellectual responsibilities, international jurists are unlikely to engage in the self-criticism necessary for revitalizing their field. In its absence, the discipline risks deepening its condition of intellectual impoverishment and perpetuating the systemic habit of injustice.

## Objective Deprivation as Middle Term: The Empirical Synthesis

It has been demonstrated that in federal and multiethnic states, the connection between the international right to self-determination and constitutional law cannot be established through the lens of social contracts between peoples and governments, as commonly argued by international legal scholars (McWhinney 2007, 12; M. Weller 2008, 31). Social contracts, being metaphorical and abstract, fail to meet the logical standards required for valid syllogisms, as the use of figurative and metaphorical language constitutes a fundamental logical error. In syllogistic logic, terms, including middle terms, must be unambiguous and precisely defined (Jevons 1948, 127). I delved into these fundamental principles of syllogistic logic, elucidating how equivocation leads to the fallacy of the ambiguous middle. To ensure the validity of legal syllogisms, all terms must be rigorously defined (Minto 1915, 84). Given that the concept of the social contract falls short of these logical standards and no alternative middle term is readily available from legal theory, the process of induction was employed to derive a connecting term.

The process of expanded inductive reasoning facilitated an exploration into the general phenomenology of rights. Drawing on Aristotle's expanded induction and Husserl's phenomenology, rights were conceptualized as abstract potentialities that are actualized through concrete acts of deprivation. Such acts transition rights from potentiality and inertia to actuality and claim. To ascertain how constitutional acts of deprivation might impact collective identities and consequently actualize the international right to self-determination, the expanded induction chapters drew upon relevant psychological, psychoanalytical, and hermeneutic social theories to elucidate the psychological mechanisms through which acts of deprivation and loss can traumatize collective identities. Subsequently, empirical and ethnographic data were examined, highlighting the historical instances of collective deprivation before, during, and after the decolonization process. These historical cases illustrated how collective deprivation has disrupted communal narratives and traumatized the collective identity of various groups, including the Cherokee people, the Nauruans, the Greek and Turkish Cypriots, the Jewish people, the Palestinians, and the Kosovar Albanians.

From the above examinations, two distinct forms of collective deprivation have emerged: relative deprivation and objective deprivation. Relative deprivation, as defined in the book, denotes the subjective, collective sense of discontent arising from comparisons with other peoples and reference groups within a liberal framework. Unlike objective deprivation, relative deprivation does not entail actual removal or loss; rather, it involves the subjective evaluation of one's position relative to others, leading to perceptions of advantage or disadvantage. Essentially, what the relatively deprived perceive as 'loss' is not actual, tangible loss but rather a constriction of freedom—an abstract limitation of potentiality (Hull 2007, 47–50).

The psychological, phenomenological, and empirical analyses revealed that while relative deprivation generates feelings of envy and resentment through unfavorable comparisons, objective deprivation can inflict profound traumas on collective identities by activating deep psychoanalytical and psychological mechanisms of grief, anxiety, and frustration. However, given the varied dynamics of identity, determining the phenomenology of objective deprivation requires an examination of the relative significance of the deprived object in the consciousness of the affected collective. This additional step ensures a safer conclusion regarding whether an act of deprivation has indeed disrupted communal narratives or inflicted trauma on collective identity.

This final, synthetic chapter concludes the rational dialectic and proceeds to a logical reconstruction of the international legal framework based on the phenomenology of objective deprivation. This reconstruction suggests that the normative relationship between the international right to self-determination and constitutional law should not be sought in abstract social contracts, but rather in tangible constitutional amendments, administrative actions, and governmental or judicial decisions that lead to objective deprivation and detrimentally impact communal narratives and collective identities of peoples, communities, and indigenous populations. In contrast, collective feelings of relative deprivation arising from unequal or unsatisfactory constitutional arrangements are not encompassed by this middle term. Consequently, the international right to self-determination is not invoked by collective discontent stemming from such inequalities. For instance, the sense of relative deprivation experienced by English-speaking Canadians due to language legislation in Québec favoring French as the official language does not constitute a violation of the international right to self-determination for English-speaking Québecois according to this model (Taylor and Moghaddam 1994, 135).[6]

Constitutional and administrative laws often incorporate provisions that implicitly or explicitly acknowledge the distinctiveness of a people or group, including their connection to a particular land, their entitlement to government and political rights, their right to preserve and promote their language, religion, and cultural practices, as well as their autonomy in local governance and administration. These provisions encompass various aspects of collective life, such as land cultivation, educational practices, religious worship, cultural expression, and traditional customs. Any violation, unilateral amendment, or withdrawal of such provisions by public authorities warrants scrutiny. Moreover, standard administrative practices that establish legitimate expectations or public policies of non-interference in collective life hold moral significance. Therefore, sudden modifications to such policies, whether through legislative measures, judicial decisions, or the implementation of harmful actions (such as excessive police violence against religious, racial, or ethnic groups), are likely to provoke collective disturbance. International jurists should view these actions as instances of objective deprivation that can potentially harm the communal narratives and collective identities of affected peoples or groups.

Throughout history, several such measures and policies have been observed. For example, Serbian legislative authorities enacted numerous administrative laws targeting the Kosovar Albanians with the aim of altering the demographic composition of Kosovo. These measures included the prohibition of Kosovar Albanian mass media, the renaming of streets, the imposition of Serbian curricula in education, the dismissal of thousands of Kosovar Albanians from public sector positions, the provision of financial incentives for Serbs to immigrate to Kosovo, and the imposition of property restrictions on Kosovar Albanians (Independent International Commission on Kosovo 2000, 41–2). Most significantly, the Serbian Assembly's decision to strip Kosovo of its legislative competencies and revoke its constitutional autonomy in 1990 constituted the most severe form of political objective deprivation against the Kosovar Albanians.

In the case of the Cherokee Nation, the Hopewell agreements concluded with the United States ensured the tribe's continued use of its land while also preserving their right to control entry and settlement within their territory (Garrison 2002, 15). Additionally, the Northwest Ordinance, passed by the US Continental Congress, guaranteed that the tribes' lands and property would not be taken without their consent and that they would not be subject to invasion or disturbance except "unless in just and lawful wars authorized by the Congress" (Garrison 2002, 16). However, the state of Georgia violated these international agreements, which had become integral parts of the American constitutional legal order. Georgia enacted state legislation that "annexed the Cherokees lands, abolished the Cherokee government and courts, and nullified the laws promulgated by the Cherokee National Council" (Garrison 2002, 3). Following Georgia's lead, Alabama, Tennessee, and Mississippi pursued similar removal policies and extended their jurisdictions over Indian lands (Garrison 2002, 3). The federal government's involvement in objective deprivation became evident with the passage of the Indian Removal Act by the American Congress in 1830. This legislation granted President Andrew Jackson the authority to negotiate removal treaties with the tribes, thereby formalizing the process of forced removal (Garrison 2002, 3).

The most contentious constitutional case arises from the situation in Cyprus. As outlined in the historical section, following Cypriot independence in 1960, significant constitutional and statutory challenges surfaced, attributed in part to the intricate complexity and inflexibility of the Cypriot Constitution (Chrysostomides 2000, 30–2).[7] This led to a state of constitutional stagnation. According to one legal commentator, despite substantial goodwill from both communities, the constitution was inherently flawed, stating that "the scheme never had any chance of lasting success. . . . The documents of the 1960 settlement [were] incredibly detailed, often repetitious, and occasionally ambiguous" (Ehrlich 1974, 38). The failure of both sides to collaborate in implementing the 1960 Constitution, formulated based on the Zurich-London accords, exacerbated the situation. Peremptory inter-communal cooperation on crucial matters such as municipal delimitation, tax collection, and the structure of the Cypriot police and army became unattainable (Hoffmeister 2006, 13). Additionally, there was significant inter-communal disagreement over the enforcement of the 70:30 Greek Cypriot-Turkish Cypriot ratio for the public sector stipulated in the Zurich-London accords. Greek Cypriots argued that the percentage was unjust given the true 80:20 population ratio, while Turkish

Cypriots maintained that the 70:30 ratio protected their interests and restored equality in the public service (Joseph 1997, 25–6). These constitutional conflicts remained unresolved, impeding the functionality of the state.

The constitutional impasse prompted President Makarios to propose 13 amendments to the 1960 Cypriot Constitution. These amendments included the abolition of veto powers held by the president and vice president of Cyprus, the elimination of provisions requiring separate majorities for the election of the Greek president and Turkish vice president, as well as the enactment of laws and the consolidation of municipalities and security forces, among others (Chrysostomides 2000, 33).[8] However, Turkey and the Turkish Cypriots interpreted these proposals as nullifying the 1960 Treaties and rejected them outright (Chrysostomides 2000, 34). Subsequently, following Makarios' constitutional proposals, Turkish Cypriot Vice President Küçük and all Turkish Cypriot members of the House of Representatives withdrew from the Cypriot government, declaring that "the Cyprus Government . . . lost its legality" (Hoffmeister 2006, 17). Turkish Cypriots then established a General Committee to administer Turkish Cypriot affairs within areas under their *de facto* control. All Turkish Cypriot civil servants were instructed by their leadership to resign from their public positions, which they did (Hoffmeister 2006, 17, 26, 28–9).

The peculiarity of the Cypriot constitutional case lies in the fact that constitutional deprivation against the Turkish Cypriots was not overtly inflicted due to the 13 proposed amendments. Instead, it was only formally articulated through a constitutional proposal submitted by President Makarios to Vice President Küçük. However, had this proposal been passed or enforced by the Greek Cypriot majority, it would have likely stripped the Turkish Cypriots of most of their veto powers and worsened their constitutional position. Although not inherently illegal, Makarios' proposal must be interpreted as a clear rejection of the Zurich-London terms, which, according to the 1959 accords, formed the unamendable legal foundation for the 1960 Constitution (Hoffmeister 2006, 22). Such significant constitutional revisions could only have been enacted through the same multilateral process that birthed the 1960 Constitution, namely, via a new international treaty among the three Guarantor powers and the Cypriot Republic, which at the time seemed improbable (Hoffmeister 2006, 22). Therefore, it is reasonable to conclude that while not constituting an act of objective deprivation, the proposal as such likely caused distress to the Turkish Cypriots, who still regarded the Zurich-London terms as applicable between the two communities.

Regarding the relationship between self-determination and constitutional law, the Cypriot constitutional case provides a clear illustration of why the social contract theory is too abstract to serve as a sound middle term. This theory fails to offer a concrete method for verifying the existence or absence of a genuine agreement between parties. Is the mere external act of signing sufficient, or should one also consider the internal will of the parties? And if so, how does this internal will indicate a genuine agreement? In other words, what specific characteristics or motives of the will signify a conscious and voluntary commitment to a binding arrangement? The social contract theory does not provide satisfactory answers to these questions.

On the contrary, a phenomenological examination of the constitutional landscape in Cyprus before 1964 exposes a reality where the will of the two communities was not genuinely driven by a collective desire for peaceful constitutional coexistence, at least not within the framework of the Zurich-London terms. Neither party fully embraced the Constitution because neither had truly accepted the conditions of constitutional partnership and cohabitation. For the Greek Cypriot leader, the Constitution was imposed on Cyprus, resulting in a situation where constitutional and political development was stunted, and the sovereignty of the Republic was constrained (Ehrlich 1974, 46). Similarly, for the Turkish Cypriots, the constitutional order of the Republic of Cyprus did not represent a voluntary and mutually desired constitutional partnership but, in fact "a compromise between the opposing claims of Greek and Turkish Cypriots" (Necatigil 1989, 102).

As outlined in the preceding chapters, the two communities held markedly divergent views on self-determination. While Greek Cypriots initially viewed self-determination as a struggle for *enosis* and later as the quest for international independence through the creation of a unitary Cypriot state based on majority rule, Turkish Cypriots saw self-determination as a pursuit of absolute inter-communal equality despite numerical disparities. The 1960 Cypriot Constitution thus served as a diplomatic endeavor to strike a delicate balance between these opposing conceptualizations. To this end, the Constitution formalized many of the liberal aspirations of the pre-1960 era: recognizing the independence of a unitary Cypriot state to appease Greek Cypriots while affording Turkish Cypriots the principle of political equality and the illusion of geographical division through provisions such as extensive veto powers for the vice president, the principle of separate majorities, and the establishment of separate municipalities.

The Cypriot constitutional order was destined for failure as it inherently perpetuated and institutionalized the inter-communal antagonism that existed before 1960. The underlying Greek Cypriot and Turkish Cypriot agendas aimed at the annulment of the Cypriot Constitution further underscore this conclusion. The Greek Akritas plan, purportedly supported by Makarios (Hoffmeister 2006, 21) envisioned the gradual abolition of the Cypriot constitutional order in favor of *enosis*. Similarly, a Turkish Cypriot ministerial document from 1963, drafted before the constitutional crisis later that year, asserted that the Turkish Cypriot side only accepted and signed the Zurich-London terms as a temporary stopgap before partition, viewing it as an interim measure rather than a permanent solution. According to Turkish Cypriots, any attempt at a final solution under the existing terms would result in the "extermination of the Turks on the island" (Chrysostomides 2000, 515). These documents reveal a lack of genuine intent from both Greek Cypriots and Turkish Cypriots to adhere to the Zurich-London accords and the 1960 constitutional order. The 1960 Constitution was essentially imposed on all Cypriots by the three guarantor powers, with coercion tactfully obscured and justified under the principle of *pacta sunt servanda*. This principle has been rigorously invoked by the majority of international jurists studying the Cypriot question since the constitutional breakdown of 1963.[9]

Throughout the three years of political coexistence, no true constitutional equilibrium was ever attained. Unlike the constitutional cases of the Cherokee Nation and Kosovo, the pre-1964 Cypriot constitutional order failed to achieve political stability, operational co-governance, or an effective government. It did not establish a sense of political normalcy or lasting cohabitation conducive to the development of standard constitutional practices, the challenge or alteration of which would lead to objective deprivation.

It becomes evident that the 'unworkability' of the constitutional order stemmed not so much from the complexity of the Cypriot Constitution but rather from it becoming a stage for constant inter-communal bargaining. Both communities entered the new constitutional order without a sincere desire to cooperate and without relinquishing their liberal aspirations and conflicting interpretations of self-determination. This dynamic defined subsequent political developments on the island. Greek Cypriots, dissatisfied with the 70:30 ratio in the public service, postponed its implementation, prompting Turkish Cypriots to exploit the provision on separate majorities by refusing to extend British taxation laws (Ehrlich 1974, 43). Constitutional stagnation served as a pretext for Greek Cypriots to demand revision of what they deemed unjust constitutional terms, to which they had never truly consented (Ehrlich 1974, 39). In the likely event of Turkish Cypriot rejection of the 13 amendments, Makarios intended to involve the United Nations (Ehrlich 1974, 54). Consequently, the 13 amendments served as a convenient excuse for Turkish Cypriots to denounce constitutional cooperation with Greek Cypriots, withdraw into enclaves, and establish their *de facto* administration, as they desired.[10] Both communities acted in bad faith, seeking to undermine the constitutional order by sabotaging each other and exploiting resulting deadlocks to their advantage.

During the period between 1960 and 1963, no established constitutional practices or overall normalcy existed between the two communities. However, post-constitutional breakdown, despite Turkish Cypriots' bad faith withdrawal from public posts, the "Hellenization project" proposed in 1965 by Greek Cypriot Members of the Council of Ministers and Makarios was not entirely irrelevant in terms of objective deprivation (Ehrlich 1974, 91). Although overall constitutional normalcy had not been achieved in the initial three-year period, Turkish Cypriots had nonetheless engaged in, and become accustomed to, certain practices. For example, they enjoyed unrestricted access to governmental buildings and courts and participated in votes without intrusion or harassment. Despite withdrawing from the Cypriot government, Turkish Cypriots continued cooperation with Greek Cypriots in the judicial field (lower courts) (Hoffmeister 2006, 18). Therefore, Greek Cypriot measures post-1964 that challenged these established practices, such as blockades and restrictions on freedom of movement preventing certain Turkish Cypriot judges from performing their duties, as well as imposing preconditions on Turkish Cypriot members of the House of Representatives to attend ministerial meetings (even if they did not wish to participate or vote), must be considered acts of objective deprivation against Turkish Cypriots (Hoffmeister 2006, 29–30).

## From the Logical Synthesis to the Wider Morality of Political Guardianship and Corrective Justice

Before advancing to the logical reconstruction of the international legal syllogism, it is imperative to summarize our phenomenological findings on deprivation and subsequently delineate a comprehensive method of legal reasoning. This method will enable jurists to determine whether, in a given constitutional legal framework, the international right of a people or group to self-determination has been infringed upon. This legal reasoning method comprises four distinct tests:

1. Deprivation due to removal of a constitutional object, or due to disturbance of a constitutional habit (objective deprivation), and not due to comparisons (relative deprivation): Furthermore, the jurist must evaluate the relative significance of the deprived constitutional right, object, or practice to the collective identity of the affected people or group. Genuine, collective attachment to the constitutionally protected entity must be established. It is crucial to discern between true attachment and mere collective expectations stemming from comparisons, such as a collective desire for more or equal treatment (e.g., Québec), which are influenced by wants rather than intrinsic attachment and habit.
2. Phenomenology of the constitution, new vs. old rights and practices: Element 1) typically necessitates a phenomenological analysis of the constitution. For instance, consideration should be given to whether the constitution was democratically drafted (e.g., Canada) or imposed (e.g., Cyprus). In cases of imposition, it is reasonable to anticipate that the constitution would be more detached from the collective lifeworld of the affected peoples, meaning their existing habits and practices. However, even in the context of a new constitution, the element of attachment is not automatically precluded. It is essential for the jurist to further investigate whether the new constitution upholds and acknowledges old rights and practices or introduces entirely novel circumstances. It is improbable that new rights and practices would immediately foster a constitutional habit or engender genuine attachment. In instances of imposed constitutions (e.g., Cyprus), new rights and practices often reflect political compromises among various competing claims rooted in intergroup comparisons. Consequently, the elements of genuine attachment or habit are likely to be absent. Similarly, a constitution may emerge from an international agreement among leaders representing different peoples (e.g., Yugoslavia). Even in cases where constitutions are the result of consensus, a distinction must be made between provisions that establish new circumstances and those that reflect and institutionalize existing habits and practices. Any subsequent withdrawal,

breach, or amendment of the latter should be scrutinized as potentially harmful to the collective identities of the affected peoples (e.g., the American Constitution in the case of the Cherokee people).

3. New provisions that create constitutional habits and establish political normalcy: Even in cases where a constitution introduces new rights and practices, the jurist should delve deeper to ascertain whether these rights and practices foster political normalcy. This entails the emergence of new constitutional habits and an undisturbed communal rhythm, wherein there is a reasonable expectation that the related constitutional practices and rights will persist (e.g., Kosovo). Political normalcy denotes a state where various claims gradually diminish, giving way to an established environment of calm cohabitation. If the new constitutional habits and established practices are intertwined with the collective identity of peoples (e.g., constitutional recognition of autonomy or self-government, permission for the operation of separate schools), any subsequent public acts that disrupt these practices should be scrutinized as potentially harmful and an infringement of the right to self-determination.
4. Deprivation that leads to injury: Finally, it is crucial to assess whether the conduct of public authorities disrupts the aforementioned constitutional habits and practices in a manner that traumatizes the identities of the affected peoples or groups. While presented last for systematic clarity, the test of deprivation and injury is, in reality, paramount. As elucidated in the previous chapters, deprivation serves as the phenomenological catalyst, propelling the international right to self-determination from potentiality and inertia to actuality and claim.

The term 'public authorities' used in this section encompasses judicial authorities, the legislature, and the government/administration of a state. While Aristotle's theory on corrective justice predates Montesquieu's tripartite principle for the separation of powers outlined in *L'Esprit des Lois*, Aristotle's political framework in the *Politics* offers insights into the organizational structure of the state.

Aristotle did introduce a distinction of powers in the *Politics*, delineating between the general assembly, public officials, and the judiciary, which roughly correspond to the legislative, executive, and judicial organs of the modern state. However, this distinction served systemic and pedagogical purposes, and Aristotle did not advocate for a strict division of powers (Fairlie 1923, 393;

Radin 1938, 860). In fact, he viewed the legislature and the executive as largely intertwined and overlapping (Fairlie 1923, 393). For Aristotle, the government of a state constitutes an organic whole comprising three elements: the deliberative element, the executive element, and the judicial element (Aristotle 1995, 175, 184). He regards the deliberative element, corresponding to the legislature, as the supreme element (Aristotle 1995, 176, 179). This deliberative function is exercised by either the legislature or the executive, namely, magistrates elected through a vote or by lot (Aristotle 1995, 177). Aristotle underscores the importance of virtue and justice in governance, asserting that a good government must prioritize justice as the perfect virtue. Governments that prioritize the common interest and adhere to principles of justice are considered true forms, whereas those that prioritize the interests of rulers are deemed defective and perverted forms, akin to despotism (Aristotle 1995, 114).

Modern administrations indeed embody Aristotle's deliberative element by executing legislation through individual or collective administrative acts, exercising discretion, and sometimes even assuming legislative functions when delegated such authority by national or federal legislative bodies (Smith and Brazier 1994, 20). Administrative law, along with constitutional law, constitutes a significant aspect of public law, encompassing both the horizontal relations among public bodies and the vertical relationship between public bodies and individuals or collectivities (Le Sueur and Sunkin 1997, 5). National courts serve as the judicial dimension of Aristotle's government and are thus also bound by principles of corrective justice. For instance, in the case of *Worcester v. Georgia*, Chief Justice Marshall's ruling declared Georgia's extension and removal laws unconstitutional and void. Therefore, by disregarding this ruling, the southern American courts perpetrated an injustice against the Cherokee people.

It follows from the above that, from the perspective of corrective justice, the international legal syllogism on self-determination and constitutional law must involve the behavior of states as *Aristotelian wholes*. Accordingly, deprivation acts from the judicial, legislative, and governmental/administrative bodies that infringe the constitutional rights of peoples and traumatize their collective identities must be considered as violating the latter's international right to self-determination. The international legal syllogism on the relation between self-determination and constitutional law in federal or multiethnic states must therefore be reconstructed as follows:

P1: In federal or polyethnic states, all rights to self-determination (S) are [arise from] serious disruptions of constitutional rights (M);
P2: In federal or polyethnic states, all serious disruptions of constitutional rights (M) are cases of objective collective deprivation (P);
C: In federal or polyethnic states, all rights to self-determination (S) are [arise from] cases of objective collective deprivation (P).

Again, the syllogism is Barbara for it follows the form "All S is M; all M is P; therefore, all S is P." Our expanded induction produced the definition of the minor premise (P2) and particularly the middle term (M). It then replaced the logically unsound concept of social contract with the phenomenology of objective collective deprivation. This narrow syllogism, however, is only a small fraction of a wider political morality that is neither constituted by, nor contained in, the various federal or state laws.

Corrective justice is essentially political because it pertains to, and is enacted within, the *polis* (Aristotle 1995, 12; Heyman 2003, 473). However, its manifestation in concrete legal frameworks does not imply that it originates solely from the laws of the *polis* (Schroeder 2003, 44). Corrective justice serves as the moral benchmark for both constitutional and international law, as the overarching purpose of law is to mirror natural justice (Schroeder 2003, 44). Consequently, beyond the individual and collective rights explicitly safeguarded by constitutional and administrative laws, national or federal legislators, governments, and administrations bear a broader moral responsibility to prevent and rectify all injustices suffered by the peoples and citizens within their jurisdiction. This moral imperative is linked to the objective political duty that governments and legislators owe to their constituents, whom they are entrusted to protect, since they are specifically tasked with the ethical mission of corrective justice.

It should not be assumed that legislative, governmental, or administrative acts of objective deprivation against peoples or groups always manifest as formal and overt actions carried out directly by official state authorities. In reality, behaviors such as governmental encouragement or tolerance of inter-communal conflict, deliberate or unintentional legislative failure to implement protective measures, or the overlooking of hostile actions against peoples or groups by other parties all exhibit distinct moral failings. An illustrative example of such behavior is Turkey's treatment of the Greek community in Istanbul during the 1955 pogroms. As detailed in the historical section, Turkey responded to Britain's diplomatic pressure regarding the Cypriot self-determination debate by seeking to leverage its position. This included implicating the Orthodox Patriarchate of Istanbul in a political exchange, which Britain accepted (Holland 1998, 69). Subsequently, when the tripartite conference on Cyprus broke down, hostile declarations by Turkish officials led to severe emotional reactions and numerous acts of brutality against the Greek community in Istanbul (Holland 1998, 75). During these events, acts of deprivation perpetrated by Turkish individuals, such as rapes of Greek women and the destruction of Greek property and places of worship, occurred amidst governmental and administrative inaction. Despite the violence, the Turkish police chose not to intervene in the riots, demonstrating a passive stance from the authorities (Holland 1998, 75).

From the standpoint of corrective justice, the political motivations driving acts of deprivation hold no relevance. What matters in terms of moral assessment is the actual impact and moral gravity of these actions or omissions themselves (Aristotle 1926, 291). Therefore, whether the legislative body or administration responsible for deprivation was legitimately elected, whether they represent a specific population or not, or whether they operate within a democratic or despotic framework is inconsequential in the evaluation of moral responsibility. The moral imperative of corrective justice is objective, demanding that all legislators and governments, irrespective of their political ideologies, take affirmative steps to prevent and address acts of objective deprivation against their populace and citizens. Consequently, administrative hostility or indifference toward individual and collective harm is inherently immoral, as it signifies a breach of the moral duty derived from principles of ethical guidance and political guardianship. Indeed, such an omission can be characterized as a double injustice. According to Arthur Schopenhauer:

> [double injustice] is loathed and detested as something revolting and outrageous, as a monstrous crime, and ἄγος, at which the gods, so to speak, cover their faces. This double injustice occurs when anyone has expressly undertaken the obligation to protect someone else in a definite respect; consequently, the nonfulfillment of the obligation would in itself be an injury to the other person, and thus a wrong; but in addition, he now attacks and injures the other man at the very spot where he should protect him. (Schopenhauer 1995, 156)

The failure to fulfill a moral obligation constitutes a moral wrong in itself. However, the situation escalates into a double injustice when a legislator's or government's neglect or breach of their objective moral duties of ethical guidance and political protection results in harm to the very people they are tasked to protect. This dynamic is exemplified by the collapse of the mandate system in the case of Nauru. Designed to safeguard the interests of indigenous peoples and foster their well-being until they were deemed 'ready' for self-governance, the Nauru Island Agreement, where Australia, New Zealand, and the United Kingdom obtained all rights to Nauruan phosphate at a minimal cost, manifested a case of double immorality. These mandate powers, charged with protecting the Nauruans, instead exploited them economically.

A notable instance that explicitly invoked the principle of political guardianship is *Worcester v. Georgia*, where Chief Justice Marshall asserted that, through bilateral treaties, the United States had effectively guaranteed the sovereignty and territorial rights of Indian tribes. Marshall elevated the moral principle of political guardianship to a legal doctrine, integrating it into the fabric of the US Constitution (Garrison 2002, 186).

In the case of Palestine, the Arab population's discontent with the British Mandate escalated into riots during the early 1920s, primarily due to the British administration's passivity in the face of Zionist expansionism led by figures like Ben-Gurion and the consequent upheaval in rural Palestine (Pappe 2006, 97–8). The Zionist policy during this period involved acquiring land from large landlords and displacing tenants without compensation, a practice that provoked widespread dissent and objections from British agricultural experts (Pappe 2006, 98–9). However, the United Kingdom failed to respond effectively to this ongoing collective deprivation experienced by the Arab population.

While some have argued that the Arab Committee, though disorganized and ineffective, should have played a more proactive role in safeguarding Arab interests (Pappe 2006, 103), the primary moral responsibility lay with the British colonial power. It was the duty of the United Kingdom, as the colonial authority, to address and mitigate the impacts of Zionist expansionism through preventive and remedial measures. The burden of curtailing the Zionist project should not have fallen on the Arab leadership alone. Similarly, the British Government's decision not to pursue the UN partition plan outlined in Resolution 181, which proposed a Jewish State encompassing 56 percent of Palestine, was justifiable despite humanitarian appeals made by the UN General Assembly (Dowty 2012, 89).

The British withdrawal from Palestine in 1948, which inadvertently led to the devastating Arab-Israeli conflict, and the subsequent transfer of Palestinian public assets to Israel in the early 1950s, constituted acts of collective deprivation by the

British administration. These actions resulted in a situation of double injustice against the Arab populations of Palestine (Pappe 2006, 134). If the British had taken measures to prevent or rectify this double injustice, the Palestinians might not have felt compelled to assume a vigilante identity and resort to *intifadas* and systematic guerrilla warfare to address the injustice inflicted upon them by the Israelis (Dowty 2012, 101). As a consequence, Israel cannot be perceived as a trustworthy political guardian or ethical educator by the Palestinian minority within Israel. In the collective consciousness of the Palestinian people, Israel is seen as the oppressor, representing and embodying historical injustice.

The British administration's failure to address enosist demands of the Greek Cypriots did not constitute an injustice against them, as intergroup comparisons of relative deprivation fall outside the scope of the objective, moral responsibility that governments bear toward their peoples by virtue of corrective justice. However, after the Second World War, the British promised self-government to Cyprus, raising the expectations of the Greek Cypriot majority (Holland 1998, 13). Therefore, by subsequently retracting this promise and effectively excluding the option of self-determination for Cyprus due to strategic considerations in Palestine and the Middle East, the British caused a disturbance to the Greek Cypriots. While this disturbance did not amount to actual deprivation and thus did not harm the collective identity of the Greek Cypriots, it did impact their collective psychology (Holland 1998, 16). Although the Greek Cypriot right to self-determination was not violated, the behavior of the British administration cannot be deemed morally acceptable, especially given its role as a political guardian and ethical educator of the Cypriot communities.

A double injustice against the Greek Cypriots occurred when Governor Harding declared a state of emergency, implementing harsh measures such as prolonged curfews and the arbitrary arrest and release of Greek suspects near Turkish villages. These practices cannot be justified as part of the ethical mission of the British administration, as they did not aim to educate the Greek Cypriots but rather punish them en masse for the actions of EOKA. Additionally, after the British renewed the promise of partition, Turkish Cypriot leaders initiated a policy of ethnic cleansing with the goal of *de facto* partitioning the island (Holland 1998, 263). Despite Greek Cypriot requests for protective and remedial measures, Prime Minister Macmillan dismissed them (Holland 1998, 263). This denial to apply corrective justice by the British led EOKA to redirect its guerrilla actions from solely targeting British to targeting both British and Turkish

Cypriots. Essentially, after the British failed to apply corrective justice, EOKA took matters into its own hands, assuming the role of the administration.

The deportation and forced exile of Makarios constituted another act of double immorality. The British deported Makarios, depriving the Greek Cypriot community of their political and religious leader, to further their own interests. Their aim was to promote an interim constitutional structure for Cyprus that would ease the Greek Cypriot demand for self-determination and appease the Turkish side with constitutional advantages. This act of immorality cannot solely be assessed based on the concrete act of deportation and the responsibility that a government bears toward its people by virtue of corrective justice. It also stems from the role of the colonial administration as a political guardian.

Aristotle posited that a good government must not only protect and educate its people but also pursue policies that serve the common interest, as governments that prioritize the interests of rulers are defective and despotic (Aristotle 1995, 114). Unlike the neutral stance of corrective justice, when evaluating the morality of political guardianship, motives hold moral significance. Similarly, the British decision to involve Turkey in the dispute solely to preserve their own geostrategic interests in the region was inherently wrong. The principle of political guardianship encompasses a broader moral concept than corrective justice, as it includes, but is not limited to, the remedial and ethical mission of corrective justice. Therefore, evaluating actions within the framework of political guardianship requires considering the moral worth of motives and the alignment of actions with the common interest of the community.

The possible covert Greek involvement in EOKA's activities and Turkey's overt manipulation of the Turkish Cypriot leadership toward the *de facto* partition of Cyprus (Holland 1998, 229) can indeed be considered as governmental acts of moral demerit, though not necessarily as acts of double injustice. From the perspective of political guardianship, neither Greece nor Turkey can be held politically accountable for the situation on the island before the signing of the Zurich/London agreements in 1959. Until 1959, the United Kingdom held sole responsibility for Cypriot affairs and thus sole administration of corrective justice. However, in 1959, Greece and Turkey became guaranteeing powers of Cyprus, sharing a moral burden akin to that of the United Kingdom regarding the well-being of Cypriot populations. The behavior of Greece and Turkey after the Zurich/London accords must therefore be scrutinized in this light.

After 1959, both Greece and Turkey violated their moral duties of political guardianship, inflicting double injustices against the two ethnic communities.

Turkey's actions included the bombardment of Greek Cypriot towns (Hoffmeister 2006, 17), support of the paramilitary TMT, military invasion of 1974, killing and displacement of Greek Cypriots, and continuous military occupation of a significant portion of Cypriot territory (Chrysostomides 2000, 37; Hoffmeister 2006, 37). Greece inflicted a double injustice by openly supporting paramilitary operations against Turkish Cypriots and against Makarios (O'Malley and Craig 1999, 134), exporting arms to Cyprus (Crawshaw 1978, 398), organizing a coup against Makarios, and establishing a pro-enosist puppet regime under Nicos Sampson's control. Since the Zurich/London accords remain in force (Hoffmeister 2006, 98), the moral duties arising from three-partite political guardianship of local ethnic populations are still valid. Therefore, Turkey's continuous military occupation of Northern Cyprus, withholding of information regarding missing persons, and facilitation of illegal Turkish immigration from Anatolia to Northern Cyprus constitute acts of double injustice against the Greek Cypriot community.

From the perspective of political guardianship, one must evaluate not only governmental activity but also political omission. Since good governments are tasked with serving the common interest and well-being of their peoples, the overall diplomatic inactivity of the United Kingdom and Greece in the post-Attila era, their diplomatic non-engagement, or insubstantial diplomatic engagement, must be considered as omissions of double injustice against the local populations, assuming that these contribute to a potentially injurious diplomatic stagnation.

Similarly, from the standpoint of corrective justice, the situation in Palestine mirrors this dynamic. The absolute diplomatic disengagement of the United Kingdom and all UN member-states that voted in favor of General Assembly Resolution 181 and the 1947 partition plan must be deemed immoral, as all these states contributed to Palestinian deprivation. Consequently, all these states bear the specific moral responsibility to correct the collective wrongs they have contributed to. Hence, the diplomatic abandonment of the Turkish and Greek Cypriots, as well as the Palestinians and Israelis, to the voluntary and unequal process of direct talks, even if 'charitably' mediated by entities like the United States, the UN, or the EU, does not rectify the immorality stemming from injurious governmental acts or omissions.

Similarly, political guardianship partially justifies Turkey's initial military intervention in Cyprus (Attila I), presuming it was conducted solely to secure peace on the island and protect the Turkish Cypriot community from potential

Greek aggression in light of the Greek coup d'état. However, the second Turkish intervention (Attila II) is not justifiable from the perspective of political guardianship, as it occurred well after the restoration of the Cypriot constitutional order. This moral argumentation aligns with the mainstream interpretation of the Treaty of Guarantee (Hoffmeister 2006, 46).

In considering the direct moral responsibility between Israelis and Palestinians, as well as the two local administrations in Cyprus—the legitimate Greek Cypriot government and the illegitimate but *de facto* Turkish Cypriot administration—it is crucial to note that while the political reality in Gaza, the West Bank, and the *de facto* dichotomization of Cyprus may suggest that the element of political guardianship does not apply equally to all these ethnic administrations concerning the opposite ethnic community, they are all morally bound and accountable to each other from the perspective of corrective justice. This is because corrective justice belongs to the *polis* but does not arise solely from the *polis*; it exists by nature (Schroeder 2003, 44). Although all ethnic administrations must, within their respective areas of jurisdiction, give concrete legal form to corrective justice, corrective justice *per se* is independent of any such laws and political divides.

The occurrence of collective deprivation and loss is indeed a historical fact, and the corresponding moral responsibility for restitution is a moral fact. It is crucial to acknowledge that our world encompasses both physical and moral dimensions, with physical and moral truths coexisting.[11] In the cases of Cyprus and Palestine, the moral truths dictate that all ethnic administrations are accountable to each other and have the moral obligation not to cause further harm to their compatriots. They must also make proper arrangements for the restitution of the collective wounds and damages that they have inflicted during intercommunal and interethnic conflicts.

The expulsion of Palestinians by Israelis from their land, the damages and casualties during Greek and Turkish Cypriot paramilitary operations, and the inter-communal strife of 1963–1968 are all wrongful acts of objective deprivation. Similarly, the isolation, commercial restrictions, and economic pressure systematically exercised on Turkish Cypriot enclaves by the Greek Cypriot administration after the constitutional breakdown constitute wrongful acts (Crawshaw 1978, 368). Furthermore, any cooperation between Greek Cypriot officials and paramilitary troops that led to injustices represents a form of double injustice. As long as Turks and Turkish Cypriots continue to occupy the northern part of Cyprus and deprive Greek Cypriots of their homes, cities, and villages, and as long as Israel expands its operations and illegal settlements without acknowledging historical injustices and negotiating a right of return for Palestinian refugees, corrective justice remains disregarded.

Disregarding corrective justice has serious ethical implications. Since corrective justice serves not only a remedial function but also an educational and ethical mission, the failure of an administration to apply it properly sends the wrong moral signals to its people. This mismanagement of corrective justice can lead to moral confusion, moral indifference, and *anomie*, fostering the erroneous impression that certain forms of wrongfulness are socially and morally acceptable. This perpetuates a vicious cycle of individual and collective immorality, as it instructs individuals and collectives that certain injurious acts are morally permissible, thereby contributing to a culture of impunity and moral degradation.

## Notes

1 But also Miller 2003, 311.

2 According to Alasdair MacIntyre: "There is no expression in any ancient or medieval language correctly translated by our expression 'a right' until near the close of the Middle Ages: the concept lacks any means of expression in Hebrew, Greek, Latin or Arabic, classical or medieval, before about 1400, let alone in Old English, or in Japanese even as late as the mid-nineteenth century" (Miller 2003, 311).

3 For instance, a tort might be actionable even where the claimant has not suffered actual loss or injury, if to a certain wrongful act the legislator has attached a presumption of injurious effect (Calnan 1997, 132).

4 Thucydides was the first to introduce a theory on equality and justice in his History of the Peloponnesian War. In the Melian dialogue, the Athenians asked the Melians to surrender instead of them having a military encounter on the island of Melos. The Athenians pledged: "we both know that decisions about justice are made in human discussions only when both sides are under equal compulsion; but when one side is stronger, it gets as much as it can, and the weak must accept that." However, as one commentator suggests, the Athenians did not suggest that "might makes right." Instead, they argued that justice is relevant only where "both sides [. . .] feel the force of law." At some later point, the Athenians added, "Remember what is usually the best course: do not give way to equals, but have the right attitude

toward your superiors and use moderation toward your inferiors" (Thucydides 1993, 103, 108)

5 Paraphrasing Nietzsche, good is the useful (to the powerful) and not the valuable (to all) (Nietzsche 1994, 12).

6 However, while instances of unequal constitutional treatment may not fall within the realm of corrective justice, they should still be scrutinized from the domestic perspective of distributive justice. In the case of English and French-speaking Quebecers, this entails ensuring governmental adherence to distributive constitutional criteria established by the Canadian legislature.

7 An article from *The Economist* in 1964 reads: "The snag was that this most bizarre and complicated of constitutions needed more than the normal injection of tolerance, good-will, common sense and mutual give-and-take to make it work. Some of the provisions [were] . . . unrealistic from the start . . . [and] wildly impractical. . . . Among both Greek and Turkish Cypriots there are moderates who do want to try to make the Zurich settlement work. In both communities there are extremists who want it to fail and who are prepared to resort to open violence. The constitution's creaking performance so far has naturally played into the hands of the extremists on both sides" (Adams 1966, 488).

8 It has been suggested that Makarios' 13 amendments were essentially the first stage of the 1963 Akritas plan, a "hidden agenda" which would presumably lead to Greek Cypriot self-determination through the gradual abolition of the constitutional and international restrictions "imposed" on Cyprus during the Zurich/London talks (Hoffmeister 2006, 21).

9 Unlike the Greek Cypriots who lean primarily on the invalidity of the Zurich-London accords and, secondarily, on the legal argument of *rebus sic stantibus*, Turkey and Turkish Cypriots have been persistently invoking the *pacta sunt servanda* principle. According to Zaim Necatigil, former Attorney General of the TRNC and legal consultant at the Ministry of Foreign Affairs of Turkey, "The way in which the 1960 Constitution was drafted does not only imply a difference in procedure or form, it actually represents documentary evidence proving that the 1960 Constitution was one based upon the *agreement* of the parties concerned. The 1960 Constitution comprised, on the basis of *agreement* between the parties concerned, certain solutions and institutions which differed from those contained in other existing constitutions. This Constitution was based on principles *agreed* upon by the parties concerned rather than on precedent existing in other constitutions. Every article of the Constitution was drawn up after *agreement* was reached between the sides concerned." (Necatigil 1989, 11). The same author argues that "the Greek side did not want to implement certain articles of the Constitution which underlined the partnership. . . . Archbishop Makarios and many other

Greek Cypriots did not like the rights accorded to the Turkish Cypriots in the Constitution which were intended as safeguards against any attempt at Greek Cypriot hegemony" (Necatigil 1989, 17–18).

10 According to the Turkish Cypriot Ministerial document, the plan of the Turkish Cypriots "We shall profit from the blunders and mistakes of the Greeks and, once we have prepared better in the time gained, we shall wait for the day when they decide to abrogate the agreements, whereupon we shall obtain our full freedom" (Chrysostomides 2000, 515).

11 "That the world has only a physical and not a moral significance is a fundamental error, one that is the greatest and most pernicious, the real perversity of the mind" (Schopenhauer, Parerga and Paralipomena: Short Philosophical Essays 1974, 201).

# Conclusion

## Corrective Justice and the Future of International Law

The conclusion of the dialectic surrounding the tracing and application of the middle term should not be understood as a neo-Marxist attempt to emancipate legal meaning. Rather, the aim of this book has been to respond to the modernist dismissal of metaphysics by drawing attention to, and reviving, a largely overlooked—if not altogether discarded—form of induction. This form of reasoning, it is suggested, holds the potential to illuminate the underlying essence of legal concepts, theoretical frameworks, and the structural dimensions of law more broadly.

In this concluding section, two significant meta-questions arise that require attention: one practical and one theoretical. The practical meta-question pertains to the ongoing self-determination conflicts in Cyprus and, particularly, Palestine. Given the unlikely reversal of irrationality and injustice in the near future—absent a radical overhaul at both the institutional level of international law and, most critically, at the individual level of rationality and ethics—is there any possibility for corrective justice in bilateral and/or mediated negotiations to at least mitigate the historical harm, namely, the inflicted traumas on identity and collective narrative?

The second meta-question, though theoretical in nature, carries significant practical implications and is no less important than the first. If legal academics, jurists, judges, and international officers were to undergo the kind of rational and ethical transformation that would enable them to distinguish clearly between the rational and the irrational, the just and the unjust, how should this legal intelligentsia then go about envisioning and advancing meaningful reforms in international law? What operative strategy should they adopt in order to revise international legal reasoning in both logical and moral terms? What form of struggle—intellectual or otherwise—ought this legal elite to pursue in order to discredit and dismantle the coercive and amoral elements that continue to underpin much of international legal doctrine? The response to this meta-question ultimately hinges on whether legal professionals can, in practice, extricate themselves from the gravitational pull of their national, cultural, or institutional contexts and engage freely in such moral activism.

The preceding chapters have framed the theoretical meta-question suggesting a compelling need to develop a direct form of moral activism aimed at, eventually, establishing a global administrator of corrective justice. I advance this discussion by contrasting the moral activist thesis with the most pertinent moral, cultural, and post-modern counter-proposals, most notably: (a) the methodology of the Critical Legal Studies movement (CLS); (b) Allen Buchanan's moral theory of remedial secession; and (c) Nathaniel Berman's exploration of post-modern cultural fantasies (Berman 2012) . I contend that these approaches fail to satisfy because they are either logically flawed, overly abstract for the necessary moral reform, or they inadequately reflect the principles of corrective justice. This discussion is primarily addressed to legal philosophers, theorists, and practitioners, as well as to political and international relations theorists, governmental officials, and diplomats—professions crucial in influencing both bilateral or mediated negotiations and the broader development of international law. For structural reasons, I commence with the second meta-question concerning alternative proposals and conclude with the first meta-question, which probes the role of corrective justice in an era dominated by capitalist Realpolitik and legal–political careerism.

As I see it, legal activism and the CLS movement stand in sharp ideological opposition. While CLS has undoubtedly brought important critiques to the surface, its tone, marked by rhetorical excess and an often paralyzing pessimism, renders it an ineffective vehicle for moral reform. To draw on Hegelian language, the CLS method exemplifies what Hegel terms "Skeptical Consciousness," the condition in which "the empirical person . . . is everlastingly subject to many definite, unjustifiable convictions" (Hegel 2005, 524). This form of consciousness is relentlessly suspicious, engaging in chains of "reasonings and counter-reasonings [that] are like the arguments of children concerned to contradict one another and always to have the last word" (Hegel 2005, 524). What CLS ultimately denies is the possibility of essential meaning. In doing so, it becomes self-contradictory, rejecting any stable point of reference—any truth-value—from which a coherent critique might be launched. Even though CLS scholars recognize the Hegelian Master–Slave dialectic and acknowledge their own internal contradictions, they refuse to affirm truth as anything more than "confused, variable and distorted" (Hegel 2005, 524). The result is a kind of syllogistic instability, in which the critique implodes under the weight of its own relativism. Ironically, while CLS denounces the dogmatism of legal modernity, it replicates its most conservative feature: a deep suspicion of induction.

The systematic exclusion of truth-values from CLS's critical syllogisms presents a profound problem. From a Hegelian perspective, the CLS scholar's Skeptical Consciousness inevitably devolves into what Hegel termed the "Unhappy Consciousness"—a condition of intellectual paralysis, caught in a cycle of repetitive, esoteric, and ultimately self-referential critique. While the CLS movement has succeeded in exposing many of the underlying prejudices and contradictions of the legal mainstream, its methodology functions more as a heuristic device than a genuine path toward legal transformation (Carty 2007, 8). Scholars within CLS frequently find themselves entangled in the paradoxes of international law, employing "rhetorical devices which are neo-positivist and neo-naturalist," yet without fully committing to the foundational premises of either school. They vacillate between these paradigms, adopting their terminology but not their structure (Carty 2007, 8). This reluctance to engage meaningfully with induction and particularly the pre-emptive dismissal of its capacity to reveal essential truths reveals a deeper problem: a fractured understanding of the international legal system that ultimately enables that very system to absorb and defang the CLS critique. What results is a "broadly effective critique of arbitrary structures" that, as Habermas observed, never quite forces a real confrontation with legal doctrine (Habermas 1988, 84).

In the final analysis, the CLS movement does not succeed in substantively challenging international legal doctrine. It lacks the philosophical coherence and methodological rigor necessary to mount a serious challenge to the foundational structures of the field. Its critique remains largely academic—bourgeois in its distance from practical reform—often more invested in self-referential deconstruction than in articulating a viable alternative legal vision. By contrast, even the cautious *de lege ferenda* proposals occasionally advanced by mainstream legal scholars, however limited, tend to be more earnest and pragmatically engaged. As Arthur Schopenhauer observed, "[t]he pretence of the impartial investigation of truth, with the resolve to make the established religion the result, indeed the measure and control, of truth, is intolerable; and such a philosophy, tied to the established religion like a dog to a chain, is only the vexatious caricature of the highest and noblest endeavor of mankind" (Schopenhauer 1974, 143).

From a broader critical perspective, the assumption that legal meaning can be emancipated solely through Habermasian discourse theory falls short when it comes to the ethical demands of corrective justice. Rational and moral reform in international law requires more than the continuous exposure of bias and contradiction within its doctrines. It demands explicit moral judgment: a deliberate and uncompromising rejection of coercive norms, rooted in universally intelligible logical and ethical principles. The path to realizing corrective justice in international relations lies not in perpetual debate but in decisive moral action and the cultivation of legal virtue. As Aristotle argued, habituation begins with action; virtue emerges only when individuals repeatedly choose to act well. Thus, for international law to develop a new ethos of rationality and justice, international jurists must first cultivate these inclinations in their own professional conduct. Through consistent rational and ethical practice, the jurist becomes a model of integrity: one capable of transmitting this new moral habit to future generations. Only then can a transformative legal culture take root.

A proactive stance by such a rationally and morally mature legal intelligentsia represents the sole path forward. It is not surprising that political theorists and interdisciplinary scholars have been markedly more 'imaginative' in proposing innovative and creative ways to apply corrective justice in international relations. Unlike legal theorists, these scholars tap into a broader pool of empirical data and engage with a more extensive network of theories and ideas. This exposure enables them to make numerous and considerably wide-ranging inductions. However, most of these theorists remain classical modernists at heart, in that they stop short of acknowledging essential meanings or insights as valid forms of reasoning.

Allen Buchanan emerges as a prominent political theorist and advocate for a version of corrective justice in international relations, which unfortunately represents a significantly distorted interpretation. Buchanan has formulated a moral theory positing that the "primary moral goal of the international legal system" should be to promote basic human rights and ensure that "all persons have access to institutions of justice" (Buchanan 2004, 73). According to Buchanan's moral theory, induction cannot yield absolute truth-values. Achieving justice within the so-called international legal order involves negotiating and agreeing upon the minimum protections that must be extended to peoples and individuals. This process entails an academic elite determining the specifics of this minimum protection, essentially defining the content of basic human rights as spheres of interests (Buchanan 2004, 186, 128). In Buchanan's framework, international legitimacy does not depend on the principle of state consent, grounded in the realistic expectation that states may, and often do, infringe upon these basic rights (Buchanan 2004, 289).

In addressing the international right to self-determination, Buchanan puts forward two key strategies. First, he argues that international law must move beyond colonial-era rhetoric and explicitly affirm a right to remedial secession as a measure of last resort in response to grave injustices in post-colonial contexts. Second, he recommends the pursuit of alternative solutions to secessionist demands, such as arrangements for internal self-governance, coupled with a sustained effort to improve compliance with established human rights norms (Buchanan 2004, 331). Buchanan conceptualizes remedial secession as a claim-right, allowing a people to attempt the formation of a fully independent and primary political unit, one that would ideally receive recognition from the international community (Buchanan 2004, 334). This right, in his view, is triggered only under extreme circumstances—specifically, when a state engages in or permits: (a) acts of aggression or illegitimate annexation; (b) genocide or systematic violations of fundamental human rights; and (c) serious, ongoing breaches of intrastate autonomy agreements (Buchanan 2004, 335, 351–2). Importantly, Buchanan makes clear that the existence of this right does not entail an automatic obligation on other states to recognize the seceding entity as a sovereign state under international law. Instead, recognition remains a matter of discretion, resting with individual states (Buchanan 2004, 334–5).

There are several issues with Buchanan's Remedial Right Only theory. As might be expected, his enumeration of moral justifications that presumably warrant a right to remedial secession is not comprehensive. This list is subject to revision and updates as new empirical data emerge, potentially revealing new forms of injustice. Buchanan introduced point c), the persistent violations of intrastate autonomy agreements, as a novel justification for remedial secession in his work *Justice, Legitimacy, and Self-determination: Moral Foundations for International Law* (Buchanan 2004). He acknowledged this addition as a significant enhancement to his prior theory on secession, which he admitted was "seriously flawed" (Buchanan 2004, 352). This flaw, however, was predictable. By rejecting the possibility of essential meaning, Buchanan inevitably confronts the typical challenge of formal induction: the issue of probability.

Formal induction dismisses insight as an 'unscientific' psychological or even metaphysical phenomenon. By relying solely on formal induction, Buchanan is confined to utilizing the available empirical data to draw probable conclusions—

conclusions that may be later amended or even falsified based on new empirical evidence that could complement or contradict the initial inductive syllogism. The addition of persistent violations of intrastate autonomy agreements as a new moral basis for secession in Buchanan's theory was prompted by the dramatic developments in Kosovo. The chaotic constitutional situation in Kosovo, coupled with Serbia's failure to manage the constitutional and humanitarian crisis, led Buchanan to draw crucial analogies with the situations in Sudan, Eritrea, and the Kurds of Northern Iraq. He concluded that deprivation of autonomy should be recognized as a valid ground for remedial secession. Buchanan noted that these cases shared a common sequence: "[w]hat these otherwise disparate cases have in common is the following sequence of events: Pressures from a minority group eventually result in the state agreeing to an intrastate autonomy arrangement; the state breaks the agreement; in response to the broken autonomy agreement autonomists become secessionists; and then the state violently attempts to suppress the secession" (Buchanan 2004, 357). Buchanan's moral reasoning is empirical and entirely descriptive, dependent solely on the empirical analogies he draws between disparate events. By employing formal induction, he is unable to discern the *fundamentum relationis*, the essential connection among these instances. This limitation highlights why the Remedial Right Only theory requires revisions to address its shortcomings effectively.

Another significant limitation of Buchanan's Remedial Right Only theory is its lack of an account of collective identity, a critical oversight given that the theory constructs moral claims on the rights of groups and peoples. While Buchanan makes an incidental reference to the necessity of supplementing his moral account with a theory that clarifies the territorial claims of seceding entities (Buchanan 2004, 337), he seems entirely dismissive of the existence of any plausible theory: "[u]nless a theory can provide a plausible account of the validity of the claim to territory by those to whom it ascribes the right to secede, it fails" (Buchanan 2004, 337). In Buchanan's framework, peoples possess "ascriptive" characteristics, attributes ascribed to individuals regardless of their choice (Buchanan 2004, 352). In his critique of nationalist Primary Right theories—which advocate that all nations should have the moral right to form their own independent states irrespective of past injustices—Buchanan counters by arguing that the concept of national identity itself is highly controversial. He cites Margalit and Raz's definition of nations as anonymous, large-scale "encompassing cultural groups" that share a common culture and character, significantly influencing many aspects of life. Membership in these groups partly depends on mutual recognition, is crucial for self-identification, and represents belonging rather than achievement (Buchanan 2004, 380). However, not all national groups that engage in nationalist discourse constitute "distinct cultural groups in any significant sense" according to Buchanan (Buchanan 2004, 381). He does not provide a detailed explanation of what he considers significant in this context. For example, he contends that in the case of Scottish nationalism, there is no "distinct Scottish culture" and in the context of Northern Ireland, the terms "Catholic" and "Protestant" do not denote distinct cultural groups. Buchanan summarily states that national groups are not cultural groups "in any interesting sense" (Buchanan 2004, 381).

Buchanan's treatment of national identity as an abstract, anonymous entity requiring some form of "significant" or "interesting" cultural distinctiveness to substantiate a self-determination claim neglects the potential for a people to exhibit actual psychological characteristics, a communal narrative, and genuine emotional ties to a specific land. This omission appears driven by a typical liberal bias: the belief that peoples must be controlled due to their presumed irrational nationalist passions, which purportedly drive them to claim space and redraw boundaries whenever possible. Indeed, Buchanan dismisses ascriptivist Primary Right theories on the basis that their institutionalization would "only exacerbate ethno-national violence, along with the human rights violations that it inevitably entails" (Buchanan 2004, 382). He also suggests that his Remedial Right Only theory needs bolstering through an "impartial international adjudicative procedure" to minimize the risk of groups attempting unilateral secession under unmet conditions (Buchanan 2004, 359).

Interestingly, despite criticisms, Buchanan aligns with the phenomenological distinction between objective and relative deprivation, rejecting the latter (Primary Right theories) as a valid basis for secession while acknowledging the "moral demerit" of the former (Remedial Right Only theory). One might question why this is the case, especially since Buchanan has relied on formal rather than the expanded Aristotelian induction (*ἐπαγωγή*), the latter exposing essential meanings through insight.

To understand this, a revisit to our expanding induction chapters is necessary, where it is explained how intuition is an indispensable inductive step that remains largely beyond control or instrumentalization because it is part of a natural mental process (Jevons 1948, 1). It appears that traces of this intuitive process influenced Buchanan's articulation of his moral theory on remedial secession, albeit through a liberal lens focused on individual human rights.

Despite unconsciously taking this intuitive step, Buchanan failed to develop a mature phenomenological insight. A major reason for this shortfall is his inability to set aside his liberal assumptions.

Ironically, the most significant error in Buchanan's Remedial Right Only theory lies not in its logic but in its moral implications. The theory essentially functions as a self-help mechanism, greenlighting oppressed (and even not-so-oppressed) groups to assert and enforce their conceptions of justice. Buchanan defends this moral stance by arguing that a remedial right to secession, as a self-help measure, would be subjected to scrutiny by an impartial, international adjudicative body. He also notes that "even if the unilateral right to secede is to be a 'self-help' device, international society has a legitimate interest in imposing some constraints on the recourse to self-help" (Buchanan 2004, 360). However, there is a profound difference between imposing constraints on self-help actions and institutionalizing a legal right to self-help that supersedes traditional concepts of self-defense. Institutionalizing such a right encourages arbitrary self-administration of international justice and fundamentally contradicts the purpose of corrective justice, which aims to educate men, states, and governments about the harms of certain deprivations. Institutionalizing a legal right to self-help essentially concedes the absence of an international legal order. The identification and correction of wrongful acts, along with the ethical mission of corrective justice, cannot be left solely to the discretion of the perpetrator or the victim. For corrective justice to be effectively realized within the so-called international legal order, an international authority is required to ensure its proper implementation. Only with such governance can justice become a virtuous habit among peoples and states.

It is also important to note that Buchanan's proposal for remedial secession is not entirely novel. The concept was considered as early as 1920 by the International Commission of Jurists, who recognized that "the separation of a minority from a State of which it forms part" could be deemed "an altogether exceptional solution, a last resort when the State lacks either the will or the power to enact and apply just and effective guarantees" (in Cassese 1995, 360). This view is similarly held by Antonio Cassese, a notable mainstream legal theorist on self-determination, who supports the remedial option for certain oppressed groups. By means of a *de lege ferenda* approach to international law he suggests that, in exceptional cases, the post-colonial exercise of external self-determination must be allowed:

> [a]llowance should . . . be made for exceptional cases where factual conditions render internal self-determination impracticable. When, in a multinational State, armed conflict breaks out and one or more groups fight for secession, it may be that it is too late to plead for a peaceful solution based on internal self-determination. Similarly, when the central authorities of a multinational State are irremediably oppressive and despotic, persistently violate the basic rights of minorities and no peaceful and constructive solution can be envisaged, it seems difficult to imagine that those central authorities would be willing to grant autonomy or participatory rights. (Cassese 1995, 359)

The International Commission of Jurists and Antonio Cassese employ precise language when they characterize remedial secession, framing it as an "allowance" rather than a legal right. This distinction is crucial because it indicates that the *de lege ferenda* perspective does not support the establishment of an *a priori*, positive legal right to secede. Instead, it favors an *a posteriori* approach that relies on specific criteria for legitimacy. These criteria include (a) international recognition of the newly formed entity if it successfully separates from the oppressing mother-state or (b) authorized international intervention or supervision in cases where the entity cannot achieve independence but is facing, for example, a severe humanitarian crisis. This approach denotes a preference for treating secession as a conditional measure, reserved for exceptional circumstances rather than a universally applicable right.

The *de lege ferenda* view primarily focuses on the international management of severe civil war crises and aligns with Buchanan's moral theory in advocating for instances of remedial secession to be placed under direct international supervision. However, while Buchanan's approach centers on preventing conflicts through the institutionalization of an international judiciary to assess claims to remedial secession, the *de lege ferenda* perspective adopts a therapeutic approach. This involves suggesting, negotiating, and establishing alternative constitutional structures in areas considering secession. These alternatives may include new forms of association, federation, confederation, and both international and intra-state cooperation. The primary aim of the *de lege ferenda* approach is pragmatic: to mitigate the demands for secession and reduce pressures on central authorities. This perspective envisions international supervision not just as a regulatory or corrective mechanism but as a constructive force that can reshape and stabilize regions facing secessionist tensions.

The conceptualization of this view in legal consciousness can be further elucidated through the psychoanalytic, post-modern lens of Nathaniel Berman's work. Berman explores the intricate interplay of nationalist passions, cultural fantasies, and international law, providing a deeper understanding of the emotional and cultural dynamics that influence legal outcomes in international contexts. This brings us to the critique of the last theoretical proposal concerning potential moral reforms of international law, as discussed in Berman's analyses.

Nathaniel Berman has argued that international law and European nationalism formed an implicit alliance in legal consciousness following the First World War, particularly during the Paris Peace Conference (Berman 1994, 456). This conference, he contends, was designed to create a new world order that would accommodate the aspirations of emerging nationalist movements (Berman 1992–1993, 1794). In Berman's interpretation, the outcome of this effort was the emergence of a "legal fantasy" he terms "international legal modernism," a framework that sought to affirm and imaginatively reconcile competing nationalist energies (Berman 1992–1993, 1798). This modernist vision, he explains, was energized by a fusion of Enlightenment rationalism—especially its ideal of freedom—and the emotive forces of nationalist solidarity (Berman 1992–1993, 1810). The product of this fusion, which Berman describes as the "double origin" of international legal reasoning, gave rise to a characteristic "modernist ambivalence," wherein international law continuously attempted to harmonize rational concepts of legitimacy with the passionate energy of popular nationalism (Berman 1992–1993, 1811).

During the interwar years, Berman observes, legal imagination flourished. International law became a site of experimentation, marked by a range of innovative proposals that embraced rather than suppressed nationalist sentiment (Berman 1994, 458). Many of these experimental legal ideas were subsequently absorbed into mainstream doctrine, including principles such as the right to self-determination, the protection of minorities, human rights, mandates, trusteeships, plebiscites, and supranational governance structures (Berman 1995–1996, 825). He singles out internationalization projects in regions like the Saar, Danzig, and Upper Silesia as emblematic of this period's creative momentum. In these cases, international law functioned as what Berman calls an "autonomous creator of institutions," stepping in to replace the state as the central unit of legal order, while simultaneously promoting historical nations as symbolic carriers of cultural identity (Berman 1992–1993, 1874). These projects, he maintains, were remarkably effective in reconciling the nationalist passions of all parties involved.

However, Berman contends that this creative legal spirit was abandoned in the aftermath of the Second World War. The horrors of Nazism, he suggests, severed the perceived alliance between nationalism and international law. In his view, a kind of "survivor's guilt" took hold within legal doctrine—a psychological analogue to the trauma experienced by survivors of concentration camps—which led international jurists to disavow the nationalistic roots of international law (Berman 1992–1993, 1902). Since then, legal thought has moved toward functionalism and realism, privileging pragmatic peace-building processes over the bold imaginative planning that once characterized legal approaches to geopolitical challenges, such as the situation in Palestine.

Drawing on Derrida's notion of the dangerous supplement, Berman characterizes the relationship between legal ideas and nationalist passions in paradoxical terms. In his account, legal concepts serve as a necessary but ultimately subordinate supplement to the real energies of nationalist sentiment. These ideas, while inert on their own, act as a corrective or stabilizing force to passion, and yet paradoxically come to supplant the very energy they are meant to supplement (Berman 1992–1993, 1811). For Berman, this dynamic reinforces the idea that international law cannot replace the nation, understood as a primordial force, because the state itself is always a secondary and problematic construct. Consequently, state-based, sovereignty-centered proposals by international jurists are, in his view, incapable of capturing the authentic nationalist energies that drive historical and political change.

Berman expresses admiration for the creativity and flexibility of international legal proposals during the interwar period, pointing to United Nations General Assembly Resolution 181 on the partition of Palestine as a prime example. He argues that this resolution embodied "the entire range of international legal solutions for the problem of nationalism," from self-determination and minority protections to supranational integration (Berman 1995–1996, 825).

Berman also critiques the moral language of wrong and redress adopted by some theorists, suggesting that this framing incorrectly assumes the superiority of reality over idea. He contends that any effort to redress a perceived historical wrong inevitably requires contesting an established reality that others consider legitimate, thereby leading to a confusion of competing normative claims. In his analysis, such disputes reflect clashing nationalist visions, each asserting its own moral legitimacy (Berman 1995–1996, 827–8).

From Berman's perspective, legal formalism is similarly flawed. It presumes that nationalist actors are rational legal subjects, capable of balancing rights within frameworks adjudicated by neutral authorities—an assumption he finds deeply mistaken. Issues like the status of Jerusalem, he argues, cannot be reduced to technical questions of secular law, as they are shaped by deep, irreconcilable nationalist attachments. For Berman, addressing such conflicts requires a cultural and imaginative legal approach—one that permits full expression of all competing nationalist visions. He regards this as the most "accurate" way to grasp the complex relationship between international law and nationalism (Berman 1995–1996, 832).

Ultimately, Berman suggests that international law must be structurally reimagined to "make room for fantasy," arguing that enduring legal solutions will be those capable of integrating disparate nationalist dreams within a single framework (Berman 1995–1996, 832). In contrast to ethical or rationalist strategies, his proposed response to Kierkegaard's either/or dilemma is to embrace the aesthetic dimension of law, particularly in the case of Palestine, where he recommends an imaginative, integrative legal vision over moral rigidity or procedural formality. Berman's argument asserts that there is no foundational logical or moral truth that international lawyers can use as a basis for framing their legal reasoning. When Berman uses the term reason, he is not referring to logic in a strict sense, but rather to abstract rational ideas of the Enlightenment, such as concepts of legitimacy and human freedom. His post-modern interpretation of international law suggests that justice is merely one idea among many that exist solely in the mind of the international jurist.

One significant self-contradiction in Berman's theory occurs in his *de lege ferenda* proposal to international jurists. He suggests that to devise a viable plan for Palestine, jurists must harness their legal imagination and draw upon the creative spirit of the interwar period, acknowledging the natural alliance between international law and nationalism. Yet, while Berman views the State as a dangerous supplement to real nationalist passions, he paradoxically believes in the possibility of an exceptionally inventive legal mind—a Dworkinian Hercules of legal imagination—that could integrate all these 'real passions' into a single legal framework. This highlights a contradiction between the supposed 'inflexibility' of the State and the 'flexibility' of alternative institutional solutions, where Berman appears to opt for what he considers the lesser of two evils. The notion of (in)flexibility serves merely as a rational compromise to mask this contradiction.

Berman's post-modern account also raises several moral issues. Even assuming his theory is rational and non-contradictory, his idea of accommodating conflicting passions through a highly creative plan inevitably leads to the notion of diplomatic agreement or compromise. However, unless such a legal plan is either imposed or voluntarily accepted in totality by all parties, it is difficult to envisage how peoples with deeply conflicting nationalist passions could coexist peacefully. Historical examples, such as the 1960 Cypriot Constitution, demonstrate that formalist legal consciousness often legitimizes inequality and coercion as components of valid legal agreements. Furthermore, Berman suggests that international law should make room for fantasy within its structure, but he does not address the rest of the structure characterized by established practices and legal habits. Moreover, there is nothing to guarantee that in Berman's utopic plans, the nationalist passions of one side will not dominate those of the other. This oversight highlights the potential for imbalance and conflict within his proposed framework.

Berman's post-modern narrative significantly overlooks the crucial concepts of identity and collective memory, as well as the entire discipline of social psychology. This field provides insights into how experiences of deprivation, separation, and loss can profoundly stigmatize popular fantasy and disrupt the communal narratives of peoples in ways that could prevent the alignment and coexistence Berman imagines under a single legal framework, no matter how creative or visionary it may be. Even from Berman's perspective, which rejects the dichotomy between reality and idea as expressions of the same underlying passions, the effects of collective deprivation and trauma must inevitably manifest as a nationalistic passion for rectification. For Palestinians, this passion is symbolized by the figure of the Palestinian fighter or *fida'i*, who strives to correct the historical wrongs of the Palestinian catastrophe or *al-nakba*. For Greek Cypriots, it is captured in the *δεν ξεχνώ*—'I do not forget' rhetoric, which has internalized and eternalized the traumatic memory of the Attila invasion within the Greek Cypriot collective consciousness. Unless Berman's avant-garde plan for Palestine incorporates elements of rectification, the Palestinian passion for redress will not simply dissipate.

Corrective justice transcends the subjective, nationalistic fantasies of what might be considered right, contrary to what Berman seems to imply. It serves as an essential truth by offering actual relief to the traumatic memories of deprivation and loss. Without a concrete proposal for rectifying historical injustices, Berman's aesthetic plan for Palestine is inherently flawed. His approach presupposes that peoples can instantly forget their historical traumas and cooperate in good faith, which is both utopian and dismissive, failing to acknowledge the significant role of collective psychology. This oversight undermines the driving force behind what Berman labels 'nationalistic passions' and ignores the central place of trauma in a people's memory and collective identity. Corrective justice has a profound ethical function, not merely a symbolic one. It aims to address social fear, re-establish trust among peoples, and lay the groundwork for the realization of a vision like Berman's, but with a grounded and realistic approach that genuinely respects and integrates the deep-seated traumas and historical narratives of the communities involved.

In the philosophy of tort, the central concept is moral responsibility rather than culpability. Corrective justice, accordingly, is not about assigning moral labels but rather instructing perpetrators—and, by extension, all potential perpetrators—that certain acts of deprivation are inherently harmful, immoral, and must be avoided. If such acts do occur, corrective justice mandates their rectification based on the objective moral responsibility we inherently hold toward each other. Jules Coleman articulates this notion, stating, "[c]orrective justice connects agents with losses by the criterion of responsibility" (Coleman 1994, 59). In the distinct realm of international law, this connection is often inadequately established or entirely missing.

Given the ethical mission of corrective justice is typically delegated to legislators, the significant structural deficiencies of international law suggest that this moral responsibility should extend to all international legal professionals, including judges, arbitrators, legal practitioners, and academics. The pathologies of international law necessitate that the moral responsibility of corrective justice permeates all individual and collective levels, especially within international legal authorship and practice which are proximate to governmental structures and capable of exerting significant influence on political and diplomatic decision-making centers.

The moral responsibility of international jurists can manifest in the promotion of legal rhetoric that champions logical rules and explicitly delegitimizes all international and state practices contradicting corrective justice. Once such legal rhetoric gains mainstream acceptance and authority, a gradual paradigm shift can be expected toward legal rationality and corrective justice.[1] This shift, essentially a reversal of the habits of irrationality and injustice in international legal reasoning, can be achieved through individual legal activism, akin to that demonstrated by Chief Justice Marshall in *Worcester v. Georgia*, which challenged prevailing legal theories and established case law of his time.

Whether and how this moral and rational transformation of international law might influence international relations is uncertain. However, it is highly unlikely that the majority of governments will easily deviate from the conventional norms of international legitimacy. Since adherence to legitimacy is crucial for maintaining international and domestic political stability, a newly established mainstream understanding of legitimate state behavior will inevitably compel states, and their legal advisors, to either overtly reject international law, thereby acknowledging a state of nature in international affairs, or conform to the new normative framework.

In the context of the proposed legal paradigm shift toward corrective justice in international relations, this new norm should eventually entail the institutionalization of an international administrator with absolute authority to exercise corrective justice in international relations. Although detailing the structure of this hypothetical institution is way beyond the scope of this book, it is imperative to highlight that the individuals composing this new international body should be selected and appointed based on stringent criteria. These criteria should prioritize suitability, ethical behavior, and intellectual merit. This raises a significant philosophical question about the feasibility of such an elite: Can intellectuals genuinely detach themselves from their national, cultural, or professional contexts?

Echoing Schopenhauer's views on the independence required for genuine philosophical inquiry, the most crucial characteristic for an intellectual, especially in this context, is to be an original and independent thinker, devoted unconditionally to the pursuit of truth. Schopenhauer suggests that "in order to pay absolute homage to truth and really to philosophize, so many conditions have to be fulfilled, but there is also one that is almost indispensable, namely that we stand on our own feet and recognize no master" (Schopenhauer 1974, 194). This implies that true intellectuals must not philosophize with a predetermined goal in mind; rather, they must think autonomously and independently. Philosophers and intellectuals who are to be part of this international body must, first and foremost, think for themselves and not for others (Schopenhauer 1974, 152).

The distinction between an academic and a true intellectual is pivotal in the context of pursuing a legal paradigm shift toward corrective justice in international relations. According to Schopenhauer, *φιλοσοφία μισθοφόρος* (paid philosophy) often hinders the critical spirit and independence of the mind. Academic philosophers and scholars, under the pressures of institutional agendas, tend to align their thoughts with the research projects of their superiors and the goals of their institutions, which stifles their critical faculties essential for the quest for truth (Schopenhauer 1974, 151). Additionally, the capitalist fragmentation and commercialization of knowledge into specialized fields and degree-assets, along with the valuation of academic merit based on publication metrics like journal impact factors, foster a regrettable scholarly rivalry. Under these circumstances, the pursuit of true knowledge becomes subordinate to professional ambitions. The maxim "*primum vivere deinde philosophari*" (first to live, then to philosophize) suggests that knowledge becomes conventional, maintained within a closed circle of prominent academics and journal editors who set and preserve the criteria of academic merit. Nothing is deemed of intellectual value unless recognized by this select group of illuminati. In such a dystopian academic environment, it is challenging for a free mind to emerge and confront the *norma conventionis* (Schopenhauer 1974, 149).

However, even Schopenhauer, perhaps the most pessimistic of philosophers, believed that through a rare anomaly, original and independent minds devoted to the truth—the "egoists in the noblest sense of the word"—can arise against all odds and challenge the fallacies of conventional wisdom (Schopenhauer 1974, 152). My thesis for the legal paradigm shift places its hope on this anomaly, asserting that it is through these exceptional individuals that long-term change can be catalyzed. Independent minds, by standing out, can exert significant academic and social influence. Moral activism from such an intellectual elite entails that these independent intellectuals could historically become opinion-makers. They can influence academics, public officials, and legal advisors to adhere to logical and ethical standards (Carty 2007). Such an elite can lay the groundwork for a transformative synchrony of logical thinking and ethical acting, necessary for effectuating a paradigm shift in international legal doctrine.

The question of whether an intellectual elite can effectively detach itself from its national and cultural contexts is secondary to the broader capabilities such an elite might possess. As noted, "we are all embedded in national, linguistic, historical communities," and while Husserl's notion of absolute transcendental bracketing might not be wholly realistic, an independent intellectual can still employ tools from ethnography and cultural anthropology (Carty 2007, 18). These tools aid in understanding how one's national and cultural backgrounds influence perceptions of facts and ideas. This approach aligns with Alasdair MacIntyre's perspective that understanding one's moral identity is crucially framed "in and through" one's family and community memberships. This does not necessarily mean accepting moral limitations from such affiliations. Instead, as MacIntyre suggests, "without those moral particularities to begin from there would ever be anywhere to begin; but it is in moving forward from such particularity that the search for the good, for the universal, consists" (MacIntyre 2007, 221).

In terms of the practical meta-question regarding the abstractness of the current canon of international and constitutional self-determination, which often leads to comparisons and produces *anomie* or diverse 'fantasies' about what is just, the task for international legal academics is to reformulate existing norms. This reformulation should focus on excluding relative deprivation and centering solely on the phenomenology of objective deprivation. In the cases of Cyprus and Palestine, a proper application of corrective justice would ideally translate into imposing a non-negotiable solution on all parties involved. However, the entrenched habits of irrationality and injustice in international law indicate that such an imposition might be a quixotic utopia.

Nevertheless, this challenging context does not diminish the moral responsibility of international jurists. In the ongoing negotiations in Cyprus and Palestine, there is an opportunity for jurists to exercise *phronesis,* i.e.practical wisdom in judgment and action, particularly considering the historical traumas involved. The moral responsibility of corrective justice is especially incumbent upon those jurists who oversee and contribute their legal expertise to these negotiation processes. They are positioned to influence outcomes not merely through legal technicalities but through a deep engagement with the ethical dimensions of these conflicts.

The phenomenology of objective deprivation extends beyond acts of collective deprivation themselves to include actions that attempt to distill, finalize, formalize, and/or legitimize such acts of deprivation *ex post facto*. Therefore, international jurists involved in negotiations must pay careful attention to specific negotiation chapters that could perpetuate injustice. These include discussions on the annexation of territories, the expansion or demolition of illegal settlements, the immigration of illegal settlers, and the negotiation of the status of refugees, particularly regarding their confiscated properties and right of return. It is crucial that negotiations prioritize assessing the psychological impact of proposed solutions on the collective identity of the affected peoples, groups, or communities. Any constitutional or international legal proposal that legitimizes and solidifies acts of traumatic deprivation *ex post facto* is inherently flawed. Such proposals are likely to unconsciously revive the initial trauma of separation and loss, thereby resulting in a renewed violation of the right to self-determination. Furthermore, tactfulness in the negotiation process is indispensable. Proposals that fail to address a people's traumatic memory with the requisite seriousness and respect should not be presented at all. Historical examples such as the Annan Plan for Cyprus, which proposed absolving Turkey of any liability, and Ehud Olmert's suggestion to Mahmoud Abbas of a symbolic return of a maximum of 15,000 Palestinian refugees to Israel (Dowty 2012, 248), demonstrate a profound lack of tact and respect.

The practical meta-question concerning the moral responsibility of contemporary international jurists has been answered affirmatively. Ultimately, whether an international jurist will assume this moral responsibility is a matter of personal choice, grounded in one's own understanding and ethical conscience.

## Note

1 It is important to clarify that the term paradigm shift, as employed in this context, should not be understood in the subjectivist sense associated with Thomas Kuhn's account of scientific revolutions (Kuhn 1970). Rather, the phrase legal paradigm shift refers here to a deliberate and reflective process—an intentional effort to reverse entrenched habits of irrationality and injustice within international law. The aim is to foster a rational and ethical transformation in legal reasoning.

# Bibliography


Acierno, Silvia, and Julio Baquero Cruz. 2005. "The Order of the Spanish Constitutional Court on the Proposal to Convert the Basque Country into a Freely Associated Community: Keeping Hands Off Constitutional Politics." *International Journal of Constitutional Law* 3 (4): 687–695.

Adams, T. W. 1966. "The First Republic of Cyprus: A Review of an Unworkable Constitution." *Western Political Quarterly* 19 (3): 475–490. https://doi.org/10.2307/444709.

Adelman, Howard. 1994. "Refugees: The Right to Return." In *Group Rights*, edited by Judith Baker. Toronto: University of Toronto Press.

Agnew, Robert. 1997. "The Nature and Determinants of Strain: Another Look at Durkheim and Merton." In *The Future of Anomie Theory*, edited by Nikos Passas and Robert Agnew. Boston: Northeastern University Press.

Allott, Philip. 2002. *The Health of Nations: Society and Law Beyond the State*. Cambridge: Cambridge University Press.

Amselek, Paul. 1973. "The Phenomenological Description of Law." In *Phenomenology and the Social Sciences*, edited by Maurice Natanson. Evanston: Northwestern University Press.

Anderson, Benedict. 1991. *Imagined Communities: Reflections on the Origin and Spread of Nationalism*. London: Verso.

Aquinas, Thomas St. 1920. *The Summa Theologica, Part I, QQ LXXV.—CII, Treatise on Man*. London: Burns Oates & Washbourne Ltd.

Arbitration Commission. January 11 and July 4, 1992. Opinions on Questions Arising from the Dissolution of Yugoslavia. Conference on Yugoslavia, 31 I.L.M. 1488.

Aristotle. 1926. *Art of Rhetoric*. Vol. XXII. Cambridge, MA: Harvard University Press.

Aristotle. 1926. *The Nicomachean Ethics*. Edited by H. Rackham. Cambridge, MA: Harvard University Press.

Aristotle. 1960. *Posterior Analytics*. Edited by Hugh Tredennick. Cambridge, MA: Harvard University Press.

Aristotle. 1960. *Topica*. Edited by E. S. Forster. Cambridge, MA: Harvard University Press.

Aristotle. 1995. *The Politics*. Edited by R. F. Stalley. Oxford: Oxford University Press.

Aristotle. 1998. *The Metaphysics*. Westminster: Penguin Books.

Aspremont, Jean d.' 2011. *Formalism and the Sources of International Law: A Theory of Ascertainment of Legal Rules*. Oxford: Oxford University Press.

Aspremont, Jean d.' 2012. "Wording in International Law." *Leiden Journal of International Law* 25: 575.

Baka, Anna Irene. 2022. "The Logic of Absence in Customary International Law: An Open System Approach." In *The Theory and Philosophy of Customary International Law and its Interpretation*, edited by Panos Merkouris, Jörg Kammerhoffer, and Noora Arajärvi. Cambridge: Cambridge University Press.

Barron, James. 1992. *Interface of Psychoanalysis and Psychology*. Washington, DC: American Psychological Association.

Berman, Nathaniel. 1992–1993. "But the Alternative is Despair: European Nationalism and the Modernist Renewal of International Law." *Harvard Law Review* 106.

Berman, Nathaniel. 1994. "Between 'Alliance' and 'Localization': Nationalism and the New Oscillationism." *New York University Journal of International Law and Politics* 26.

Berman, Nathaniel. 1995–1996. "Legalizing Jerusalem or, of Law, Fantasy, and Faith." *Catholic University Law Review* 45.

Berman, Nathaniel. 2012. *Passion and Ambivalence: Colonialism, Nationalism, and International Law*. Leiden: Martinus Nijhoff Publishers.

Billig, Michael. 1976. *Social Psychology and Intergroup Relations*. London: Academic Press.

Bix, Brian. 1993. *Law, Language and Legal Determinacy*. Oxford: Clarendon Press.

Bordens, Kenneth, and Irwin Horowitz. 2008. *Social Psychology*. Madison, WI: Freeload Press.

Bourdieu, Pierre. 2001. "The Force of Law: Toward a Sociology of the Juridical Field." In *Sociological Perspectives on Law*, vol. I, edited by Roger Cotterrell. London: Ashgate.

Bowlby, John. 1969. *Attachment and Loss*. Vol. 1. London: Penguin Books.

Brinkmann, Klaus. 2002. "The Deduction of Intersubjectivity in Fichte's Grundlage des Naturrechts." In *New Essays on Fichte's Later Jena Wissenschaftslehre*, edited by Daniel Breazeale and Tom Rockmore. Evanston: Northwestern University Press.

Bryant, Rebecca. 2009. "The Many Cyprus Problems." *Middle East Report* 251.

Buchanan, Allen. 1991. *Secession: The Morality of Political Divorce from Fort Sumter to Lithuania and Quebec*. Boulder: Westview Press.

Buchanan, Allen. 2004. *Justice, Legitimacy, and Self-Determination: Moral Foundations for International Law*. Oxford: Oxford University Press.

Buchdahl, G. 1951. "Induction and Scientific Method." *Mind, New Series* 60.

Buchheit, Lee. 1978. *Secession: The Legitimacy of Self-Determination*. New Haven: Yale University Press.

Budding, Audrey Helfant. 2008. "Nation/People/Republic: Self-Determination in Socialist Yugoslavia." In *State Collapse in South-Eastern Europe: New Perspectives on Yugoslavia's Disintegration*, edited by Lenard J. Cohen and Jasna Dragovic-Soco. West Lafayette: Purdue University Press.

Cagaptay, Soner. 2004. "Race, Assimilation, and Kemalism: Turkish Nationalism and the Minorities in the 1930s." *Middle Eastern Studies* 40.

Calnan, Alan. 1997. Justice and Tort Law. Carolina Academic Press.

Campel, Yolanda. 2001. "Group Psychology, Society, and Masses." In *On Freud's "Group Psychology and the Analysis of the Ego,"* edited by Ethel Spector Person. New Haven, CT: Yale University Press.

Carty, Anthony. 1991a. "Critical International Law: Recent Trends in the Theory of International Law." *European Journal of International Law* 2 (1): 1.

Carty, Anthony. 1991b. "Liberalism's Dangerous Supplements: Medieval Ghosts of International Law." *Michigan Journal of International Law* 13: 161.

Carty, Anthony. 1994. "Interwar German Theories of International Law: The Psychoanalytical and Phenomenological Perspectives of Hans Kelsen and Carl Schmitt." Cardozo Law Review 16: 1235.

Carty, Anthony. 2007. *Philosophy of International Law*. Edinburgh: Edinburgh University Press.

Carty, Anthony. 2011. International Law and the Spirit of Anti-Colonialism: Europe Fights Back. Review Article of The Decolonization of International Law by Matthew Craven. Modern Law Review 74: 135.

Carty, Anthony. 2012. "Language Games of International Law: Koskenniemi as the Discipline's Wittgenstein." *Melbourne Journal of International Law* 13.

Carty, Anthony, and Anna Irene Baka. 2017. "Sources in the Meta-History of International Law: From Liberal Nihilism and the Anti-Metaphysics of Modernity to an Aristotelian Ethical Order." In The Oxford Handbook of the Sources of International Law, edited by Jean D'Aspremont and Samantha Besson. Oxford: Oxford University Press.

Cassese, Antonio. 1995. *Self-Determination of Peoples: A Legal Reappraisal*. Cambridge: Cambridge University Press.

Cavaletto, George. 2007. *Crossing the Psycho-Social Divide: Freud, Weber, Adorno and Elias*. Aldershot: Ashgate.

Chapman, Bruce. 1995. "Wrongdoing, Welfare, and Damages: Recovery for Non-Pecuniary Loss in Corrective Justice." In Philosophical Foundations of Tort Law, edited by David G. Owen.

Chelstrom, Eric. 2013. *Social Phenomenology: Husserl, Intersubjectivity, and Collective Intentionality*. Lanham: Lexington Books.

Chrysostomides, Kypros. 2000. *The Republic of Cyprus: A Study in International Law*. The Hague: Martinus Nijhoff Publishers.

Chryssochoou, Xenia. 2004. *Cultural Diversity: Its Social Psychology*. Malden, MA: Blackwell Publishing.

Cohen, Albert. 1997. "An Elaboration of Anomie Theory." In *The Future of Anomie Theory*, edited by Nikos Passas and Robert Agnew. Boston: Northeastern University Press.

Cohen, Jonathan. 1989. *An Introduction to the Philosophy of Induction and Probability*. Oxford: Clarendon Press.

Coleman, Jules. 1994. "Corrective Justice and Property Rights." In *Foundations of Tort Law*, edited by Saul Levmore. New York: Oxford University Press.

Coleman, Jules. 1995. "The Practice of Corrective Justice." In Philosophical Foundations of Tort Law, edited by David G. Owen, 53.

Conant, James. 1998. "Wittgenstein on Meaning and Use." *Philosophical Investigations* 21 (3): 222.

Copeland, Charlton. 2009. "Ex Parte Young: Sovereignty, Immunity, and the Constitutional Structure of American Federalism." *The University of Toledo Law Review* 843.

Crawford, James. 1988. *The Rights of Peoples*. Oxford: Clarendon Press.

Crawford, James. 2006. *The Creation of States in International Law*. Oxford: Clarendon Press.

Crawshaw, Nancy. 1978. *The Cyprus Revolt: An Account of the Struggle for Union with Greece*. London: George Allen & Unwin.

Demirtaş-Bağdonas, Özlem. 2008. "The Clash of Kemalisms? Reflections on the Past and Present Politics of Kemalism in Turkish Political Discourse." *Turkish Studies* 9.

Derrida, Jacques. 1997. *Of Grammatology*. Baltimore: Johns Hopkins University Press.

Dovidio, John. 2000. "Group Identity and Intergroup Relations." 17.

Downes, David, and Paul Rock. 2007. *Understanding Deviance: A Guide to the Sociology of Crime and Rule-Breaking*. Oxford: Oxford University Press.

Dowty, Alan. 2012. *Israel / Palestine*. Cambridge: Polity Press.

Dubrow, Heather. 1999. *Shakespeare and Domestic Loss: Forms of Deprivation, Mourning, and Recuperation*. Cambridge: Cambridge University Press.

Durkheim, Émile. 1951. *Suicide: A Study in Sociology*. New York: Free Press.

Ehrlich, Thomas. 1974. *Cyprus 1958–1967: International Crises and the Role of Law*. Oxford: Oxford University Press.

Ellemers, Naomi. 1999. *Social Identity, Context, Commitment, Content*. Oxford: Blackwell Publishers.

Epicurus. 1926. *The Extant Remains*. Oxford: Oxford University Press.

Fairlie, John. 1923. "The Separation of Powers." *Michigan Law Review* 21.

Feinberg, Joel. 1993. "Social Philosophy." In *The Nature and Process of Law*, edited by Patricia Smith. Oxford: Oxford University Press.

Feinberg, Joel. 1994. "The Nature and Value of Rights." In *Philosophy of Law*, edited by Jules Coleman and Anthony Sebok. New York: Garland Publishing.

Finnis, John. 2011. *Natural Law and Natural Rights*. Oxford: Oxford University Press.

Franck, Thomas M. 1992. "The Emerging Right to Democratic Governance." *The American Journal of International Law* 86 (1): 46–91. https://doi.org/10.2307/2203138

Franck, Thomas. 1993. "Postmodern Tribalism and the Right to Secession." In *Peoples and Minorities in International Law*, edited by Catherine Brolmann. Dordrecht: Martinus Nijhoff Publishers.

Franck, Thomas. 2000. "Legitimacy and the Democratic Entitlement." In *Democratic Governance and International Law*, edited by Brad Roth and Gregory Fox. Cambridge: Cambridge University Press.

Freud, Sigmund. 1945. *Group Psychology and the Analysis of the Ego*. London: Hogarth Press.

Freud, Sigmund. 1989. *The Freud Reader*. Edited by Peter Gay. New York: W. W. Norton & Company.

Friedmann, Wolfgang. 1973. "Phenomenology and Legal Science." In *Phenomenology and the Social Sciences*, edited by Maurice Natanson. Evanston: Northwestern University Press.

Garrison, Tim Alan. 2002. *The Legal Ideology of Removal: The Southern Judiciary and the Sovereignty of Native American Nations*. Athens: The University of Georgia Press.

Gewirth, Alan. 1996. *The Community of Rights*. Chicago: University of Chicago Press.

Golding, Martin. 2007. *Legal Reasoning, Legal Theory and Rights*. Aldershot: Ashgate.

Gorman, Jonathan. 2003. *Rights and Reason: An Introduction to the Philosophy of Rights*. Durham: Acumen Publishing.

Green, Leslie. 1994. "Internal Minorities and Their Rights." In Group Rights, edited by Judith Baker, 103–125. Toronto: University of Toronto Press.

Griffin, James. 2008. *On Human Rights*. Oxford: Oxford University Press.

Groarke, Louis. 2009. *An Aristotelian Account of Induction: Creating Something from Nothing*. Montreal & Kingston: McGill-Queen's University Press.

Groarke, Paul. 2004. *Dividing the State: Legitimacy, Secession and the Doctrine of Oppression*. Aldershot: Ashgate.

Grzegorczyk, Christophe. 1991. "Legal System and Reality: A Discussion of the Autopoietic Theory of Law." In *Controversies about Law's Ontology*, edited by Paul Amselek and Neil MacCormick. Edinburgh: Edinburgh University Press.

Habermas, Jürgen. 1988. *Legitimation Crisis*. Cambridge: Polity Press.

Hart, H. L. A. 1982. *Essays on Bentham: Studies in Jurisprudence and Political Theory*. Oxford: Clarendon Press.

Hart, H. L. A. 2007. "Positivism and the Separation of Law and Morals." In *Law and Morality: Readings in Legal Philosophy*, edited by David Dyzenhaus, Sophia Reibetanz Moreau, and Arthur Ripstein. Toronto: University of Toronto Press.

Hart, H. L. A. 2009. "Positivism and the Separation of Law and Morals." In *Arguing about Law*, edited by Aileen Kavanagh and John Oberdiek. London: Routledge.

Hegel, G. W. F. 2005. *Phänomenologie des Geistes. Vorrede: Hegel's Preface to the Phenomenology of Spirit*. Princeton: Princeton University Press.

Heidegger, Martin. 1962. *Being and Time*. London: SCM Press.

Heyman, Steven J. 2003. "Aristotle on Political Justice." In Aristotle and Modern Law, edited by Richard O. Brooks and James Bernard Murphy, 472.

Higgins, Rosalyn. 1993. "Postmodern Tribalism and the Right to Secession: Comments." In *Peoples and Minorities in International Law*, edited by Catherine Brolmann. Dordrecht: Martinus Nijhoff Publishers.

Higgins, Rosalyn. 1994. *Problems and Process: International Law and How We Use It.* Oxford: Clarendon Press.

Hoffmeister, Frank. 2006. *Legal Aspects of the Cyprus Problem: Annan Plan and EU Accession*. The Hague: Martinus Nijhoff Publishers.

Hohfeld, Wesley Newcomb. 1913. "Some Fundamental Legal Conceptions as Applied in Judicial Reasoning." *Yale Law Journal* 23: 16.

Holland, Robert. 1998. *Britain and the Revolt in Cyprus 1954–1959*. Oxford: Oxford University Press.

Honore, Tony. 1995. "The Morality of Tort Law – Questions and Answers." In Philosophical Foundations of Tort Law, edited by David G. Owen.

Hull, Richard. 2007. *Deprivation and Freedom: A Philosophical Enquiry*. London: Routledge.

Husserl, Edmund. 1931. *Ideas: General Introduction to Pure Phenomenology*. Edited by W. R. Boyce Gibson. London: George Allen & Unwin LTD.

Husserl, Edmund. 1970a. *Krisis der Europäischen Wissenschaften und die Transzendentale Phänomenologie: The Crisis of European Sciences and Transcendental Phenomenology: An Introduction to Phenomenological Philosophy*. Evanston: Northwestern University Press.

Husserl, Edmund. 1970b. *The Shorter Logical Investigations*. London: Routledge.

Independent International Commission on Kosovo. 2000. *The Kosovo Report: Conflict, International Response, Lessons Learned*. Oxford: Oxford University Press.

Janoff-Bulman, Ronnie, and Andrea Berger. 2000. "The Other Side of Trauma: Towards a Psychology of Appreciation." In *Loss and Trauma: General and Close Relationship Perspectives*, edited by John H. Harvey and Eric D. Miller. Philadelphia: Brunner-Routledge.

Jevons, Stanley W. 1948. *Elementary Lessons in Logic: Deductive and Inductive*. London: Macmillan and Co.

Joseph, H. W. B. 1916. *An Introduction to Logic*. Oxford: Clarendon Press.

Joseph, Joseph. 1997. *Cyprus Ethnic Conflict and International Politics: From Independence to the Threshold of the European Union*. London: Macmillan.

Judah, Tim. 2008. *Kosovo: What Everyone Needs to Know*. Oxford: Oxford University Press.

Kamenka, Eugene. 1988. "Human Rights, Peoples' Rights." In *The Rights of Peoples*, edited by James Crawford. Oxford: Clarendon Press.

Kant, Immanuel. 1991. The Metaphysics of Morals. Translated by Mary Gregor. Cambridge: Cambridge University Press.

Kant, Immanuel. 1998. *Critique of Pure Reason*. Cambridge: Cambridge University Press.

Karlsson, Gunnar. 2010. *Psychoanalysis in a New Light*. Cambridge: Cambridge University Press.

Kaymak, Erol. 2009. "The Turkish Cypriot Views on Annan V." In *Reunifying Cyprus: The Annan Plan and Beyond*, edited by Andrekos Varnava and Hubert Faustmann. London: I.B. Tauris.

Kedar, Nir. 2006. "The Political Origins of the Modern Legal Paradoxes." In *Paradoxes and Inconsistencies in the Law*, edited by Oren Perez and Gunther Teubner. Oxford: Hart Publishing.

Kelsen, Hans. 1971. *What is Justice? Justice, Law, and Politics in the Mirror of Science: Collected Essays by Hans Kelsen*. Berkeley: University of California Press.

Kelsen, Hans. 1973. *Essays in Legal and Moral Philosophy*. Dordrecht: Reidel Publishing Co.

Kennedy, Duncan. 1998. "Freedom and Constraint in Adjudication: A Critical Phenomenology." In *Evolution and Revolution in Theories of Legal Reasoning*, edited by Scott Brewer. London: Taylor & Francis.

Kili, Suna. 1980. "Kemalism in Contemporary Turkey." *International Political Science Review* 1.

Kingsbury, Benedict. 2001. "Reconciling Five Competing Conceptual Structures of Indigenous Peoples' Claims in International and Comparative Law." In *Peoples' Rights*, edited by Philip Alston. Oxford: Oxford University Press.

Kojève, Alexandre. 2000. *Outline of a Phenomenology of Right*. Lanham: Rowman & Littlefield.

Koskenniemi, Martti. 1989. *From Apology to Utopia: The Structure of International Legal Argument*. Helsinki: Lakimiesliiton Kustannus.

Krahé, Barbara. 1996. "Aggression and Violence in Society." In *Applied Social Psychology*, edited by Gun Semin and Klaus Fiedler. Thousand Oaks, CA: Sage Publications.

Krämer, Gudrun. 2008. *A History of Palestine: From the Ottoman Conquest to the Founding of the State of Israel*. Princeton: Princeton University Press.

Kuhn, Thomas. 1970. *The Structure of Scientific Revolutions*. Chicago: University of Chicago Press.

Le Sueur, Andrew, and Maurice Sunkin. 1997. *Public Law*. London: Longman.

Lefebvre, Alexandre. 2011. "Law and the Ordinary: Hart, Wittgenstein, Jurisprudence." *Telos* 154: 99.

Lohmar, Dieter. 2012. "Language and Non-Linguistic Thinking." In *The Oxford Handbook of Contemporary Phenomenology*, edited by Dan Zahavi. Oxford: Oxford University Press.

Loizides, Neophytos, and Marcos Antoniades. 2009. "Negotiating the Right of Return." *Journal of Peace Research* 46.

Lyons, David. 1998. "Legal Formalism and Instrumentalism: A Pathological Study." In *Evolution and Revolution in Theories of Legal Reasoning: Nineteenth Century Through the Present*, edited by Scott Brewer. Taylor & Francis.

MacCormick, Neil. 1978. *Legal Reasoning and Legal Theory*. Oxford: Clarendon Press.

MacIntyre, Alasdair. 2007. *After Virtue: A Study in Moral Theory*. Notre Dame: University of Notre Dame Press.

Mallinson, William. 2009. "Cyprus, Britain, the USA, Turkey and Greece in 1977: Critical Submission or Submissive Criticism?" *Journal of Contemporary History* 44.

Martin, Rex. 1993. *A System of Rights*. Oxford: Clarendon Press.

McCrudden, Christopher. 2010. "Legal Research and the Social Sciences." In *Legal Theory and the Social Sciences*, Vol. II, edited by Maksymilian Del Mar and Michael Giudice. Aldershot: Ashgate.

McGoldrick, Dominic. 2000. "The Tale of Yugoslavia: Lessons for Accommodating National Identity in National and International Law." In *Accommodating National Identity: New Approaches in International and Domestic Law*, edited by Stephen Tierney. The Hague and Boston, MA: Kluwer Law International.

McWhinney, Edward. 2007. *Self-Determination of Peoples and Plural-Ethnic States in Contemporary International Law: Failed States, Nation-Building and the Alternative, Federal Option*. Leiden: Martinus Nijhoff Publishers.

Mellon, James. 2006. "Islamism, Kemalism and the Future of Turkey." *Totalitarian Movements and Political Religions* 7.

Merton, Robert K. 1996. "Social Structure and Anomie." In Social Deviance, edited by Erich Goode, 78–94. Oxford: Blackwell.

Mill, John Stuart. 1950. *Philosophy of Scientific Method*. New York: Hafner Publishing Company.

Miller, Fred D. 2003. "Aristotle's Theory of Political Rights." In Aristotle and Modern Law, edited by Richard O. Brooks and James Bernard Murphy.

Minto, William. 1915. *Logic Inductive and Deductive*. London: John Murray.

Morris, Clarence. 1960. "Justice and Scientific Method." *Columbia Law Review* 60: 60.

Necatigil, Zaim. 1989. *The Cyprus Question and the Turkish Position in International Law*. Oxford: Oxford University Press.

Neimeyer, Robert, and Heidi Levitt. 2000. "What's Narrative Got to Do with It? Construction and Coherence in Accounts of Loss." In *Loss and Trauma: General and Close Relationship Perspectives*, edited by John Harvey and Eric Miller. Philadelphia: Brunner-Routledge.

Neyzi, Leyla. 2002. "Remembering to Forget: Sabbateanism, National Identity, and Subjectivity in Turkey." *Comparative Studies in Society and History* 44.

Nietzsche, Friedrich. 1994. On the Genealogy of Morality, edited by Keith Ansell-Pearson, translated by Carol Diethe. Cambridge: Cambridge University Press.

Nietzsche, Friedrich. 1999. *The Birth of Tragedy and Other Writings*. Cambridge: Cambridge University Press.

Norman, Wayne. 2001. "Secession and (Constitutional) Democracy." In *Democracy and National Pluralism*, edited by Ferran Requejo. London: Routledge.
Noyes, Reinold. 1940. "The Law and Scientific Method." *Political Science Quarterly* 55: 55.
O'Malley, Brendan, and Ian Craig. 1999. *The Cyprus Conspiracy: America, Espionage and the Turkish Invasion*. London: I.B. Tauris Publishers.
Oeser, Erhard. 2003. *Evolution and Constitution: The Evolutionary Self-Construction of Law*. Dordrecht: Kluwer Academic Publishers.
Oliver, Peter. 2000. "Canada's Two Solitudes: Constitutional and International Law in Reference Re Secession of Quebec." In *Accommodating National Identity: New Approaches in International and Domestic Law*, edited by Stephen Tierney. Kluwer Law International :The Hague and Boston .
Papadakis, Yiannis. 2008. "Narrative, Memory and History Education in Divided Cyprus: A Comparison of Schoolbooks on the 'History of Cyprus.'" *History and Memory* 20.
Pappe, Ilan. 2006. *A History of Modern Palestine: One Land, Two Peoples*. Cambridge: Cambridge University Press.
Passas, Nikos. 1997. "Anomie, Reference Groups, and Relative Deprivation." In *The Future of Anomie Theory*, edited by Nikos Passas and Robert Agnew. Boston: Northeastern University Press.
Pavković, Aleksandar. 1997. *The Fragmentation of Yugoslavia: Nationalism in a Multiethnic State*. London: Macmillan Press.
Pavković, Aleksandar, and Peter Radan. 2007. *Creating New States: Theory and Practice of Secession*. Aldershot: Ashgate.
Perez, Oren. 2006. "The Institutionalisation of Inconsistency: From Fluid Concepts to Random Walk." In *Paradoxes and Inconsistencies in the Law*, edited by Oren Perez and Gunther Teubner. Oxford: Hart Publishing.
Philippou, Stavroula, and Andrekos Varnava. 2009. "Constructions of Solution(s) to the Cyprus Problem: Exploring Formal Curricula in Greek Cypriot State Schools." In *Reunifying Cyprus: The Annan Plan and Beyond*, edited by Andrekos Varnava and Hubert Faustmann. London: I.B. Tauris.
Pomerance, Michla. 1982. *Self-Determination in Law and Practice: The New Doctrine in the United Nations*. The Hague: Martinus Nijhoff Publishers.
Posner, Richard A. 1995. "Wealth Maximization and Tort Law: A Philosophical Enquiry." In Philosophical Foundations of Tort Law, edited by David Owen, 108.
Radan, Peter. 2002. *The Break-Up of Yugoslavia and International Law*. New York: Routledge.
Radin, Max. 1938. "The Doctrine of the Separation of Powers in Seventeenth Century Controversies." *University of Pennsylvania Law Review and American Law Register* 86.

Raes, Koen. 1994. "Legalisation, Communication and Strategy: A Critique of Habermas' Approach to Law." In *Sociological Theories of Law*, edited by Kahei Rokumoto. Aldershot: Dartmouth Publishing Company.

Ramet, Sabrina. 2005. *Thinking About Yugoslavia: Scholarly Debates About the Yugoslav Breakup and the Wars in Bosnia and Kosovo*. Cambridge: Cambridge University Press.

Rank, Otto. 1973. *The Trauma of Birth*. New York: Harper & Row Publishers.

Raphael, Beverley, and Matthew Dobson. n.d. "Bereavement." In *Loss and Trauma: General and Close Relationship Perspectives*, edited by John Harvey and Eric Miller, 2000. Philadelphia: Brunner-Routledge.

Rawls, John. 1999. *The Law of Peoples with "The Idea of Public Reason Revisited."* Cambridge: Harvard University Press.

Raz, Joseph. 2009. "Legal Positivism and the Sources of Law." In *Arguing About Law*, edited by Aileen Kavanagh and John Oberdiek. Oxford: Oxford University Press.

Raz, Joseph. 2010. "Human Rights without Foundations." In *The Philosophy of International Law*, edited by Samantha Besson and John Tasioulas. Oxford: Oxford University Press.

Réaume, Denise. 1994. "The Group Right to Linguistic Security: Whose Right, What Duties?." In *Group Rights*, edited by Judith Baker. Toronto: University of Toronto Press.

Rehman, Javaid. 2000. *The Weaknesses in the International Protection of Minority Rights*. The Hague: Kluwer Law International.

Ricoeur, Paul. 1989. *The Conflict of Interpretations: Essays in Hermeneutics*. London: Continuum.

Ricoeur, Paul. 2004. *Memory, History, Forgetting*. Chicago: University of Chicago Press.

Ricoeur, Paul. 2013. *Hermeneutics: Writings and Lectures*. Cambridge: Polity.

Ritchie, A. D. 1945. Scientific Method in Social Studies, *Philosophy* 20: 3.

Roth, Brad. 1999. *Governmental Illegitimacy in International Law*. Oxford: Clarendon Press.

Runciman, W. G. 1966. *Relative Deprivation and Social Justice: A Study of Attitudes to Social Inequality in Twentieth Century Britain*. Aldershot: Gregg Revivals.

Russell, Bertrand. 1995. *An Inquiry into Meaning and Truth*. London: Routledge.

Sajó, András. 2005. "Constitution without the Constitutional Moment: A View from the New Member States." *International Journal of Constitutional Law* 3: 235–45.

Samuel, Geoffrey. 2010. "Is Law Really a Social Science? A View from Comparative Law." In *Legal Theory and the Social Sciences*, vol. II, edited by Maksymilian Del Mar and Michael Giudice. Aldershot: Ashgate.

Schacht, Richard. 1994. *The Future of Alienation*. Urbana: University of Illinois Press.

Scheler, Max. 1961. *Man's Place in Nature*. New York: The Noonday Press.

Schlag, Pierre. 1996. "Rights in the Postmodern Condition." In *Legal Rights: Historical and Philosophical Perspectives*, edited by Austin Sarat and Thomas R. Kearns. Ann Arbor, MI: University of Michigan Press.

Schmitt, Carl. 2004. *Legalität und Legitimität: Legality and Legitimacy*. Durham: Duke University Press.

Schopenhauer, Arthur. 1974. *Parerga and Paralipomena: Short Philosophical Essays*. Oxford: Clarendon Press.

Schopenhauer, Arthur. 1995. *On the Basis of Morality*. Oxford: Berghahn Books.

Schroeder, Donald. 2003. "Aristotle on Law." In *Aristotle and Modern Law*, edited by Richard Brooks and James Bernard Murphy. Aldershot: Ashgate.

Schutz, Alfred. 1966. *Collected Papers III: Studies in Phenomenological Philosophy*. The Hague: Martinus Nijhoff.

Schütz, Alfred. 1967. *The Phenomenology of the Social World*. Evanston: Northwestern University Press.

Schwarzenberger, Georg. 1965. *The Inductive Approach to International Law*. London: Stevens & Sons.

Sidanius, Jim, and Felicia Pratto. 1999. *Social Dominance: An Intergroup Theory of Social Hierarchy and Oppression*. Cambridge: Cambridge University Press.

Smith, Patricia. 1993. *The Nature and Process of Law: An Introduction to Legal Philosophy*. Oxford: Oxford University Press.

Smith, Stanley De, and Rodney Brazier. 1994. *Constitutional and Administrative Law*. London: Penguin Books.

Stern, Laurence. 1975. "Bitter Lessons: How We Failed in Cyprus." *Foreign Policy* 34.

Strauss, Leo. 1959. *What is Political Philosophy?* Chicago: The University of Chicago Press.

Suksi, Markku. 1998. *Autonomy: Applications and Implications*. The Hague: Kluwer Law International.

Sunstein, Cass. 1996. *Legal Reasoning and Political Conflict*. Oxford: Oxford University Press.

Sunstein, Cass. 2001. *Designing Democracy: What Constitutions Do*. Oxford: Oxford University Press.

Taşpınar, Ömer. 2006. "Islam, Secularism, and Nationalism in Modern Turkey: Who Is a Turk?" *Middle East Journal* 60.

Taylor, Donald, and Fathali Moghaddam. 1994. *Theories of Intergroup Relations: International Social Psychological Perspectives*. Westport, CT: Praeger.

Teubner, Gunther. 1994. "Substantive and Reflexive Elements in Modern Law." In *Sociological Theories of Law*, edited by Kahei Rokumoto. Aldershot: Dartmouth Publishing Company.

Thucydides. 1993. On Justice, Power, and Human Nature: Selections from the History of the Peloponnesian War, translated by Paul Woodruff. Indianapolis: Hackett Publishing Company.

Trubek, David. 1994. "Max Weber on Law and the Rise of Capitalism." In *Sociological Theories of Law*, edited by Kahei Rokumoto. Aldershot: Dartmouth Publishing Company.

Tuck, Richard. 1979. *Natural Rights Theories: Their Origin and Development.* Cambridge: Cambridge University Press.

Turp, Daniel. 2003. "Québec's Right to Secessionist Self-Determination: The Colliding Paths of Canada's Clarity Act and Québec's Fundamental Rights Act." In *Secession and International Law: Conflict Avoidance—Regional Appraisals*, edited by Julie Dahlitz. The Hague: T.M.C. Asser Press.

Vater, Michael. 2006. "Schelling's Aphorisms on Natural Right (1796/97): A Comparison with Fichte's Grundlage des Naturrechts." In *Rights, Bodies and Recognition: New Essays on Fichte's Foundations of Natural Right*, edited by Daniel Breazeale and Tom Rockmore. London: Routledge.

Villey, Michel. 1991. *Controversies about Law's Ontology.* Edited by Paul Amselek and Neil MacCormick. Edinburgh: Edinburgh University Press.

Waldron, Jeremy. 2010. "Two Conceptions of Self-Determination." In *The Philosophy of International Law*, edited by John Tasioulas and Samantha Besson. Oxford: Oxford University Press.

Wall, John. 2002. "Moral Meaning: Beyond the Good and the Right." In *Paul Ricoeur and Contemporary Moral Thought*, edited by Paul Ricoeur. London: Routledge.

Walzer, Michael. 1980. "The Moral Standing of States: A Response to Four Critics." *Philosophy & Public Affairs* 9 (3): 209–229. Princeton, NJ: Princeton University Press.

Weeramantry, Christopher. 1992. Nauru: *Environmental Damage Under International Trusteeship*. Oxford: Oxford University Press.

Weller, Marc. 2008a. *Escaping the Self-Determination Trap*. Leiden: Martinus Nijhoff Publishers.

Wellman, Carl. 1997. *An Approach to Rights: Studies in the Philosophy of Law and Morals*. Dordrecht: Kluwer Academic Publishers.

Weinrib, Ernest J. 2003. "Corrective Justice." In Aristotle and Modern Law, edited by Richard O. Brooks and James Bernard Murphy, 446.

Williams, John. 1998. *Legitimacy in International Relations and the Rise and Fall of Yugoslavia*. London: Macmillan Press.

Williams, Robert. 2002. "The Displacement of Recognition by Coercion in Fichte's Grundlage des Naturrechts." In *New Essays on Fichte's Later Jena Wissenschaftslehre*, edited by Daniel Breazeale and Tom Rockmore. Evanston: Northwestern University Press.

Willke, Helmut. 1991. "The Autopoietic Theory of Law: Autonomy of Law and Contextual Transfer." In *Controversies about Law's Ontology*, edited by Paul Amselek and Neil MacCormick. Edinburgh: Edinburgh University Press.

Wittgenstein, Ludwig. 1974. *Philosophical Grammar*. Edited by Rush Rhees. Oxford: Basil Blackwell.

Wittgenstein, Ludwig. 2009. *Philosophical Investigations*. Oxford: Blackwell Publishing.

Wright, Richard W. 1995. "Right, Justice and Tort Law." In Philosophical Foundations of Tort Law, edited by David G. Owen, 166.

Young, Iris Marion. 2001. "Two Concepts of Self-Determination." In *Human Rights: Concepts, Contests, Contingencies*, edited by Austin Sarat and Thomas R. Kearns. Ann Arbor: University of Michigan Press. [Original source: https://studycrumb.com/alphabetizer]

# Index

Note: Page numbers followed by 'n' indicate note number(s).

# About the Author

**Anna Irene Baka** is a legal philosopher and human rights lawyer. Her work focuses on the philosophy of law and human rights, as well as the right of peoples to self-determination, explored from both international and constitutional perspectives. She is a Senior Researcher at Charles University, Faculty of Law, Institute for Interregional Study of Constitutionalism, Prague, Czech Republic. She has held the prestigious Marie Skłodowska-Curie Global Fellowship at Harvard University's Faculty of Arts and Sciences and at the Department of Philosophy and Cultural Heritage at Ca' Foscari University of Venice, where she led the EU-funded project RIGHT, developing a cross-cultural foundation for human rights dialogue between the EU and China. Dr. Baka also served as human rights lawyer at the Greek National Commission for Human Rights, the country's UN-accredited national human rights institution. Her recent research explores constitutionalism and collective identity, law and Aristotle, law and phenomenology, and the cultural foundations of justice in Western and Chinese traditions. She is also deeply interested in interdisciplinary approaches to law, including the intersections of law and ethics, law and logic, law and language as well as law and psychology. Her forthcoming monograph, *From Passion to Reason: Aristotle and the Foundations of Rights*, rethinks the foundations of rights through a neo-Aristotelian lens. Fluent in five languages and active across three continents, Dr. Baka is committed to bridging legal cultures through philosophically informed scholarship, institutional cooperation, and public dialogue.

www.ingramcontent.com/pod-product-compliance
Ingram Content Group UK Ltd.
Pitfield, Milton Keynes, MK11 3LW, UK
UKHW020215290926
15470UKWH00001B/208

9 781666 965155